Teaching Linguistics

Other books by Koenraad Kuiper

Formulaic Genres
Bounty

Koenraad Kuiper and W. Scott Allan
Introduction to English Language: Word, Sound and Sentence

Allan Bell and Koenraad Kuiper (editors)
New Zealand English

Li FuYin and Koenraad Kuiper (editors)
Semantics: A Course Book
Timepieces
Smooth Talkers
Mikrokosmos
Signs of Life

Teaching Linguistics

Reflections on Practice

Edited by Koenraad Kuiper

Published by
Equinox Publishing Ltd
UK: 1 Chelsea Manor Studios, Flood Street, London SW3 5SR
USA: DBBC, 28 Main Street, Oakville, CT 06779

www.equinoxpub.com

First published 2011

British Library Cataloguing-in-Publication Data

A catalogue record for this book is available from the British Library.

ISBN 978 1 84553 686 2 (hardback)
978 1 84553 687 9 (paperback)

Library of Congress Cataloging-in-Publication Data

Teaching linguistics : reflections on practice / edited by Koenraad Kuiper.
p. cm.
Includes bibliographical references and index.
ISBN 978-1-84553-686-2 (hb) -- ISBN 978-1-84553-687-9 (pbk.) 1. Linguistics--Study and teaching. I. Kuiper, Koenraad.

P51.T373 2010
410.71--dc22

2010020269

Typeset by Steve Barganski, Sheffield
Printed and bound in Great Britain by Lightning Source UK Ltd, Milton Keynes

I will teach you my townspeople
*how to perform**

Contents

Contributors

Laurie Bauer, Victoria University of Wellington

Kate Burridge, Monash University

Andrew Carstairs-McCarthy, University of Canterbury

Sandra Chung, University of California, Santa Cruz

Wes Collins, Summer Institute of Linguistics

Susan Foster-Cohen, Champion Centre, Burwood Hospital, Christchurch

Jen Hay, University of Canterbury

Janet Holmes, Victoria University of Wellington

Brian D. Joseph, The Ohio State University

Harold Koch, Australian National University

Koenraad Kuiper, University of Canterbury

Diana Van Lancker Sidtis, New York University

David Mendelsohn, York University

Miriam Meyerhoff, University of Auckland

Barbara H. Partee, University of Massachusetts at Amherst

Christopher Potts, Stanford University

Paul Warren, Victoria University of Wellington

Alison Wray, Cardiff University

Foreword

Reading this book on linguistics education, fittingly enough, is an education in itself, for this linguist at least, and surely it will be so for any linguist (just as writing for it, even just a foreword, is a genuine honour for me).

And, at the same time, again for me at least, reading this was also in part a trip down memory lane, as it summoned up images of my own education in linguistics some 35 years ago at the hands and mouths of some extraordinarily gifted teachers whom I am proud to name here: Judith Aissen, Jorge Hankamer, Jay Jasanoff, Susumu Kuno, Gregory Nagy, David Perlmutter, Haj Ross, Joki Schindler and Calvert Watkins. These scholar-teachers taught me vast amounts of content about their particular areas of specialization within our field, but they also imparted to me the intricacies of our field's methodology, focusing especially on argumentation and on critical evaluation. But also, through their excellent teaching and their enthusiasm for the subject matter and for disseminating knowledge, they taught me about crafting lectures, about leading discussions, about asking questions, and so on. I have tried in my own way to carry on the high standard for excellence in teaching that they modelled so well for me.

The present collection of 17 essays, plus an introduction, dealing with various aspects of the teaching of linguistics, offers remarkable insights into the teaching process, viewing not only its practical side, but also the philosophical side, the planning side and even the personal side. There are serious reflections on teaching in general, 'tricks' that have worked in the classroom, carefully designed syllabi, ways of blending analysis of data with development of theory, statements of desiderata that we should all try to live up to, and the like. Some are more curricular in nature, some are technique-oriented, some come complete with materials to use, but all are engagingly written and, quite appropriately, all are highly instructive.

There are some common themes that emerge from the collection taken as a whole. For instance, several of the authors stress learning by doing, that is, 'active learning', as opposed to learning by being told. Many of the course designs that we read about are built around this premise, and all are backed by successful experiences with this approach. Another recurring theme is the importance of engaging our students, giving them a voice in the class and listening to them, though not mindlessly praising everything they do, and thus giving them a chance to make mistakes and learn from those mistakes. Several chapters also address assessment and grading, an inevitable aspect of our trade but one that can be applied fairly and judiciously and turned into a learning experience of its own for students. Finally, all speak of opportunities and challenges, challenges not only to the instructors in devising classes and executing lesson plans, but also for the students, the thinking being that students want to be intellectually challenged and to be involved in learning and discovery; in that case, we as instructors should not shrink from offering our students challenging material – for the most part, they will thrive with it, assuming *we* do our job right in terms of how we present it to them.

Importantly, too, even though most of the chapters focus on the classroom setting, the volume recognizes learning outside the classroom and in particular the learning that goes on via the advising process and the supervision of theses and major research projects, especially undergraduate honours theses, MA theses and PhD dissertations. I consider this dimension to be significant, as the one-on-one advising that thesis supervision requires is indeed a form of instruction that all too often does not get the attention, value or recognition that it deserves.

Each chapter is written by a skilled and talented practitioner who has perfected the teaching trade over many years of dishing out wisdom to students, of receiving insight from their students, of discussing classes with colleagues, and, significantly, of learning themselves when they were students in the classroom with skilled and talented teachers of their own (as their somewhat unconventional but highly entertaining bio-blurbs tell us). Many reflect on their own days as students, just as I was moved to do above. We can infer from this that good teaching begets good teaching, and learning (by students) encourages good teaching (by instructors).

This volume is, as best I can tell, the first of its kind in the vast literature on linguistics, or at the very least it is one of the few such collections around. I found myself agreeing with the authors repeatedly on point after point, and so it is clear to me that this is a work that all of us should turn to again and again for inspiration and insight.

BRIAN D. JOSEPH
Columbus, Ohio

Acknowledgments

I acknowledge the stimulus given to this book by the death of my friend and colleague Scott Allan. His voice sounds in my inner ear often. 'Get real!' he says. Alison Wray thought this book was a good idea and gave me a shove just at the right time to move me and it forward. Andrew Carstairs-McCarthy went through the whole volume meticulously noting areas for improvements. I thank them.

1 Introduction

Koenraad Kuiper

If you are a linguist then it is likely that you had a committed teacher or teachers of linguistics somewhere in your past, and that you have colleagues who are committed to their teaching. I had a number of gifted teachers who taught me linguistics. I worked for many years with other gifted teachers including Scott Allan, a man in love with his subject and with the joy of sharing that love with his students. The last time I saw him, little of him then remaining, he was still thinking about how he might teach linguistics. When he died soon after, generations of students to come were deprived; generations of the students he taught remembered.

How does one celebrate people like Scott? Not by the normal festschrift presented on an aging scholar's birthday (or some time thereafter) with homage to his (almost always his) research. But maybe by a book like this.

Almost no one I approached to write about their teaching turned me down. Almost everyone asked: How long did I want their contribution to be? What was I looking for? What approach should they take? I was evasive. Just write about what turns you on, what you think is significant, what you find works, just reflect on your own teaching practice. That is it. That is what is in the following pages. The writers are themselves. They have written what they wanted to write. With no template, no preconceived outcomes, at first the results seem wonderfully, anarchically unacademic. And yet the writers have given me and I hope will give you, the readers, pause to think about the nature of teaching. Also, and entirely by accident, they have covered so much of what concerns teachers: selecting the right texts, how to put things in the best order, how to engage students, how to make learning enjoyable, what kinds of learning outcomes does one want from a course, how to put your personal research into a course, how to have a course generate personal and student research projects.

These chapters show just how personal teaching is. So they falsify the notion that there is some box of tricks that any dog, old or new, can learn about how to teach. Yes, there are hints here for good practice, gems and germs of ideas that might be adapted, but every writer shows that they have evolved their own way to profess their subject. They have their strongly felt predilections. Each teacher has her or his ways of seeing their subject, their obligations to their students. So to be a teacher you must be an interesting and interested person. There is no prescription for that.

The chapters also show that there is no substitute for experience. Given how painfully it is sometimes acquired, that is as well. A good teacher is a good learner, and not just about what they teach but also about how they teach. You do get to know your subject better over time and you get your personal store of experiences in that subject. Also, every year there is a new set of students. They change. You change. When I started being taught, those who taught often wore academic gowns and addressed students by their title and surname. 'Now, Mr Kuiper, would you please translate the next passage (from Beowulf) starting at line 1251.' (You do remember these moments.) Now we are on first-name terms, the 18-year-olds and me. It makes a difference. Quite what that difference is, is hard to say, but certainly social distance has decreased. We, the teachers, are, I think, more caring of our students. That makes a difference. Student-centred teaching is not so difficult. You just have to think how your students are going to learn, given where they are, rather than given where you are. The teachers who have written for this book have all asked themselves that, and have all worked out their own answers. Those answers evolve.

Each domain of linguistics presents its own challenges. The fact that we, the teachers, have overcome some of these challenges can make us aware of what our students still have to overcome. Hearing distinctive features in a language not your own is tricky. Why do so many students have trouble with complementary distribution when it is such a painfully obvious idea? How do you explain that we can all find syllable boundaries in our native languages when there is nothing much in the speech signal that announces syllable boundaries? How do you get across that deixis is pragmatically interpreted, that *here* here and *here* there are, like allophones, both the same and different? These questions need a teacher to think as hard as a teacher as they do as a researcher.

Another thing is clear reading each chapter. Every teacher teaches in their own institutional back yard. What you can do in the UK with students who have a preselected major and who have been selected for your programme is rather different than what can be done with students in Australia who are doing a general degree, who do not have any clear notion of what their major might be and who are trying things out. Degree structures differ. Bologna universities with a three-year first-degree programme and North American universities with a four-year undergraduate degree make different demands on a curriculum.

The curriculum itself is often a strong influence. A teacher works within a team with others, and a curriculum is communally constructed. It too evolves. Not everyone gets to teach what they might like. And yet there is a job to be done.

All teachers have colleagues. Some people team-teach. Some people take sole charge of a course. Both have an influence on what gets taught and how it gets taught.

Affect is central. All the teachers who have written for this volume have emotional attachments. Some of them are strong. They feel about particular issues. That explains, in part, what lectures have to offer over websites. In lecturing to students, teachers are not just presentational conduits. They are living affect. They like certain topics. They find others less interesting. All this is taught.

All teachers have their academic bailiwicks. We are not just linguists; we are also phonologists, psycholinguists, experts on case. The connection between teaching and research is clear in many of these chapters even if it isn't foregrounded in all. Sometimes research finds its way into teaching and sometimes teaching finds its way into research.

So it has been a privilege working with the contributors to this book. Thank you. I hope what they have had to say will be seen as provocative of the same kind of practice: personal, thoughtful, inspirational. While research extends our subject into new domains, and offers new explanations, it would hardly exist if it were not for teachers who challenge the next generation of linguists, train the school teachers, the latter-day mendicants teaching English around the planet, the spell-check creators, the voice recognition software engineers, the people who want to know.

2 A toolbox for teaching phonetics

Jen Hay[*]

2.1 Introduction

Phonetics is my favourite topic to teach. I think this is because it has such a high 'wow' factor – the scope for fun and impressive demonstrations is vast. This makes the students particularly easy to engage.

In developing my introductory phonetics teaching, a lot of effort has gone towards collecting fun but useful demonstrations which can be done in the classroom. I have encountered many of them as, I am sure, has anyone else who has attempted to teach in this field. And I have settled on my own personal favourites. This chapter describes my own 'phonetician's toolbox' – the ingredients which are packed into my phonetics teaching drawer, and which do dutiful service each year. I write this in the hope that itemizing the objects may provide a useful service for people who are new to the teaching of phonetics, or for more experienced people looking for a toolbox refresher.

My contribution here is solely one of compilation and documentation. None of the demonstrations I describe in this article are of my own invention, but I am afraid the chain of inheritance is so long and so lost that it is impossible to credit anyone appropriately. I have observed some of these tricks in other people's lectures, I have read about some of them on the Web or in books, and many of them have been related to me by fellow phoneticians. Hopefully readers will forgive the paucity of citations.

When teaching phonetics, a lot of the best learning happens in the lab, and there is a sense in which excellent lab exercises are the very best arsenal you can have. Luckily these days no special equipment is required, at least at introductory level. In fact, one does not even need a lab, as there is excellent free available software such as Praat, which students can download onto their own machines. Students enjoy being asked to work with unknown languages – even from very early in the phonetics course, and they also very much enjoy working with their own voices. In my introductory course, a successful assignment involves recording all of the students, and then asking them to analyse their own voice: produce a vowel plot, measure their Voice Onset Times, assess the length difference between their 'short' and 'long' vowels. From a teaching perspective, this is much more engaging and successful than having all the students measure a single voice. It does, however, present its own challenges in terms of the increased grading burden.

As students become increasingly advanced, it is my preference to make my phonetics teaching increasingly lab based. However, at the beginning there is basic content to be covered, and lecturing to be done, and this is where the box of tricks is invaluable.

Our introductory course at Canterbury covers both articulatory and acoustic phonetics. Students inevitably find the acoustic phonetics material more difficult, and often slightly overwhelming. I have found an approach which weaves together the two approaches throughout the course more successful than one which has a strictly separate 'acoustics' component. This way they have had several weeks to digest – for example – what a waveform is, before we get on to complex wave forms and resonant frequencies.

Now, onto the contents of the toolbox.

2.2 Two empty beer cans and a straw

Sometime early in an introductory phonetics class, I teach about the voicing mechanism, and attempt to convey how the passage of air through the vocal folds causes them to vibrate. This – I relate to the students – consists of several phases. First, the air builds up below the closed vocal folds until the pressure is high enough to push the vocal folds apart. As the air rushes through the vocal folds, the increasing velocity of air eventually causes the vocal folds to spring back together. On this last point, I invariably lose the students, whose foreheads wrinkle in eerie unison. Out come the trusty beer cans for a demonstration of the Bernoulli Effect.

To do this, position two empty cans quite close together on a desk – with about 5 mm or so between them. My cans are battered 'Canterbury Draught' cans, which I like to think endows me with extra street credibility amongst my students. I then wave a straw at the students and ask what will happen if I use the straw to blow air between the cans. New Zealand students are very consistent in their response: The air will force the cans to move away from one another. When asked for a show of hands, the majority of the class seems to agree on this point. But – lo and behold – when I blow through the straw, the exact opposite happens. The cans snap together in a pleasing demonstration of the Bernoulli Effect. Moving air creates low air pressure. Objects move from areas of higher air pressure to areas of lower air pressure. This makes planes fly, and vocal folds vibrate. I also remind students of the demonstration later in the course, when we discuss the mechanisms of trills. It is always satisfying to demonstrate something that seems to run completely counter to students' intuitions. And precisely because it is counter to their intuitions, the demonstration is important. The element of surprise seems to make the principle memorable.

Of course, the same point can be made by holding a piece of paper vertically below one's mouth and blowing (causing the paper to rise up to horizontal position). But this doesn't involve beer cans, and so is inherently less interesting.

The presence of the straw in your inventory can come in handy for other means, as well. For example, in combination with a glass of water, it can be used to demonstrate different degrees of airflow produced by different types of sound.

2.3 A balloon for each student

This demonstration has some slight educational value, but I mainly like it because it makes the students laugh. It is very loud and is guaranteed to break down any preconceptions students may have about the lecture theatre being a non-interactive environment. I use it early – directly after teaching about voicing, when I am teaching about pitch. The puzzle: how do we use our articulators to increase or decrease the pitch of our voices?

I give every student a balloon, and ask them to blow it up and then slowly let out the air such that the balloon emits a rather annoying squeaky noise. They seem to have to do this at least once or twice to get over the apparent humour involved in the chorus of a classroom of 40 students emptying balloons simultaneously.

In collaboration with their neighbours they are then asked to figure out the various ways in which they can change the pitch of their deflating balloon. With luck, there are two families of response. One involves changing the tautness with which the mouth of the balloon is held. This can be directly related to the tightness of the vocal folds. The second involves the velocity of air through the balloon – manifest in two ways. One is simply the observation that as there is progressively less air in the balloon, the pitch of the balloon decreases. The second is that a sudden squeezing of the balloon results in a corresponding rise in pitch. From the resulting discussion the students are usually able to infer that a change in the pitch of an individual's voice relates to a change in the speed of vibration of the vocal folds. The speed of vibration can be controlled in two ways: (1) by manipulating how tightly the vocal folds are stretched, and (2) by manipulating the speed of airflow through the vocal folds. I usually suggest to the students that they can test this latter point at home by attempting to voice a constant pitch while having their flatmate or sibling punch them in the stomach. I'm not sure whether any of them have actually conducted this experiment.

2.4 A lollipop for each student

The tongue is not as sensitive as one might think, and students seem to have surprising difficulty knowing what position their tongue is in when they produce various sounds. And instructing them to put their tongue in a particular position to create a new sound is more or less doomed to failure. A tried and true method for connecting the tongue with the brain is the use of the lollipop. I first came across this technique while visiting Ohio State as a graduate student. It is crucial for its success that it is a classic, round, flat lollipop with a nice long stick. The modern spherical lollipops of the chuppa-chups generation are no good at all.

I distribute lollipops when I am teaching vowels. They can be placed flat on the body of the tongue, and then the movement of the stick reveals relative differences of the position of the tongue. For example, if you can get the students producing a high front /i/, then you can issue instructions such as: 'Attempt to slowly lower your tongue without moving it backwards'. The lollipop stick should lower, but not retract (or, at least, as little as possible). This gives them the concept of moving from high to low front vowels. Once they are producing a low front vowel, they can be asked to keep the lollipop stick as low as it is, but retract their tongue so the stick moves back as far as possible. This enables them to 'feel' the difference between front and back low vowels. Producing various vowels while holding the lollipop stick gives relatively concrete feedback about the position of the tongue. Of course, and rather unfortunately, the presence of the lollipop in the mouth rather distorts the acoustics of the vowel, and also the ability of the tongue to get into the highest positions. This activity, of course, needs to be optional, as there are occasionally students who have dietary restrictions prohibiting lollipop consumption. For such students, it is useful to note that the activity works just as well with the lollipop 'backwards' – so that the stick is in the mouth and the plastic-covered lolly is held outside the mouth. The degree to which this approach provides a hygiene hazard may depend on the initial packaging of the lollipop.

2.5 Slinkies

Slinkies are invaluable for the demonstration of various properties of waves. I have two – a large one and a small one. One useful demonstration involves the difference between transverse and longitudinal waves. This works best with a relatively large slinky, so students can quite clearly see the movement of the individual coils for the longitudinal wave. I also often use members of the class for this demonstration, setting up a transverse (Mexican) wave along one row of the classroom, and a longitudinal wave along another (where a student starts the wave by rocking left to right, and bumping into their neighbour).

When questioned about what kind of wave sound is, many students believe it is transverse. This no doubt comes from the standard method of diagramming sound waves, which looks very similar to a transverse wave. So I find it is very important to drum home the fact that the sound waves are longitudinal, and to carefully explain how a diagrammed waveform relates to differing air pressure during the wave.

The slinky also comes in handy for various other demonstrations. By holding it fixed at each end, it is useful to demonstrate different modes of vibration, in discussions of harmonics. Once one gets to the third mode of vibration, one needs to be quite practised, unless in possession of a relatively small slinky. I keep two different sizes on hand for different demonstrations.

And when teaching the acoustics of consonants, I often return to the slinky in an attempt to demonstrate a non-periodic wave. I do this by attempting to introduce chaos into the slinky. Having broken two slinkies during such demonstrations (by getting them irreparably tangled), my non-periodic slinky waves are now produced in a relatively restrained manner.

2.6 Pendulums and tubes

Pendulums are invaluable for illustrating the notion of a resonant frequency. They do not need to be fancy – but there does need to be more than one. Mine are simply pieces of string with dog clips on the end. Simple pendulums have a simple resonant frequency – a frequency at which they like to swing. For each pendulum, you can demonstrate that, no matter how much or little energy you put into it, it likes to swing at the same rate. Showing two pendulums of different lengths side by side demonstrates that this rate is different for different pendulums – changing the length of the string changes the resonant frequency of the pendulum. It is impossible to get the two different length pendulums swinging in parallel (though it is easy to amuse the students while trying).

What is important is that in order to keep each pendulum swinging nicely, you have to inject energy into it at its own resonant frequency. As long as you do this, the swings will get bigger and bigger. However, if you try and inject energy at a different frequency, this energy will be damped out, and the pendulum will not swing nicely, but rather will wobble in a chaotic, non-pendulum-like manner. This is very useful for talking about resonant frequencies and sound. Sound components near the vocal cavity's resonant frequencies will be amplified, and others will be damped.

In order to demonstrate that different-shaped cavities have different resonant frequencies it is handy to have at least two different lengths of tube on hand. Mine are simply cardboard tubes which have been cut to different lengths from the inner tube of a roll of paper towels. Hum, whistle or speak through each tube to show that the tube changes the perceived quality of the voice. The input to each tube is the same, but the sounds are filtered by the different tubes, each of which has its own resonant frequency.

2.7 A teaspoon

I do happen to know the original source of this particular trick. Peter Ladefoged, in *A course in phonetics* (1982: 174-75), suggests various ways of learning to 'hear' the resonant frequencies of the vocal tract (i.e. the formants). A good way to hear the second formant is to whisper the vowels. A good way to hear the first formant is to produce the vowels in creaky voice. Another way of hearing the first formant, suggests Ladefoged, is to create a glottal closure, and then flick the side of the neck with your fingernail. If you silently create different vowels, the sound created by the flick has remarkably different acoustics.

This last demonstration can make quite an impression on students, and so is worth putting some effort into perfecting it. One tool which I find indispensible in this respect is a metal teaspoon. I have found that hitting the side of your neck with the back of a spoon provides a much louder, more satisfying and uniform tone than the mere flick of a fingernail.

This skill can be useful in other respects as well. I was once required to attend a farewell party for a friend which took the form of an 'everyone participates' talent quest. As I am completely talentless, this presented rather a challenge. I ended up studying the 'glottis and spoon' technique sufficiently that I could approximately assign each of my vowels to musical notes, enabling me to perform 'Auld Lang Syne' and other classics at the party. I was an unexpected hit. If you are dedicated enough to perfect the glottis and spoon as an instrument, such performances also go down a treat in the classroom. However, I recommend that you confine your practice sessions to the comfort of your home, where an unusually scarlet neck is unlikely to raise any eyebrows.

2.8 A lighter

A common way of teaching about allophones and phonemes is to discuss the different phonetic variants of voiceless plosives. Beginning phonetics students are unaware, for example, that /t/s in different positions contain different degrees of aspiration. One way to convince them of this is to have them hold the palm of their hand in front of their mouth and produce paired words such as 'tan' and 'stan'. But, as with many demonstrations, this demonstration is made more dramatic if it involves fire.

I use a long gas lighter, which has a nice big flame. If you practice ahead of time, you will be able to figure out the optimal distance from your mouth to hold the lighter. This is the distance at which all 'tan's, no matter how subdued, extinguish the flame. On the other hand, no matter how much effort is put into giving the /t/ in 'stan' some legs, the /t/ cannot extinguish the flame. Hold the flame at this distance for your demonstration. It appears to be strangely entertaining for students to watch someone try in vain to put out a flame with their post-fricative /t/s.

2.9 IPA bingo

From http://www.cascadilla.com/ipabingo.html you can download and print IPA bingo. I keep this on call as a reliable standby, if the students need some revision, or perhaps a break from the onslaught of new information. Sometimes I sneak it into a tutorial. I like to have it on hand in my toolkit, because of my recurring paranoia that one day my lecture will finish prematurely early, and I will be left gaping with nothing to say. In practice, I tend to suffer from the opposite problem, and am constantly running slightly behind schedule. For this reason, while I keep it on hand throughout the course, we often do not have time for it at all.

It seems to require some panache to pull off in style. It was most successful the year I was able to exploit the skills of Andrea Sudbury, a seasoned caller from the bingo-halls of the northern hemisphere. She put impressive effort into devising 'bingo'-type embellished descriptions for various IPA categories, and called the cards with spookily professional intonation.

2.10 Computer tricks

It is very handy to be able to spontaneously record people and then immediately examine their speech. I take a head-mounted microphone to class, so that I can record onto my laptop and open the recording directly in Praat. This is particularly interesting if you have students from different language backgrounds in your class. For example, when I am teaching about pitch, I usually ask a speaker of a tonal language to record a few phrases, and then open this in Praat to show students how to read a pitch tracker. I usually also record myself or a student saying /t/ both initially and post-fricative, as part of the demonstration following the flame. Students can see or feel the difference in aspiration, but it is nonetheless very difficult for them to hear it. If you can play 'stan' without the /s/, they instantly realise how very /d/-like the sound is.

There are a number of good interactive IPA charts available. I keep them bookmarked, and access them over the internet when necessary. Peter Ladefoged's chart is at http://www.phonetics.ucla.edu/course/chapter1/chapter1.html. York University also has one at http://www.yorku.ca/earmstro/ipa/. You could also use the CD provided by Ladefoged in *Vowels and consonants* (2004). I find this comforting to have on hand for times when my production confidence is shaken, and I am unsure of the accuracy with which I may be producing a certain obscure sound. If you play them the sound from the interactive IPA, it provides a nice, authoritative source. Having the sound files available also means you can demonstrate what any sound happens to look like in a spectrogram, should this become relevant in the discussion.

Students seem to best develop an understanding of the component parts of speech when they are actually able to hear them separately. Using speech synthesis to demonstrate the component parts that contribute to natural sounding speech is a handy teaching device. For this purpose, I tend to lift and use Peter Ladefoged's nice 'A bird in the hand is worth two in the bush' demonstration. This is available here: http://hctv.humnet.ucla.edu/departments/linguistics/VowelsandConsonants/vowels/chapter7/abirdinthehand.html. It provides nine versions of the sentence – formants 1, 2 and 3 separately, the first three formants all together, the first three formants + higher formants, the non-periodic sounds, all of the above together, and all of the above together with pitch movement. The latter file is a reasonably convincing synthesis of a male voice producing the sentence. If you play each of formants 1, 2 and 3 separately first, students cannot make out the content. But if you play them together, they usually can. Playing them separately after students have heard them together enables the listener to tune in to the separate sounds of the different formants. And the non-periodic sounds have a funky beat-box-type effect that never fails to amuse.

A quick search of the Web also turns up many other useful demonstrations. Video demos of vocal-fold vibration are indispensable, as are X-ray videos of tongue movement. There are also a variety of online demonstrations of the McGurk effect, and of Categorical Perception tasks, which are nice and handy.

2.11 Conclusion

Obviously 'a bag of tricks' is just that, and is no substitute for good teaching. The majority of my classes are in fact much less vaudevillian than the above might suggest. But I have taken the easy way out here, as the contents of the bag of tricks is infinitely simpler to articulate than the characteristics that make for good phonetics teaching. However, I do believe that students learn better when they are able to experience a phenomenon first hand, rather than when it is explained to them in relatively abstract terms. I also believe that the degree to which one can engage the students and keep the classroom lively and interesting has a direct effect on the students' learning, and interesting demonstrations certainly help with this. I have also found that such demonstrations are effective in breaking down barriers, both between the students, and between them and me, and positively influence students' willingness to stick with me during the material that is inherently somewhat drier. These demonstrations are regularly mentioned in the positive comments on my phonetics teaching evaluations, with balloons and lollipops being particular favourites. The most negative comments usually relate to my bad handwriting and the sometimes illegible nature of my whiteboard technique. As with all things, one can only do one's best. While I have done my best to respond to this criticism, I am assured there is still room for considerable improvement.

References

Ladefoged, P. 1982. *A course in phonetics*. 2nd edn; New York: Harcourt Brace Jovanovic.

Ladefoged, P. 2004. *Vowels and consonants*. Malden, MA: Blackwell Publishing. (audio files available from: http://www.phonetics.ucla.edu/vowels/contents.html)

Notes

* **Jen Hay**

I entered Victoria University of Wellington as an undergraduate, unsure of whether I wanted to do languages, English, computer science or psychology. In the end, I embarked on a major in 'Modern Languages'. Fortunately, this major required one to take some linguistics credits. I was immediately hooked, and added in linguistics as a second major. I continued to do honours in linguistics, during which Janet Holmes presented me with a pile of pamphlets about overseas PhD programmes. In the absence of any alternative plan, I applied to a bunch of US programmes, and then settled down to write an MA thesis on 'Gender and Humour' while I waited for the outcome. I hadn't decided what I would focus on in my PhD (or really even if I wanted to do it) – and was simultaneously applying to PhDs in cognitive science and sociolinguistics.

I found myself in the PhD programme at Northwestern – a choice which was essentially a way of postponing any decision about my specialty (sociolinguistics and cognitive science were both possible options). There, I gelled with Janet Pierrehumbert, who was tremendously inspiring and tolerant, and who supervised my PhD (on 'Causes and Consequences of Word Structure'). Somewhere in the process of completing my PhD, I decided I would quite like to be an academic, if possible, although I was also dead set on returning to New Zealand, and wasn't sure if these would be compatible. Luckily, I managed to get a postdoctoral position at Canterbury in the 'Origins of New Zealand English' project, and from there moved to a permanent job in the Linguistics Department. I am still at Canterbury, where I have recently become Director of the 'New Zealand Institute of Language, Brain and Behaviour'.

I am still regularly accused of being unfocused. That there is some truth to this is indicated by the many different ways I seem to get introduced to people. I am variably introduced as a sociolinguist, a morphologist, a phonetician and a laboratory phonologist. But since I've managed to come this far without choosing a sub-discipline, I figure I should now be able to continue the avoidance indefinitely.

3 Learning phonology as a way to learn how theories are improved

*Andrew Carstairs-McCarthy**

3.1 Recent history of phonology

In some disciplines, theoretical innovations come thick and fast, even at the level of undergraduate study; in others, background assumptions remain pretty much unchanged for decades. Also, in some disciplines, a particular analytical framework can be identified, reasonably uncontroversially, as the 'mainstream' framework at any one time; in others this is not so. Many of the difficulties and the opportunities presented by teaching any discipline are affected by its settings for these two parameters (so to speak). Phonology, broadly speaking, combines rapid theoretical innovation with an identifiable mainstream.

In the early 1970s, the mainstream framework was that of Chomsky and Halle's *The sound pattern of English* (SPE) (1968). The subtitle of Anderson's *Phonology in the twentieth century* (1985) draws attention to the contrast between 'rules' and 'representations'. In the SPE framework, rules were in the ascendant. Phonological representations were relatively uninteresting. They were basically linear strings of segments and boundaries, the segments consisting of unordered matrices of binary distinctive features, each with its value (plus or minus). But, from the late 1970s on, analytical emphasis shifted in the direction of more sophisticated structuring of representations, both syntagmatic and paradigmatic.

On the syntagmatic dimension, the syllable reasserted itself, in recognition of the inadequacies of the binary feature [±syllabic]. The syllable came to be established as a unit in a hierarchy whose higher-level units were the foot and the (phonological) word. Independently, the foot and the phonological word were deriving support from new approaches to prominence and metrical structure, inspired in part by inadequacies of the binary feature [±stress]. Meanwhile, on the paradigmatic dimension, 'feature geometry' revived insights of Firthian phonology (Palmer 1970), allowing one-to-many and many-to-one links between feature values on distinct autosegmental tiers, and between these tiers and the syntagmatic units of phonology, particularly the individual segment. At the same time, the distinction between 'feature' and 'feature value' became blurred, with a new readiness to recognize non-binary features: thus, instead of a binary feature [±coronal], many phonologists now recognize a single-valued feature [coronal] in a mutually exclusive relationship with [dorsal] and [labial] and perhaps [guttural], all linked to one node for '(consonantal) place' in feature geometry's three-dimensional 'bottle-brush' structure – not hard to visualize but difficult to represent on the printed page.

The next big innovation involved the relationship between inputs and outputs, or between underlying and surface representations. The terms 'input' and 'output' conjure up an image of a factory production line, with raw materials entering at one end, being subjected to a succession of manufacturing operations ('ordered rules'), and emerging at the other end as a finished product (a pronounceable 'surface representation'). When Optimality Theory (OT) came on the scene in the mid-1990s, the production-line metaphor gave place to a metaphor of a job interview panel: the output representation is not necessarily ideal, but it is 'optimal' in terms of the priorities attached to the various criteria that the applicants are asked to fulfil (or in terms of the 'ranking' of the 'constraints' governing the 'evaluation' of the 'candidates').

The popularity of OT does not mean that students no longer need to know about earlier approaches. In particular, the concerns that gave rise to the recognition of autosegmental tiers are as valid as they ever were. The candidates in an OT tableau are typically represented not in feature-geometric diagrams, but in traditional symbols, perhaps with indication of syllable boundaries and stress – but that is largely because of the typographic difficulty of fitting anything more elaborate into the space available. And SPE-style linear rule notation has not disappeared, because it is such a convenient device for representing phonological processes informally.

Alongside these changes, phonological theory has remained in one respect stable over the last thirty years. Is the allomorphy displayed by the stems of *divine* and *divinity*, or of *leave* and *left*, something that phonology should try to account for, or should it be regarded as a purely morphological phenomenon? Notoriously, SPE treated as the business of phonology all morphophonology except gross suppletion. Most phonologists have retreated from that position now, but not in an orderly fashion. There is still an expectation that phonology should take care of as much morphophonology as possible, but determining the point at which phonology stops remains in the 'too hard' basket. A well-known alternation such as that between [t], [d] and [əd] in regular English past tense forms is typically regarded as the business of phonology, because the allomorphs are phonologically similar, the choice between them is phonologically determined, and (assuming underlying /d/) the distribution [t] and [əd] can be seen as phonotactically motivated. But what about the [t] of *kept*, *bent* and *bought*? Is it the same as the [t] (spelled *-ed*) of *seeped* and *chased*? If it is, what should we say about the differences in the past tense forms of *bend* (*bent*) and *mend* (*mended*)? If not, must we classify *-t* and the [t] allomorph of *-ed* as purely accidental homonyms? And what about the 'zero past' of some verbs that end in coronals, such as *spread*? Should these be treated as underlyingly suffixed, e.g. /spred + d/ or /spred + t/? Theorists and textbook writers alike have generally been silent on such questions in recent years.

There is thus much that students need to know about. The morphophonological issues that I mentioned last are the most difficult to handle satisfactorily at the undergraduate level. One way out for the phonology instructor is to relegate them to a separate course on morphology. For the purposes of this chapter, I will assume that that is what is done. So far as the other issues are concerned, the challenge of covering the ground can be turned into an opportunity to teach important general lessons about scientific method, as I will illustrate.

3.2 Characteristics of good theories and the nature of theoretical improvement

In any discipline, students learn about both content and method. In history, for example, students learn about what happened when, and why; they also learn about how to interpret the available evidence (documents of all kinds, oral traditions, archaeological remains, and so on). This is equally true in linguistics. An important difference between linguistics and history, however, is that the methodology of many areas of linguistics is more akin to that of so-called 'bench sciences' such as physics and chemistry. That is, it is possible in linguistics to conduct replicable experiments. An analysis of a problematic grammatical or phonological phenomenon will often entail predictions about grammatical or phonotactic acceptability that can be tested against the reactions of native speakers. A good analysis, as in physics or chemistry, will be one in which these predictions are generally confirmed, and a particularly good analysis will be one that leads to correct predictions that go beyond the original problem.

A good theory, however, is not just one that leads to valid predictions. A theory may be so accommodating that it is compatible with not merely everything that is observed, but with everything that might conceivably be observed. Karl Popper long ago pointed out that such 'theories' are not really theories at all, because they are empirically empty. A good theory is not merely compatible with as much as possible of what is observed; it is also incompatible with as much as possible of what is not observed. Theoretical improvement is often not a matter of accommodating problematic observations about things that do happen, but rather of supplying new principled reasons for why many things do not happen. One does not have to be a 'naive falsificationist' to agree with Popper on this. Even if the relationship between linguistic theory and the observed phenomena of speech is as indirect as is claimed by Chomskyan linguists, they too agree that a good theory should exclude as much as possible of what does not happen.

In phonology, there are excellent opportunities to illustrate precisely this. I will present three case studies. All of them are based on experience in the phonology section of Canterbury University's 300-level *Theory of Linguistics II* course, which I have taught regularly since 1982.

3.3 Case study 1: Linear rules, ranked constraints, and English /z ~ s ~ əz/

The English pattern of allomorphy exhibited by the regular noun plural and verbal 3rd singular suffix *-s* can easily be described by invoking two SPE-style linear rules: a rule of schwa-epenthesis between sibilants, and a voicing assimilation rule applying to clusters of obstruents. This is how the situation is described by Spencer in his textbook *Phonology* (1996: 49-55). Both of these rules seem satisfactorily 'natural' (whatever precisely that means). Yet in order to achieve the right outcome, we need to make sure that schwa-epenthesis applies before voicing assimilation. In terms of SPE-style phonology, is there a deep reason why these rules are so ordered, or is it just an accidental fact about English?

It is hard to think of any deep reason in SPE terms. Theories of rule-ordering developed in the 1970s distinguished feeding and bleeding orders; but that distinction does not help here. It was suggested then that rules should tend to apply in an order that would maximize feeding and minimize bleeding. The underlying idea seems to have been that speakers (or rather the brains of speakers) will favour a grammar in which every rule is exploited as much as possible. Yet in this English instance, to get the proper plural form for a noun such as *place* ([pleisəz], not *[pleisəs]), schwa-epenthesis must precede and thus bleed voicing assimilation. Could it be, then, that it is just an accident that no dialect of English exists in which the two rules apply in counter-bleeding order, so that the plural of *place* is [pleisəs]?

Native English speakers in my phonology classes tend to agree that a hypothetical English dialect with plural [pleisəs], and in which the plural of *piece* rhymes with *thesis*, seems unlikely. They readily agree that a version of phonological theory that would exclude such a dialect in principle would be an improvement. I therefore conclude my discussion of SPE-style phonological rules by assuring them that such a theory does indeed exist, and that they will encounter it in a few weeks' time, when I introduce Optimality Theory (OT).

In discussing how theoretical preoccupations change, I do not gloss over the influence of mere fashion. I point out that it is probably not an accident that OT began to take off at just the time when word-processing applications acquired the ability to manipulate tables more efficiently, with cells that can be shaded and within which text can be centred or left-justified. Constructing OT tableaux in the 1990s was a novel and enjoyable typographic challenge. This usually elicits a wry laugh. But twenty-first-century students too find OT tableaux fun to use.

One of my first illustrations of OT involves the /z ~ s ~ əz/ and /d ~ t ~ əd/

alternations. Let us suppose that in English a version of the Obligatory Contour Principle ranks high, enforcing 'schwa-insertion' between coda obstruents that are identical in their supralaryngeal feature values. Another high-ranked (indeed, never violated) constraint imposes voicing agreement on tautosyllabic obstruent clusters. To be precise, both these constraints outrank two 'Faithfulness' constraints: DEP-IO and IDENT-IO[voice]. Students find it easy to see that, if the input for the suffixes is /z/ and /d/ respectively, no manipulation of the ranking of these four constraints can ever yield [pleisəs] as optimal for the plural of *place*. Likewise, no manipulation can yield [weitət] as optimal for the past tense of *wait*. The question left hanging by the SPE-style analysis ('Could there ever be a dialect of English in which the plural of *piece* rhymes with *thesis*?') now receives a clear answer: 'No.'

It may seem that a question is begged by assuming /z/ and /d/ as inputs. Surface allomorphs [əs] and [ət] would indeed be possible in a dialect where the inputs for the suffixes were /s/ and /t/ rather /z/ and /d/. But such an analysis would render it hard to account for the choice of the allomorphs /z/ and /d/ after a sonorant other than the 'inserted' schwa, as in *boys*, *bells*, *played* and *called*. After all, the realization of an underlying /s/ and /t/ by [s] and [t], so as to yield, for example, [bɔis] as the plural of *boy* or [pleit] as the past tense of *play*, would be favoured not merely by Faithfulness but also by the unmarked status of voiceless obstruents generally, captured in OT by a constraint such as 'No Voiced Obstruents' or 'OBSTR[−voice]'.

The claim that OBSTR[−voice] applies in English may well provoke a protest from some students. It is good that it should do so, because answering that protest supplies another pedagogical opportunity. 'Surely English just doesn't have any "No Voiced Obstruents" constraint', the protest runs, 'because English has voiced obstruents all over the place, in codas as well as in onsets. It's silly to suggest that this constraint just happens to be ranked low in English!' A more sophisticated complainer may take a Popperian line: 'This suggestion is not just silly but cheating, because the possibility of low ranking renders it impossible in principle to show that any constraint is absent from the grammar of any language!'

The instructor may perhaps sympathize with this complaint. But the instructor is also, for the time being, a spokesperson for John J. McCarthy on behalf of OT. So would McCarthy regard this complaint as fatal? No. He would argue that even low-ranked constraints can turn out to play an active part in the phonology of a language through the phenomenon known as 'the emergence of the unmarked' (McCarthy and Prince 2004). And English supplies neat illustrations of this with respect to OBSTR[−voice]. In most varieties of English, nasal-plosive clusters in coda include [mp, ŋk], where the plosive is voiceless, but not *[mb, ŋg]. Moreover, monomorphemic items can contain voiceless obstruent clusters in coda such as [pt, kt, ps, ks] (*apt*, *act*, *lapse*, *box*), but not voiced ones (*[bd, gd, bz, gz]). In clusters, at least, voiced obstruents are disfavoured.

The determined objector may go on to say: 'But what about [nd] as a coda cluster, as in *land, mend, sound* and many other examples? And what about the voiced obstruent clusters at the end of *robbed, dragged, seethed, grubs, dogs, wreaths, loaves* and so on?' But again, the instructor can turn these examples to good account.

The availability of [nd] as a coda reflects the relatively unmarked status of coronal consonants vis-à-vis those at other places of articulation. This shows up also in two further facts that native English-speaking students can easily discover for themselves, given one or two hints. Heavy rhymes consisting of a diphthong or long vowel followed by an intramorphemic consonant cluster are possible in English, but only if the consonants in the cluster are coronal. Thus we have *wild, field, pint, paint, pound, pounce, strange* and many other such words, but no similar examples with dorsal or labial consonants. Also, the diphthongs [au] and [ɔi] as nuclei tolerate coronals in an accompanying coda, as in *loud, lout, louse, coin, quoit, owl, oil,* but not labials or dorsals (except in phonologically aberrant proper names such as *Doig*). In OT terms, this suggests that the NoCoda constraint made famous by Prince and Smolensky's pioneering analysis of Tagalog (2004: 40-45, originally published in 1993) must be treated as a family of constraints, with the unmarked status of coronals reflected in a universal ranking of NoCoda[labial] and NoCoda[dorsal] above NoCoda[coronal].

The voiced obstruent clusters in *robbed, grubs* and so on contain a morpheme boundary. They can thus be used as an opportunity to discuss how OT treats the tug-of-war in morphology and phonology between Faithfulness and Markedness. In these regularly inflected forms, Faithfulness outranks Markedness, thus yielding optimal forms that contain phonologically awkward combinations. However, in irregular inflection, phonological Markedness constraints are generally not violated: contrast *pens*, the plural of *pen*, with *pence*, the irregular plural of *penny*, and contrast the past tense forms of *ooze* and *lose*: *oozed* has both a 'long' nucleus and a voiced obstruent coda, a combination that is impossible in a syllable with no morpheme boundary, whereas *lost* has the phonological shape of monomorphemic items such as *cost*.

There are admittedly loose ends here. Precisely how are the relevant constraints to be formulated and ranked so as to take care of all these observations? And are we to assume that Faithfulness and Markedness constraints are ranked differently for different sections of the vocabulary, thus sacrificing the analytic discipline imposed by the doctrine that any one language variety observes a single uniform constraint ranking? However, these are encouraging rather than discouraging loose ends. They merely confirm what sensible students already know: that not all problems are yet solved. A few students may indeed be motivated to go on and try to solve them later in their careers. In the light of all this, students are happy to agree that, so far as those extremely familiar English suffixal alternations are concerned, Optimality Theory supplies not merely a new way of analysing the phenomena, but a way that is an improvement on earlier analyses.

3.4 Case study 2: Syllable margins, extrametricality and stress in Tibetan, Attic Greek and Latin

A common error among beginners in phonology is the assumption that the form in which a stem appears when it is on its own must be a better guide to its underlying representation than the forms in which it appears when it is affixed or part of a compound. Every instructor in phonology encounters this assumption. Standard examples used to dislodge it include German lexemes such as *Bund* 'bundle' and *bunt* 'many-coloured', both realizable as [bʊnt] but shown to be phonologically distinct by their contrasting plural forms [bʊndə] and [bʊntə].

Halle and Clements' *Problem book in phonology* (1983:105) provides a more exotic illustration that yields a satisfying 'Aha!' experience as soon as one cottons on to what is happening. In Tibetan, numerals from 11 to 19 (or, at least, such of them as are presented by Halle and Clements) take the form 'ten-one', 'ten-two' and so on, while multiples of 10 take the form 'two-ten', 'three-ten' and so on. Forming these higher numerals in Tibetan thus ought to be a simple matter of compounding the numerals corresponding to 'one' through 'ten'. Students are puzzled to find, however, that some of these compounds contain unexpected medial consonants not found in either of the two elements of the compound when they are on their own. Where do these extra consonants come from? Formulating rules to insert them turns out to be troublesome, and the rules themselves look contrived and unnatural. But what if these consonants are present in underlying representations – specifically, in the underlying representation of the second element of the compounds where they appear? The problem now becomes one of explaining not why they get inserted but why they sometimes get deleted.

The answer to this problem is simple: the first consonant in a word-initial cluster gets deleted. In SPE-style linear notation, this is easy to represent:

(1) C → Ø / #__C

In terms of syllable structure, the phenomenon is equally easy to describe: Tibetan does not tolerate complex onsets. The reason why two-consonant clusters are permitted medially is that the first of the two can be slotted into the coda of the preceding syllable. But a question now arises that is somewhat similar to our earlier question about a hypothetical variety of English in which the plural of *piece* rhymes with *thesis*. There is in principle another way in which an initial consonant cluster could be simplified, namely by deletion of the second consonant. In SPE notation, this is equally easy to express:

(2) C → Ø / #C__

So could there be a dialect of Tibetan in which rule (2) applies rather than rule (1)?

Again, invocation of post-SPE developments suggests that the answer is no. In the notation of (1) and (2), 'C' is an abbreviation for '[−syllabic]'. It therefore has no part in the newer style of representation that exploits the syllable as a structural unit. In this newer framework, let us make the usual assumption that syllable nuclei are sonority peaks and that non-peak segments are assigned to syllables on the basis of two default assumptions: (a) onsets are maximized; (b) onset maximization is subject to sonority sequencing in accordance with the sonority hierarchy (vowels, glides, liquids, nasals, fricatives, plosives). (I call these 'default assumptions' rather than 'universals' for reasons that I will explain later.) On this basis, syllabification is a matter of attaching material to sonority peaks, working outwards from syllable nuclei towards syllable margins. Any segment that is unsyllabifiable (that is, that cannot be attached to a syllable without violating the language's syllabification constraints) will be a segment that is remote from rather than close to a sonority peak. It follows that, if one of two consonants in word-initial position is left unsyllabified, it will be the first, not the second. Actual Tibetan thus behaves as expected, and the hypothetical Tibetan with rule (2) is revealed as impossible (or at least, extremely unlikely).

There are likely to be some students who question the validity of sonority sequencing as a default assumption. If there aren't, instructors themselves should take the initiative in questioning it! Sonority sequencing is violated by forms such as the Russian monosyllables *mgla* 'gloom' and *rta* 'mouth (genitive singular)', and by numerous examples in cluster-friendly languages such as Polish and Georgian. It is also violated by an English monosyllable such as *sprints*, where the initial and final [s] constitute extra sonority peaks. But the instructor can again turn these complaints to good account. In English it may not be an accident that the extra consonants that violate sonority sequencing are always coronal, and that they are often inflectional affixes too. Besides, need it be the case that all unsyllabified consonants are 'deleted'? In Tibetan, it seems, if a consonant is not in either an onset or a coda, it cannot be pronounced. However, Spencer's (1996) analysis of the final [ts] of *convicts* suggests that not all languages are so ruthless. For English, Spencer favours a kind of half-way house: a consonant can belong to a syllable as an 'appendix' at the end without being part of the coda. This raises the possibility of having two layers of syllable structure: the core syllable (consisting of onset and rhyme) and the extended syllable (consisting of onset, rhyme and appendices). Are there any other pedagogically useful phenomena that support the notion of the extended syllable – that is, phenomena which show that it is more than just a device to protect the sonority sequencing generalization? The answer is yes. Kenstowicz (1994: 264-69) cites an intriguing analysis by Steriade (1990) of certain morphological-cum-phonological data in classical Attic Greek.

In Attic Greek verbs, one can distinguish a root and a 'perfect' stem, which is derived from it in various ways. What 'perfect' means in syntactic terms does not matter for present purposes. What matters is that, from roots beginning in a consonant, some perfect stems are formed with a prefixed *e-* (the so-called 'augment') and some with reduplication. At (3) are examples of both:

(3)

Reduplicated perfects			'Augmented' perfects		
lu:	le-luk-a	'untie'	sper	e-spar-mai	'sow'
sɛ:man	se-sɛ:mɛ:n-a	'signify'	zdeug	e-zdeug-mai	'yoke'
$klep^h$	$ke\text{-}klop^h\text{-}a$	'steal'	kten	e-kton-a	'kill'
tlă	te-tla-men	'endure'	psau	e-psauk-a	'touch'
knai	ke-knɛ:s-mai	'scrape'	$smuk^h$	e-smug-mai	'smoulder'
pneu	pe-pneuk-a	'breathe'			
$grap^h$	$ge\text{-}grap^h\text{-}a$	'write'			

What determines whether a verb takes reduplication or the augment? Steriade argues that the crucial factor is sonority distance. In the examples with reduplication, the root begins either with a single consonant or with a cluster in which there is a relatively large sonority gap between the first and second consonants. On the other hand, in the examples with the augment, the root begins with a consonant cluster within which the sonority gap is small (e.g. [ps], [sm]) or nonexistent ([kt]), or in which sonority sequencing is violated ([sp]).

This is where the distinction between core syllabification and extended syllabification comes in. Let us assume that, for Greek, core syllabification requires in onset clusters a sonority gap at least as big as that between plosives and nasals. On that basis, reduplication occurs when core syllabification is able to assign the whole of any root-initial consonant cluster to a syllable onset. But if one consonant of a root-initial cluster is not syllabifiable in this way, then the perfect stem is formed with augment rather than with reduplication.

Let us consider the root *kten-* 'kill'. (In the perfect stem, the vowel is ablauted to *-o-*, which need not concern us.) Core syllabification leaves [k] out in the cold. With the addition of the augment *e-*, [k] becomes syllabifiable as a coda consonant: [ek.to.na]. What happens, however, when the stem of this verb is not preceded by an affix of any kind? This does indeed occur, for example in the present tense. No coda slot is available for the [k] here. So does Greek, like Tibetan, ruthlessly refuse to let the initial [k] be pronounced? It turns out that Greek is more tolerant than Tibetan. In forms such as [kteinɔ:] 'I kill', [k] is permitted to remain – just as, in English, segments can be pronounced even though they lie outside the core syllable (in Spencer's analysis). We may reasonably regard [ktei] here as an extended syllable, with [k] belonging to the syllable but not to its onset. Students can thus be led to see that the idea that lies behind syllable 'appendices' has an application outside English.

I mentioned earlier that the syllable as a syntagmatic phonological unit came to be seen from the late 1970s as just one unit within a prosodic hierarchy, below the foot and the phonological word. So do we find at higher levels phenomena comparable to the syllable 'appendix'? Our theory leads us to expect that peripheral units at other levels too should be able to behave as if they are somehow outside the core structure. Therefore it is satisfying to be able to present to students data that support this.

Within metrical theory, there developed at an early stage a doctrine of 'extrametricality', according to which syllables that are endmost in the phonological word may be deemed extrametrical from the point of view of foot formation. A nice illustration of this is supplied by the Latin stress rule: 'stress the penultimate syllable if it is heavy, otherwise the antepenultimate'. Here is an SPE-style formulation:

(4) $V \rightarrow [+\text{stress}] / \_\_\_ C_0 ([V, -\text{long}]\ C^1)\ V\ C_0\ \#$

But could there be a pseudo-Latin with the following stress rule instead?

(5) $V \rightarrow [+\text{stress}] / \_\_\_ C_0 ([V, +\text{long}]\ C^1)\ V\ C_0\ \#$

In this pseudo-Latin, what the parentheses require us to skip is precisely a certain kind of heavy syllable, not a light one. That seems highly improbable. Yet in SPE terms the two processes are equally easy to state. So students are easily persuaded that the SPE-style formulation is unsatisfactory.

Happily, a better way of describing things emerges once we recognize the foot as a metrical unit – provided that we permit a word-final syllable to be 'extrametrical', that is, outside any foot, just as a syllable-final consonant can be outside the syllable's coda. If we treat the final syllable in Latin words as extrametrical, then Latin word stress exactly fits the following metrical parameter settings (Spencer 1996: 250-51):

1. words are right-headed;
2. foot-formation starts at the right edge of the word;
3. foot-formation is quantity-sensitive (i.e. every heavy syllable is the head of its foot);
4. feet are left-headed;
5. feet are maximally binary.

Latin stress behaviour thus turns out to be not one of an almost infinite range of conceivable patterns, as the SPE-style rule implies. Instead, it is constrained along a number of dimensions. What is more, if the freedom implied by the SPE formulation were genuine, it would be hugely surprising if some language unrelated to

Latin were to observe precisely the same rule. On the other hand, if it is a matter of choosing settings for a small list of parameters, such a coincidence would be less remarkable. And it turns out that Bedouin Hejazi Arabic behaves just the same as Latin (or at least, that fragment of Bedouin Hejazi Arabic that is presented by Spencer as an exercise [1996: 264]).

This chain of examples has led from a problem about determining underlying representations in Tibetan to the issue of how to describe stress in Latin. The route was determined by the search for theoretical improvements, at a level readily graspable by undergraduates. The search has been broadly successful. Admittedly, there are loose ends. For example, is it really the case that settings for parameters (1)–(5) are independent? But these are (once again) loose ends of an encouraging kind. They are consistent with a view of phonological theory as illustrating how analyses that merely 'work' can be replaced by analyses that, at least in some degree, explain.

3.5 Case study 3: The distribution of final /e/ on Spanish nouns

A substantial minority of Spanish nouns end in *-e* or a consonant in the singular (e.g. *nube* 'cloud', *mes* 'month'). All of these end in *-es* in the plural (*meses*, *nubes*). Let us call these Type A and Type B respectively. An obvious question arises: Is membership of these patterns arbitrary (that is, lexically determined) or is it predictable? That is, are Types A and B really variants of a single pattern? This case study shows how students can be led to see that the distribution of nouns between the two patterns is predictable (with very few exceptions), but that stating the relevant generalizations poses frustrating problems in a rule-based framework – problems that disappear once one looks at it in terms of ranked constraints.

Here are some relevant data:

(6)

Type A			Type B		
Singular	Plural		Singular	Plural	
[ˈxefe]	[ˈxefes]	'chief'	[reð]	[ˈreðes]	'net'
[ˈsjeɾpe]	[ˈsjeɾpes]	'snake'	[mjel]	[ˈmjeles]	'honey'
[ˈnuβe]	[ˈnuβes]	'cloud'	[maɾ]	[ˈmaɾes]	'sea'
[ˈombre]	[ˈombres]	'men'	[ˈorðen]	[ˈorðenes]	'order'
[ˈpljeɣe]	[ˈpljeɣes]	'fold'	[mes]	[ˈmeses]	'month'
[ˈbuke]	[ˈbukes]	'boat'	[beθ]	[ˈbeθes]	'time'
[paˈleŋke]	[paˈleŋkes]	'palisade'			
[alˈkalde]	[alˈkaldes]	'mayor'			
[ˈpaɾte]	[ˈpaɾtes]	'part'			
[ˈpaðre]	[ˈpaðres]	'father'			

The search for a pattern can be conducted as a brain-storming exercise in class. Before long, the students will collectively conclude that the Type B nouns in the singular all end in a single coronal consonant, whereas in the Type A nouns what precedes the final [e] or [es] is anything but a single coronal consonant: a labial or dorsal consonant or else a consonant cluster. Honesty impels me at this point to admit to students that this pattern is not absolutely exceptionless: for example, the noun *reloj* [reˈlox] 'clock' belongs to Type B despite the fact that it ends in a non-coronal consonant. But students are generally willing to accept that lexical exceptionality, or else failure so far to discover interfering factors of general relevance, does not vitiate the usefulness of exploring patterns such as that involving coronal articulation here.

Now the question arises of what this pattern implies for underlying representations. Is it that the final [e] is underlyingly present in both Type A and Type B (hence [ˈxefe] and [reð] reflect /xefe/ and /reðe/), so that it gets deleted in the singular of Type B? Alternatively, is this [e] absent underlyingly, so that it gets inserted everywhere that it occurs?

I encourage students to explore first the insertion hypothesis. To take care of the plurals of both types, it is easy enough to devise an SPE-style rule that splits up a word-final cluster /Cs/, especially as Spanish lacks such clusters except in a very few learned words such as *tórax* 'thorax'. But what of the singulars of Type A? The environment for insertion is a disjunction of conditions: after a consonant cluster, or a single consonant that is labial or dorsal. In SPE notation such an environment is expressible with curly brackets. But I put to my students the widely held view that curly brackets represent an admission of defeat: a failure to find an appropriate generalization, due to a weakness in either the particular analysis or the theory itself. They are accordingly not satisfied with this analysis. Even if one's theory treats '[−coronal]' as designating a natural class of sounds – something rejected in Spencer's (1996) framework, where CORONAL, LABIAL and DORSAL are treated as single-valued features, or as three values for a feature PLACE – '[−coronal]' will not suffice here, because of examples such as [alˈkalde], [ˈparte] and [ˈpaðre], where /e/ remains after a coronal cluster.

What of the deletion hypothesis, then? It is easy enough to formulate a rule that deletes word-final /e/ after a single word-final coronal consonant. But students who have become used to recognizing the syllable as a phonological unit are rightly unsatisfied with this. After the deletion, the coronal consonant in question is necessarily syllabified in a coda. The distribution of this final [e] seems therefore to be tied closely to what is permissible in Spanish codas. The data suggest a preference in Spanish for codas to consist of a single coronal consonant. (Prima facie counterexamples such as [ˈom.bre] and [pa.ˈleŋ.ke], assuming that they are syllabified in this way, are easily accounted for in terms of assimilation by nasals to the place of articulation of a following plosive.) But there is no way to formulate as an SPE-style rule the instruction 'Delete word-final /e/ if the result would be a well-formed coda'. Even if input strings are syllabified before /e/-deletion takes place, we are no better off: input strings such as /xefe/ and /reðe/ will naturally be syllabified as [xe.fe] and [re.ðe], so that Types A and B are not differentiated, with both [f] and [ð] assigned to onsets.

What is the way forward, then? By this stage students need little encouragement to explore an Optimality-Theoretic solution. Let us assume that Spanish assigns a high rank to the already familiar constraint CODA[coronal], a member of the family of coda constraints whose patriarch, so to speak, is NOCODA. Let us assume in particular that this outranks the anti-insertion constraint DEP-IO, and that inputs for both Type A and Type B lack the final [e], as in the insertion hypothesis. It is easy to see now that CODA[coronal] and DEP-IO, thus ranked, will favour [xe.fe] and [reð] over *[xef] and *[re.ðe] as outputs for /xef/ and /reð/ respectively. To ensure that [paɾ.te] and [al.kal.de] beat *[paɾt] and *[al.kald] as the optimal outputs for /paɾte/ and /alkald/, something more is necessary; plausibly, perhaps, a high-ranked constraint NOCOMPLEXCODA (another member of the NOCODA family). Anyway, there is plenty of scope for students to work out as an exercise what constraints are needed, and with what ranking, to exclude various wrong but not implausible candidates for selected nouns belonging to Types A and B.

Yet again, there are loose ends. For example, why in particular should [e] be the vowel that gets inserted in Spanish, rather than some other vowel? And what about the rare noncoronal codas that do exist: not only in *reloj*, *tórax*, *ombre* [ˈom.bre] and *palenque* [pa.ˈleŋ.ke] but also in words such as *pacto*, *apto*, *elección* (Harris 1983: 18)? Again, however, these are loose ends that should inspire rather than discourage those students who are keen enough to explore further on their own.

3.6 Conclusion

Very few of the students that I have taught since 1982 have gone on to become phonologists by profession. But many of them, with a little encouragement, have become quite adept at hypothesis testing and at understanding the difference between a good theory and a less good theory. What happens in phonology, and why, seems to me less mysterious than what happens in syntax (a field that I know less about), and much less mysterious than what happens in morphology (a field that I know more about but still do not understand well). That is a subjective reaction. However, even instructors whose subjective reaction is different from mine may agree that there is unusual scope in phonology to look at the same body of data from the point of view of a range of theoretical approaches, and thus build students' understanding of how a science progresses

References

Anderson, S.R. 1985. *Phonology in the twentieth century: Theories of rules and theories of representations*. Chicago: University of Chicago Press.

Chomsky, N. and M. Halle. 1968. *The sound pattern of English*. New York: Harper & Row.

Halle, M. and G.N. Clements. 1983. *Problem book in phonology*. Cambridge, MA: MIT Press.

Harris, J. 1983. *Syllable structure and stress in Spanish*. Cambridge, MA: MIT Press.

Kenstowicz, M. 1994. *Phonology in generative grammar*. Oxford: Blackwell.

McCarthy, J.J. and A. Prince. 2004. 'The emergence of the unmarked'. In *Optimality theory in phonology: A reader*, pp. 483-494, ed. J.J. McCarthy. Oxford: Blackwell.

Palmer, F.R. (ed.) 1970. *Prosodic analysis*. Oxford: Oxford University Press.

Prince, A. and P. Smolensky. 2004. *Optimality theory: Constraint interaction in generative grammar*. Oxford: Blackwell. (Originally distributed in 1993 by Rutgers University Center for Cognitive Science as RuCCS TR-2.)

Spencer, A. 1996. *Phonology: Theory and description*. Oxford: Blackwell.

Steriade, D. 1990. *Greek prosodies and the nature of syllabification*. New York: Garland.

Notes

* **Andrew Carstairs-McCarthy**

It wasn't until about 1966 that a university philosophy tutor introduced me to an influential linguistic work published in 1957: Noam Chomsky's *Syntactic structures*. But as a schoolboy, I had already become fascinated by another book on linguistics published that year: *Modern linguistics* by Simeon Potter. In my early teens I also enjoyed *The loom of language* by Fred Bodmer, *The story of language* by Mario Pei, and books on etymologies and the history of English by writers such as G.H. Vallins, Ivor Brown and Ernest Weekley.

Against this background, real live academic linguistics didn't turn out to be at all what I had expected! As a postgraduate student at London University (the School of Oriental and African Studies) I learned about J.R. Firth's prosodies and phonematic units, and about American structuralism as represented in *Readings in linguistics I*. But it was in the PhD programme at MIT that I really found out how little I knew – and how little it mattered (apparently) for a linguist to have my sort of interest in languages. So in 1972 I decided that academic linguistics was after all not for me.

In 1979 I had another go. The School of Oriental and African Studies kindly let me back in as a PhD student. Theodora Bynon and Geoffrey Horrocks tolerated encouragingly my hunch that inflectional morphology was less of a muddle than most people thought, and the enthusiasm for Karl Popper that I had picked up as a philosophy undergraduate gave me a methodological angle: what a theory must account for is not what happens but what doesn't happen. That's still an important message at more than one level: both in helping undergraduates to draw sound conclusions from evidence, and in countering the strange but fashionable notion that language is only really interesting to the extent that it is 'perfect'.

4 Teaching morphology

Laurie Bauer[*]

Introductory morphology teaching is often little more than a naming of parts. The vocabulary is daunting for the introductory student (particularly once we move from 'prefix' and 'suffix' to 'morph', 'allomorph' and 'morpheme'), but the fundamental idea that words might contain meaningful parts is unlikely to come as a surprise to anyone being taught even in English – a language notoriously poor in morphology. If they are led carefully through well-selected data, most students can pick up the basic ideas fairly rapidly, though there are a few areas which are likely to cause recurrent problems: in my experience morph and allomorph, lexeme, word-form and grammatical word, and drawing tree structures for words are continual sources of difficulty for some (but not all) beginning students. I should add that many of the other notions which are introduced as being simple turn out not to be so simple on closer acquaintance, but I assume that we will in general choose examples which do not give rise to insuperable problems in the first instance.

It is once we move on from this introductory level that we have to ask where we want the student to end up. If we are going to be teaching paradigm structure morphology, we might not care very much about the niceties of morph and morpheme; if we are going to be teaching a syntax-of-words approach, we might not care much about the difference between word-forms and lexemes. While we may feel some obligation to teach even those aspects of the general background to which we do not ourselves subscribe, it is pleasant to be able to play down some awkward terminological or theoretical point if we are not going to exploit it.

But there is one area which nobody who wants to have more than a passing acquaintance with morphology can ignore: everybody needs to be able to present an analysis of a word into elements which are morphological in nature rather than purely phonological or purely semantic. Independent of their theoretical stance, all morphologists are going to agree that *poodle* does not contain a morphological element whose meaning is 'dog', and are going to agree that the syllabic structure and the morphological structure of, say, Russian *s·put·nik* (with·way·one = 'fellow-traveller, sputnik') do not coincide. Any linguist who wants to write a description of some linguistic data, and especially any linguist who wants to consider the morphology, semantics or etymology of some aspect of a given language, has to be able to determine, at least in the clear cases, what the units within the word are.

It is surprising how bad students are at this. Even advanced students will find an affix *-ness* in *governess*. While one hopes it is a slip, it appears to be a recurrent slip! And a trick question like asking for the elements in *distressing* can lead to all kinds of wonderful answers.

Part of the difficulty for the teacher here is that morphological analysis requires a certain degree of familiarity with the language to be analysed. That is why, in very elementary morphological exercises, we prefer to present data from languages in which the relevant morphology is word-based rather than stem-based (Bloomfield 1935: 225) and why we almost invariably provide information about base forms in the data for the problem. If we want to open things up completely, we need to use a language where we can presuppose some knowledge of the available forms. In courses taught in English this will largely mean English. It happens that English not only has an impoverished inflectional morphology, it is also etymologically extremely confused, with not only Germanic elements but also Romance, Latin and Greek elements. This means that problems based on English material, apart from the obvious cases of inflectional allomorphy, are likely to be focused on derivational material, and have to avoid a minefield of etymological traps. Some apparently simple questions are very difficult for beginning students to answer. Are *-ery*, *-ary* and *-ry* allomorphs of the same morpheme, and if so what is the conditioning factor? Are *-er* and *-or* allomorphs of a single morpheme? How many morphemes of form *-er* should we distinguish in English? What is the relationship between *-able* and *-ible*?

A simple example of the problems we face when dealing with English is that it is remarkably difficult to get clear cases of polysyllabic monomorphemic words in English. If we present most classes with a word like *hippopotamus*, there will be one or more students who wish to split it into several morphemes on the basis of parallels like *hippodrome*. The proliferation of cranberry morphs does not worry most beginning students. Once beginning students are introduced to the notion of morphological analysis, what we might call the folk-etymological urge takes over: they see morphs everywhere, even if they are asked to justify every morph they isolate. But if we want to make sure that they can isolate morphs when they see them, we have to test them with some monomorphemic words. A word like *dog* is not a problem; most will expect that to be monomorphemic because it is so short. But some people will see (with some etymological justification) several morphs in *quarantine*. However, it seems relevant to provide a short list of polysyllabic monomorphemic words of English for such exercises. The words in (1) seem fairly clearly to be monomorphemic. We should add that words like *bahuvrihi*, *perestroika*, *rangatiratanga*, *Schadenfreude* and *Weltanschauung* are probably to be treated as monomorphemic in English, even if they are not in their original languages.

(1) Polysyllabic words which are probably monomorphemic in English

antelope
asparagus
attitude
bagatelle
balderdash
baobab
basilica
believe
besom
blaspheme
bulletin
buttress
caravan
carpet
catamaran
chimpanzee
cummerbund
cylinder
diamond
dimple
domain
elephant
entertain
fashion
fetish
fiasco
furbelow
giraffe
guarantee
magazine
moustache
parsimony
pattern
pelican
pemmican
penguin
rostrum
sepulchre
seraglio
stupid
sturgeon
terrapin
tortoise
umbrella
verandah
yoghurt

Some of these words are more easily mistaken for polymorphemic than others, but if added judiciously to lists of words for morphological analysis, they should act to countervail the folk-etymological urge.

One point which it is difficult to communicate to students is the problem posed by unique morphs (cranberry morphs). The general rule is that morphological analysis demands exhaustivity of analysis: there should be no part of a word which is not attributed to one morph (and morpheme) or another (and equally, no part of a word which is attributed to more than one morph(eme)). However, we all know that unique morphs exist. Some words which probably contain unique morphs are listed under (2). The question is how frequent such an occurrence is.

(2) Words which may contain a unique morph

bilberry
bishopric
cartoon
clientele
curious
deciduous
demolish
fluctuate
nightingale
perdition

The general perception of phonaesthemes seems to be that they are not morphs/morphemes. One of the reasons for this is that if they were they would create far too many unique morphs. Consider *gleam*, *glimmer*, *glint*, *glisten*, *glitter*, *gloom*, which are often considered to set up a phonaestheme /gl/, connected with light. If we analyse this /gl/ as a morphological element, we imply that the remainder is also an element (or a series of elements) available for further combination. *Beam* exists and might be related to *gleam*, but *bitter*, *boom* do not seem to be related as correlates of *glitter* and *gloom* in any obvious way; *shimmer* exists, but there is no corresponding form for any of the other words; *flitter* and *twitter* do not appear to be related to *glitter*, although all might be said to share a semantic feature of frequentitiveness, which Marchand (1969: 273) attributes to a final *-er* morpheme; *bloom* is the only word which might be at all related to *gloom* on the same pattern. In other words, *-eam*, *-immer*, *-int*, *-isten*, *-itter*, *-oom* would be established as unique morphs if *gl-* were taken to be a morph. But if this is too much, there is no obvious level at which unique morphs are acceptable. Perhaps what we have to say is that no morph that is ever set up should have the effect of creating a series of unique morphs. Some of the examples in (2) might lead one to query the suitability of even this simple rule. Perhaps it should be modified to read 'no morph that is ever set up should have the effect of creating a series of unique morphs which outnumbers the number of words for which it provides a suitable explanation of the meaning of the words in which it occurs'. This is, of course, considerably weaker.

As well as the folk-etymological urge, another problem that besets the beginning analyser of words is the assumption that because a certain form has a given meaning in one place, it retains that meaning everywhere. This brings us back to the *governess* problem, although in *governess* the correct analysis should, we might think, also be clear on a superficial glance. Perhaps the irregularity in the formation of the word (why isn't it *governoress*? There do not appear to be any other examples where *-ess* is added direct to something which is clearly a verb) has a greater impact than we perceive.

As an example, consider words ending in *-er*. There is a great temptation to see these as being agentive (or, failing that, to be comparative). This is probably the most common use of this final syllable, and the *burgle* backformation from *burglar* shows how powerful it can be. Some examples where final *-er* is not (or is probably not – recall the *flitter*, *glimmer*, *twitter* examples) a suffix are given in (3).

Again, the judicious use of such examples among others in which *-er* is a suffix can be a useful pedagogical tool. Note, too, that there are generalizations to be made here. *Deter* and *inter* cannot have the expected *-er* because of the stress; they are also verbs, which is the wrong part of speech for the expected *-er* morph (though perhaps not for the frequentative one, if that is still analysable in English); some of the words in (3) are adjectives, and a similar point can be made. Although *-er* has been used as an example here, other similar instances are not hard to find: final *-al* and *-y* are obvious places to look.

(3) Words in *-er* which do not contain a suffix

aster	fever	paper
clever	hammer	patter
clover	hyper	quiver (two senses available)
clutter	inter	scatter
dagger	isomer	sever
dapper	letter (in the usual reading)	sewer (in the usual reading)
deter	litter	shelter
dicker	matter	temper (two senses available)
dither	never	utter (two senses available)
falter	otter	water
fester	over	winter

At some point in this kind of analysis, though, the question arises as to when you are dealing with two occurrences of the same morpheme and when you are dealing with two different morphemes. English abounds in such cases, and the instructor really needs some kind of guidelines available for students. Bauer (2003: Chapter 9) gives some suggestions, but the criteria provided there are not always clear-cut, and are certainly not all of equal importance. The important thing is not to allow semantic difference to become the main or only criterion. It is a very important criterion, but a semantic difference can be found between the meanings of affixes in almost any two words, and students are willing to argue for semantic differences without any thought of what might be part of the pragmatics of general use and what might be part of the definition of the affix. This criterion, therefore, if overused, simply leads to unproductive discussion in the classroom.

As an example, consider *-er* again. In *bus-driver* it denotes an agent, in *concrete-mixer* it denotes an instrument (under normal circumstances, at least). Does this mean that two morphemes are involved? Or is there a higher generalisation, namely that *-er* simply picks up on the subject argument of the verb? Dressler (1986) argues that agents and instruments are, in any case, closely linked. If a class of students has a major rule that semantic difference is sufficient to establish separate morphemes, they will inevitably conclude that there are two morphemes here, whatever the instructor wants to conclude.

Some examples of instances which can be considered within this general framework are given in (4). In some cases it might seem blindingly obvious whether one or more than one morpheme is involved, in others a thesis might be required to answer that question fully. In virtually every case, though, there are general points about morphological analysis to be made. For students at the beginning of their careers, even collecting examples which might belong to each of the two categories is likely to provide a challenge. This remains true when they are encouraged to use standard handbooks, dictionaries, and reverse dictionaries such as Lehnert (1971) or Muthmann (1999).

(4)

Affix	*Example of first use*	*Example of contrasting use*
-able	employable	marriageable
-age	parsonage	coverage
-al	parental	rebuttal
dis-	disown	disarm
-en/-ed	he has eaten	he has been eaten
-er	killer	Londoner
-ish	waspish	thirty-ish
-s	employs	hedgehogs
un-	unintelligent	untie
-y	modesty	constancy

The 'one or two morphemes?' question can be asked where there is synonymy as well as where there is homophony. In (5) there are some examples with synonymous or near synonymous, but not necessarily homophonous, morphs which may or may not belong to the same morpheme. The question of contrast becomes important here. In phonology problems, a single minimal pair will be sufficient to establish two phonemes (although whether *billow* versus *below* is sufficient to say that stress is phonemic in English is an interesting question). It is less clear that the pair *sailer* ('a boat') versus *sailor* ('a person') is sufficient to establish that *-er* and *-or* are morphs belonging to separate morphemes.

(5)

Form 1	*Example*	*Form 2*	*Example*
-able	defendable	-ible	defensible
-al	herbal	-ial	proverbial
-al	suffixal	-ual	sexual
-al	natural	-ar	polar
demi-	demigod	semi-	semitone
en-...-en	enliven	-en	brighten
-er	exerciser	-or	incisor
-ise	legalise	-ify	simplify
pre-	pre-pay	fore-	foretell

Note that some of these are excluded in classical morpheme theory from being allomorphs of the same morpheme because they do not share (enough) form. However, since there are no guidelines on what sufficient form is, in this context, and since Plag (1999: 204) argues that *-ise* and *-ify* should be seen as allomorphs, it seems worthwhile to widen the possible range of forms in exercises of this type.

Conclusion

Although English does not have a particularly elaborate morphology, it does present us with enough data to train students in many of the problems of morphological analysis. The instructor needs to take care in making clear to students just what will be accepted as evidence, and probably has to be willing to suspend his or her own judgement about what the 'correct' answer may be in any given instance; in some cases it may be sufficient for the instructor to be willing to play devil's advocate and argue against any proposed hypothesis. In the very nature of English, many phenomena which will create problems of analysis in other languages will simply never arise. But if students are used to thinking about potential objections and presenting arguments based on evidence, this should stand them in good stead.

References

Bauer, L. 2003. *Introducing linguistic morphology*. 2nd edn; Edinburgh: Edinburgh University Press.

Bloomfield, L. 1935. *Language*. London: Allen & Unwin.

Dressler, W.U. 1986. 'Explanation in Natural Morphology, illustrated with comparative and agent-noun formation'. *Linguistics* 24: 519-48.

Lehnert, M. 1971. *Rückläufiges Wörterbuch der englischen Gegenwartssprache/ Reverse dictionary of present-day English*. Leipzig: VEB.

Marchand, H. 1969. *The categories and types of present-day English word-formation*. 2nd edn; Munich: Beck.

Muthmann, G. 1999. *Reverse English dictionary*. Berlin and New York: Mouton de Gruyter.

Plag, I. 1999. *Morphological productivity*. Berlin and New York: Mouton de Gruyter.

Notes

[*] **Laurie Bauer**

Laurie Bauer did undergraduate work in linguistics at the University of Edinburgh in an attempt to avoid the formal study of literature. He met many good teachers in phonetics and linguistics, notably David Abercrombie, Gillian Brown, W.E. Jones, John Laver and John Lyons (who taught final-year morphology). On completing his MA(Hons) he went to study in Denmark for eight months, worked as a bilingual lexicographer for several months on the Collins–Robert French–English dictionary, and then returned to study for his PhD at the University of Edinburgh under the supervision of Jim Miller and Duncan McMillan. On graduating from Edinburgh, he went to Odense, Denmark, where Hans Hartvigson and Hans Basbøll were great influences. Then in 1979 he moved to Wellington, where he has been ever since. He is currently Professor of Linguistics and Dean of the Faculty of Graduate Research at Victoria University of Wellington.

5 Teaching syntax

Sandra Chung[*]

Teaching introductory syntax is simultaneously a great opportunity and an enormous challenge. I think both the opportunity and the challenge are highlighted when syntax is taught interactively, through the sustained investigation of just one language which is known to all the students in the class. Starting from the assumption that there is such a common language – whether it be English, Maori, Chinese or something else – I survey some of the thrills and spills of an intensive, hands-on, 'learn by doing' approach to teaching syntax to undergraduates. This is the approach that we use in our undergraduate syntax courses at the University of California at Santa Cruz (UCSC). Some of the complications that the approach faces in a linguistically diverse classroom are discussed near the end.

Why does teaching introductory syntax offer such a great opportunity? The answer is simple: students jump into syntax faster, more easily and more enthusiastically than into any other subfield of linguistics. For whatever reasons – perhaps including prior education, writing conventions and the size of the units involved – students are more likely to think they have direct access to sentences than to any other type of linguistic object. Every undergraduate can already recognize sentences and words, the building blocks from which sentences are constructed. So students often see syntax as more immediate, more graspable, and less abstract than, say, phonology. (Think of the struggles of teaching a beginning student to distinguish between sounds and letters.) Undergraduates are also fully aware that sentences have meaning. So they can use synonymy, ambiguity and other aspects of meaning as diagnostic tools, without having to confront any of the hard questions that arise right away in semantics. Finally, most undergraduates love the extent to which syntactic investigation directly involves *them*. When the language investigated is one that they all speak, they can be simultaneously data-generators and investigators: they can themselves produce, and judge grammatical or ungrammatical, all the sentences that they analyse.

In short, syntax is a great way to introduce undergraduates to linguistics. It is also a perfect vehicle for teaching them *how to reason* about language structure, and this is the source of the challenge. Because linguistics involves not just a body of facts and analyses, but also a distinctive mode of scientific reasoning, teaching it involves communicating a hefty number of *how to*'s. Among them: (a) how to arrive at descriptive generalizations, (b) how to form hypotheses that say why the generalizations are as they are, (c) how to use evidence to decide between competing hypotheses, and (d) how to construct a formal system for representing the conclusions.

In my experience, students learn these techniques most thoroughly and successfully when they are guided to discover them through a combination of structured problem sets and Socratic interaction in the classroom. This version of the Socratic method is labour intensive for everyone. Because students are supposed to figure out for themselves how a solution works, not 'memorize the answer', it works best if the instructor does not lecture and the students do not rely on a textbook. Instead, the instructor provides a problem set which students solve outside of class, either alone or – better – collaborating with one another. Students write up their solutions in essay-style format and submit them at the beginning of the next class. Class time is devoted to discussion of their solutions, with the instructor guiding students to assess the merits of each solution and settle on one solution as superior. At the end of class (in UCSC's intensive syntax course) or the end of the week (in our less intensive syntax course) the cycle begins again, with the instructor providing a problem set that builds on the previous problem set. And so on.

This mode of instruction is the most effective way I know to teach undergraduates how to reason about syntax. It is also the most effective way I know to teach undergraduates how to write. And because it is possible to bring students very far in a very short time, it is enormously rewarding for the instructor.

Socratic teaching is, of course, high risk. Because the instructor does not lecture and the students do not have a textbook to rely on, classroom discussion can quickly get out of control – like a symphony orchestra that has run away from the conductor. Here are some tips for those who would like to try teaching syntax Socratically and would also like to maximize the 'thrills' and avoid the 'spills'.

The fundamental goal is to guide students to discover the principles of syntax and the techniques of syntactic argumentation on their own. Therefore,

- The problem sets and their order must be very highly structured. You cannot ask students to discover subcategorization if they do not know what syntactic categories are. And you cannot ask them to analyse infinitives before they have analysed simple sentences.
- Have a flexible notion of what the optimal solution is. Otherwise, students will end up not trying to figure out the optimal solution, but rather trying to guess what *you* think the optimal solution is.

Some students find it hard to participate in class discussion, perhaps because they are shy, perhaps because they are hesitant to expose their ideas to potential criticism. For this reason,

- Try to encourage everyone to participate; do not let the discussion be dominated by just a few.
- Try to encourage members of every social group to participate: males and females, members of the majority and members of ethnic minorities, and so on.
- Every comment or observation made must be taken very seriously.
- Remember that affirming a student is different from affirming his/her ideas. It can help the dynamics of the classroom to affirm a student even when (or especially when) his/her reasoning is flawed.

Two of the more challenging concepts to teach Socratically are the difference between description and analysis, and the difference between analysis and theory. There is, I think, no way to lead students to discover these differences: they must be talked about explicitly and directly. Still, there are some indirect ways of helping the ideas to sink in:

- Aim for a relatively concrete version of syntactic analysis, not an abstract, deductive version. (The closer the analysis is to the descriptive generalizations it is supposed to explain, the easier it is for beginning students to make the leap from description to analysis. The more inductive the analysis is, the more creative students can be. As the semester progresses, you can gradually increase the level of abstractness and deductive structure, if desired.)
- Emphasize that in linguistics, as in other sciences, fundamental theoretical concepts are believed, not arrived at empirically. Once the concepts are in place, it can often be decided empirically which of two analyses is superior. But that is a different matter.

Socratic learning requires a lot of energy from everyone, including the instructor. You will want to

- Assign a lot of (essay-style) homework, and make sure it is turned in on time – before the class starts to discuss the solution.
- Grade the homework quickly, supplying as many comments as possible, so that students can learn quickly from their past performance. Comments on homework provide one important type of Socratic guidance. They are also crucial to helping students to improve their writing.
- Improvise as you teach. You will have to, because who knows what ideas or solutions will emerge from the discussion? And whatever they happen to be, you

will have to move the discussion forward. One consequence of this is that you cannot really prepare for class – at least, not in the same way you would prepare a lecture. Another consequence is that you have to (learn to) be quick on your feet.
- Laugh a lot. It will relax the students, and it will relax you.

Can the Socratic method of teaching syntax be applied to linguistically diverse classrooms – classrooms in which students have a common language but do not share a first language? I think it can. The key is to encourage dialogue, while taking steps to minimize the linguistic differences between native speakers and non-native speakers. Some steps that can be taken:

- Introduce the notion of linguistic fieldwork and its importance to the study of language structure. Encourage students who do not speak the common language natively to do fieldwork on that language; this can (and should) be the source of the new sentences they analyse in their homework. Pair a non-native speaker with a native speaker so that fieldwork is institutionalized, inside and outside the classroom.
- If there is one language spoken natively by a substantial minority of students in the class, prepare a couple of problem sets in that language. Then, for many pairs of fieldworker and native speaker, the roles will be reversed.

Throughout, the workload for the instructor is significant. But so is the level of satisfaction. It is astonishing how much students have learned by the end of the semester. It also feels great to realize that in the Socratic classroom, students can improve dramatically at any point – even in the last week of classes. It is exciting to be in the classroom: the highs and lows of Socratic teaching have to be experienced to be believed. And, no matter how long you have taught (for me, over 30 years), it is endlessly surprising to see students put an old puzzle together in a completely new way.

One of the student evaluations I value most is from the mid-1980s, just after I had started teaching syntax at UCSC. The student wrote, 'Watching her teach is like listening to jazz.' At the time, I did not understand what he meant. Now that I know more about jazz, I think of this as the highest compliment of all.

Notes

* **Sandra Chung**

Sandra Chung first encountered linguistics as a Harvard undergraduate, where she was taught syntax by Robert Underhill and George Lakoff. As a Harvard graduate student, she learned syntactic argumentation from David Perlmutter while serving as his teaching assistant in an introductory syntax course at MIT.

(The other teaching assistant was Ivan Sag.)

She began teaching at the University of California in 1975. After eleven years at UC San Diego, she moved to UC Santa Cruz, where the hands-on approach to teaching syntax had been developed to a fine art. It took one nerve-wracking quarter for her to become thoroughly committed to this style of teaching. The undergraduate introduction to syntax is still one of her favorite courses to teach.

6 On teaching formal semantics

*Barbara H. Partee**

When I was in graduate school at MIT in the early 1960s, about half of us were former math majors and the other half felt various degrees of mathematics insecurity. So I ended up designing and teaching a 'math for linguists' course there, which I have continued teaching off and on ever since; it is the source of Partee 1979 and part of the source of Partee *et al.* 1990. A lot that I learned in teaching math for linguists helped me later, both in getting into formal semantics and in teaching it. One of the first things I realized was that if I was teaching math to people who had already decided they were not going to be mathematicians, I should not teach math the way it had been taught to me, with equal parts spent on teaching the subject matter and competitive challenging to 'separate the sheep from the goats'. That 'let's see how good you are' emphasis would just drive away students with low math self-esteem. So I designed the courses to be more like the music appreciation courses I had loved in college, grateful that they could teach us a lot about music without demanding musical talent. So in my math course you could always get a decent grade by working methodically; problems that demanded some ingenuity were always optional. (It was good to include some; some students – perhaps to their own surprise – were ready for a bit more of a challenge.) General moral: it is not just the subject matter that is important, so is knowing who you are teaching.

Teaching my math course was part of what helped me understand what Montague was doing when I first encountered him and his work at UCLA in the late 1960s, and to appreciate it enough to make it my mission to integrate Montague grammar into theoretical linguistics. (I have described my perspective on the history of Montague grammar and formal semantics in Partee 2004.) Working on formal semantics and teaching it has been central to my academic life ever since.

I have been happily teaching formal semantics in a wide variety of settings for about 38 years now. Of course it was most exciting of all in the first half of the 1970s, when teaching it was also a matter of getting the field started – my first long paper comparing Montague grammar and transformational grammar (Partee 1975) went through quite a few incarnations as class notes for my first courses in the subject – at UCLA in 1971, at an institute at Santa Cruz in summer 1971, at UMass starting in 1972, and at the Linguistic Institute at UMass in the summer of 1974, with an exciting international audience, and the active participation of the students and auditors in those courses played a crucial role in the early development of formal semantics.

Those first courses were necessarily graduate-level, both because Montague grammar was hard – it required learning some higher-order intensional logic and a bit of the lambda-calculus and type theory – and because we do not usually put things into the undergraduate curriculum until they are somewhat established. Since then I have taught formal semantics both at the graduate level and at undergraduate levels in a variety of settings and in quite a few countries – sometimes in the form of a one-week 'short course', sometimes as a visiting faculty member. At UMass I have taught mainly at the graduate level; by now one can take a whole sequence of graduate courses and seminars in formal semantics (or formal semantics and pragmatics) in a PhD programme like ours.

The importance of teaching differently for different audiences was all too apparent when I had an unsuccessful experience teaching an undergraduate course in formal semantics in Leipzig in 1999. I had no trouble with the graduate course I taught there that semester, and I had had almost no trouble anywhere before that. But in Leipzig I made the mistake of using for my undergraduate formal semantics course the wonderful Heim and Kratzer textbook, which I had used the year before at UMass for the introductory graduate course. And I soon came to realize that, while that book is great for giving a very solid foundation to future formal semanticists, it is not so great for students who start off with no idea about what formal semantics is and why it might be interesting.

That experience reminded me of why that first long paper on Montague grammar and transformational grammar was organized the way it was: since Montague grammar was quite unknown to most linguists, I had to show what it could be good for if I expected them to try to do the work of understanding the logic and the formal theory. So I started with just enough of the logic to show how one can use Montague's (and Quine's before him) semantics of restrictive relative clauses to resolve a long-running debate about the syntactic structure of noun phrases with relative clauses – why compositionality needs the structure $_{DP}$[Determiner $_{NP}$[NP Relative-clause]] rather than $_{DP}$[$_{DP}$[Determiner NP] Relative-clause], that is, why a restrictive relative clause must be sister to a common noun phrase like *boy*, not to a complete noun phrase like *the boy* or *every boy*: *the* + *boy who loves Mary*, not *the boy* + *who loves Mary*. For that first part, I oversimplified the logic – I introduced lambdas but not intensions and not the whole type theory, but it meant I could show some linguistic payoff right away. And I did that bit by bit through the whole paper, motivating each new technical thing by showing something it was good for, even though it meant I had to keep revising the formalism to correct things I had over-simplified up to that point.

But by the 1980s and 1990s, students who came to UMass knew that formal semantics was one of the things we did, and were prepared to be taught it in whatever way we thought would be pedagogically best, and I would usually spend quite a bit of time teaching the lambda calculus and type theory to give them a solid grounding before moving into linguistic examples. Compare the organization of the Dowty, Wall and Peters textbook (Dowty *et al.* 1981), for instance, with the organization of my 1975 paper: Dowty, Wall and Peters introduce all the parts of Montague's logic before they present any of his syntactic and semantic rules for English; that is a much more orderly introduction, but you have to already be motivated if you are going to work through it willingly. The Heim and Kratzer book (1998) includes linguistic examples from the beginning, but the emphasis in many of the early chapters is on the logic and the choices between one formal analysis and another, good grounding for solid future research, but in many ways also working on getting the logic established first. With our graduate students these approaches went well – a number of them went on to become leaders in the field of formal semantics.

But in 1999 in Leipzig it certainly did not work! The students mostly did the work, more or less, but I realized I did not have them 'with me' the way I was used to, and it dawned on me (too late to redesign the course) that only a few of them had any sense of why we were doing what we were doing.

I drew lessons from that for my teaching in Moscow (mostly yearly since 1998, and I would say 'successfully' since about 2000), and I make sure to include real linguistic examples, if possible in Russian as well as English, from the beginning, showing their 'payoff'. And of course in 'short courses', where nothing can be done really thoroughly, the emphasis is on the 'payoff', in the hope that the students will be motivated to study more formal semantics later.

The Moscow students are also different from my students elsewhere in other ways that make a difference to my teaching: there is a tradition in Moscow that goes back almost 50 years to include quite a lot of mathematics in the linguistics curriculum. So the Moscow undergraduates can generally learn the formal parts fast and well, and the best of them have more background in logic and mathematics than many of our entering PhD students. So while I need to include some motivating examples near the beginning, I can include fairly heavy doses of logic whenever we need it without losing them.

It was also in Moscow that I most fully got into the habit of making very extensive hand-outs that are like a flexible textbook. That was out of necessity; in the US I had been happy to make use of several good textbooks in formal semantics (Chierchia and McConnell-Ginet 1990; Dowty *et al.* 1981; Gamut 1991; Heim and Kratzer 1998), but my Russian students could not afford Western textbooks, and I could not afford to buy them for them (although I did bring some copies of the user-friendly Bach 1989 with me for them to share). And they also needed hand-outs to help them follow my lectures, which were in English (everyone concerned agreed that that was best, since all the journals in the field are in English). So I got into the habit of making a very full hand-out for every lecture. (Actually, I had also done that in the math for linguists course I taught in graduate school, when it required the help of the department secretary to type them up on ditto masters and make blue ditto copies. There was no suitable textbook back then, and I did not want the students to have to spend their time taking notes, but rather to ask questions and think about examples. Those hand-outs were the foundation of my first textbook (Partee 1979).)

When I went to teach an undergraduate semantics class at the University of Canterbury in New Zealand in 2006, I really did not know quite what to expect. I made sure to give homework at the very start that would give me feedback, and I discovered that they knew much less logic than I had imagined – most of them knew none, and I needed to teach even some first-order logic methodically and give them time with it. But it worked out well, because that time I had not committed to any textbook in advance but could modify my own hand-outs, which I had developed over the years, especially in Moscow. And I could quickly make up some new hand-outs on basic logic, with exercises, and revise the linguistic topics so that we could work on things that did not demand too high a level of logic and did make use of the considerable variety of languages that students in the class knew or had worked on. I think the students and I both ended up having a great time; I know I enjoyed that class greatly.

And that reminds me of some serendipitous occasions when I happily revised course plans to take advantage of the strengths of a particular group of students. One year many years ago, I was teaching a graduate-level introduction to semantics (back when the first graduate-level course was not formal semantics, which was introduced only in the second year), and I realized that the native languages of the students in the class came from an unusually diverse number of language families. So I changed the schedule and added in a substantial unit in which we worked on the distribution of pronoun forms and pronoun meanings in different languages – null pronouns, personal pronouns, various sorts of reflexive pronouns, and meanings including indexical or deictic, 'referential-anaphoric', and bound-variable meanings. Everyone gave a brief report, and it was really exciting and fun. Some years in Russia I have managed to do similar things when I discover, for instance, that I have a class full of students who have been on fieldwork expeditions working on several of the indigenous languages of Russia. Such chances to do cross-linguistic comparisons have also seeded the beginnings of semantic typology for me and for some of the students.

Hampshire College in Amherst has a somewhat non-standard programme in several ways, and one of them is that freshmen take narrow-focus seminars, while survey courses wait until junior year. The *Invitation to Cognitive Science* textbook series edited by Daniel Osherson took a similar approach: when I was asked to write a chapter for it on 'Lexical semantics and compositionality' (Partee 1995), I was told not to survey the field but to choose a single case study and use it to illustrate some of the main issues and some of what made the field exciting. The Hampshire strategy and that textbook strategy are similar: find a story to make the subject interesting before asking the students to get into the hard work necessary to master it.

I do have some favourite case studies for getting started in formal semantics. One is the relative clause story; that one gets me excited because in my early life as a syntactician, we used to debate whether relative clauses attach to the common noun phrase or to the whole DP, and we could not find any clear arguments – both analyses are common in the literature. So the idea that semantics could help decide the issue is exciting and important: if you do not get the syntax right, you just will not be able to build a compositional semantics. So it is an argument that can appeal to anyone who already cares about syntax, and it is pretty easy to grasp.

Another favourite bunch of case studies, probably reflecting my own interests, concern quantifiers – lots of us use that domain, and you will find discussions of quantifiers in every semantics textbook. Quantifier phrases, and noun phrase semantics more generally, have been studied a great deal in formal semantics, perhaps because they fall right at the intersection of language and logic and have been studied by logicians, philosophers and linguists, the three disciplines from which formal semantics has grown. I will not review particular ones here – there are several favourites – but I know that I still get just as excited when I tell about them as I did when they were brand new results in the field. Some are included in the little bit about model-theoretic semantics in Partee *et al.* 1990, others can be found in Richard Larson's chapter in the earlier-mentioned textbook in the *Invitation to Cognitive Science* series (Larson 1995).

When I was invited to contribute a chapter to the second edition of that textbook, I had to find a different case study, since Larson had already written about quantifiers, my usual favourite; and my chapter should be not just on semantics, but on the combination of lexical semantics and compositional semantics. Lila Gleitman, co-editor of that volume, suggested I do something about the semantics of adjectives, since I had written about that topic elsewhere jointly with Hans Kamp. That had not been part of my standard 'pedagogical repertoire', but it turned out to be fun to write, and it quickly got into my own teaching – that was especially useful in Moscow, where another local feature was a long tradition of serious work on lexical semantics and much less on semantics above the word level. So my Moscow semantics classes often include a week on adjective semantics, and it is fun to get the students debating the semantic properties of Russian adjectives. One of my Moscow students got inspired to work on a topic closely related to that for her senior thesis.

Of course, for me it is always particularly exciting when a student gets turned on by some topic in semantics and does original work on it. Sometimes it is not even a semantics student, and that is exciting too – I have had two phonology students produce published papers in semantics (one a graduate student at UMass, one an undergraduate at Moscow State University, now a graduate student at Rutgers). Sometimes it starts from some homework assignment – I often make my homework assignments quite flexible: 'choose two or three of the following problems', identifying basic problems that students without much background should probably start with, and including a range of more open-ended problems for students with more background to try their hand at. And sometimes a student will come up with an idea on a homework problem which looks to me like it might actually be something new, or might lead to something new, and I will encourage them to make that into a term paper topic; I think in most of the cases where a student of mine has come out of a course with a topic they then develop into a published paper, it has started like that. (I am not counting the advanced graduate seminars, where the students are already identifying their own research problems with just occasional advice and suggestions from us.) In both of the cases of the phonology students who came up with ideas that were then developed into published papers, they had no idea that what they had written in their homework might be an original idea – that is what they need us for! (And if an idea is very good but not new, of course I give them positive feedback about that too.)

For me (perhaps for everyone?) it has always been easiest to teach the most advanced graduate courses and seminars, because the students are then closest to being junior colleagues or apprentices: the gap between teaching and doing my own research is smallest with them; they're already fully motivated and have quite a bit of background; and we are basically all working on some problems together. The introductory graduate courses are the next easiest, because even if the students do not have much background yet, they are motivated, committed and pretty highly selected. Those are important courses, because for the future semanticists we are laying the foundation for their professional development, and for those who will not specialize in semantics, we are trying to give them enough of a start so that they can appreciate semantics as it relates to their own work and to their future students' work.

A lot of what I have been writing about here is the challenges of teaching semantics to undergraduates who do not necessarily know why they should be studying it. But at least if they are in a semantics class, they have had an introduction to linguistics.

I have to tell a story on myself about the first time I had to teach a '100-level' introductory undergraduate course, the lowest level of all, designed as a 'breadth course' – not even a feeder course to the linguistics major, though students who wanted to could go from there to a higher-level introduction and onwards in linguistics. This was in my seventh and last year at UCLA; I was glad I was about to leave, because I was afraid I would do very poorly lecturing to a class of 75, mostly freshmen, who had no advance interest in the subject. I struggled through as best I could, trying to enjoy it and trying to find things to interest them. At the end of the course I was reading the evaluations with trepidation – they were not as terrible as I feared, though certainly not as favourable as those I was used to in my graduate classes – when I was struck by several students' comments to the question 'How well does the teacher know the subject?' They had written something like: 'Well, in phonology and in historical linguistics she was fine, but in syntax and semantics she often seemed unsure of herself.' How could that be?! Then I realized the answer. For phonology and historical linguistics, I was pretty much limited to classic 'textbook examples' – things I had learned when I was a graduate student, which I could retell with nice clean paradigms – and when the questions went beyond what I knew, I would say, 'Well, that's an interesting question, but it goes beyond this class'. But in syntax and semantics, in the first place I had great difficulty reducing anything I knew to 'textbook example' size, and when I did, I always knew that I was oversimplifying things, and when the students asked good questions, I would get quite engaged, and might tell them about some other ways to look at the same data, or that what they had suggested was indeed an alternative hypothesis that some scholars had argued for. Well, after reading those evaluations, I felt quite crestfallen that the parts I knew most about were parts where they thought I was 'unsure of myself'. And I carried that sense of failure for quite a number of years, until one year I ran into Wendy Wilkins, a fine and successful linguist, who told me that she had been in that class that year (with a different surname which I have now forgotten), and that that was the first time she had been given any inkling that there were open problems that people were working on – in any field – and that that was so exciting to her that she immediately switched her major to linguistics and was still entirely glad to have done so. Whew! So the lesson I got from that is that in those 100-level courses, you cannot expect to reach everyone, but it is *not* necessarily a mistake to show a bit of what the field is really like rather than try to have everything ready to present in a tidy package. My later strategy for 100-level courses boiled down to this: make very explicit and straightforward what one has to do to get a decent passing grade, and do not worry if quite a lot of the students just want to pass with the minimum effort required, but always have some things in there to potentially attract those students for whom linguistics might turn out to be a really exciting field. And although I have not had to teach too many of those courses (luckily; it never became my forte), a few more budding linguists turned up in them, and I became more comfortable in them overall.

Speaking of evaluations, we all learn what our relative strengths and weaknesses are. I think one of my strengths is that when students are having difficulty with tough stuff, I can often grasp what or how they are thinking and can find a way to explain things that clears it up; the evaluations often say that I am good at making difficult stuff clear and good at seeing where students' difficulties are coming from. And I think I am also good at being simultaneously demanding and supportive. I think one of my weaknesses is that I lecture too much, in courses at all levels, and am not good at the Socratic method, even though in principle I think it should be the best way to teach. I do invite questions, and I think I am pretty good with questions and discussion, but I do not devote as much time to seeking out questions and conjectures and class contributions as one ideally might. I try to make up for that to some degree with the homework: in all my semantics courses at all levels, I encourage the students to use homework for conversations with me. I emphasize that it is more important to get homework in on time with appropriate effort than it is to get the answers right the first time. I welcome questions on the homework, and where I spot problems I welcome 'redos' of the homework to get things straightened out. I think that's especially appropriate for a field like semantics, where one has to learn a fair amount of logic along the way – I comfort the students by telling them it took me several years to understand how lambdas work, and I am trying to teach them all about lambdas within a few weeks, so I will be understanding if they do not get all the technical exercises right the first time. So what goes on in 'homework conversations' is often somewhat Socratic, and that works well for me.

In the early years of teaching formal semantics, there was often a mix of philosophy and linguistics students in the classes; the philosophy students mostly knew lots of logic and little syntax, and vice versa for the linguistics students. Since studying semantics requires some background in both syntax and logic, I used to try to get the students to work in cross-disciplinary teams to help each other. It worked only to a limited extent – I suspect not knowing each other well and having busy schedules made that hard in practice even if welcome in principle. But it was nevertheless very nice to have linguistics and philosophy students together in class, because they asked different questions, and their questions were often educational to each other as well as to me. That is undoubtedly a challenge in any interdisciplinary subject, but also an enrichment. In Moscow it is unusual and difficult to take courses outside the established curriculum for your major field; in the US it is common, and it is really a good thing for all concerned – it always helps to have multiple perspectives on a problem, and I have always welcomed having students in my linguistics classes from philosophy, psychology, computer science or the language departments. Since my own background is interdisciplinary (a major in mathematics, minors in philosophy and Russian, then graduate work in linguistics with a little more philosophy, logic and mathematics along the way) and since all of my own education was preparing me for a field that did not yet exist at the time, I am naturally sympathetic to lots of interdisciplinary cross-fertilization.

One issue that I do not have a definite answer to concerns modifying courses over time. Sometimes I think I have been a little slow to revise some of my favourite semantics courses. I may have continued teaching Montague grammar in its classic form longer than some people. Nowadays, Montague is a historic figure in formal semantics, and it is as rare to teach his original work as it is to teach Chomsky's *Syntactic structures*. I may have been overly attached to Montague's work and the early extensions of it by linguists because I was in love with the beginnings of the field. And then when there were good textbooks to use, once I got a course well designed to coordinate with a particular textbook, it was nice to stick with it for a while. I suppose there is always some trade-off between getting certain lectures or topics polished to a 'performance' level on the one hand – some things I know I can lecture on really well – and updating so as to reflect new developments and to keep things fresh. Now that most of my semantics teaching is in Moscow and I use my own hand-outs rather than a textbook, it is easier to strike a good balance – there are three or four introductory lectures each time that do not change very much except to improve them, and then I pick some case studies to focus on that semester, with a good number of the lectures being new.

When I started teaching in Russia, one of my hopes was that my husband Vladimir Borschev and I might write a textbook on formal semantics in Russian, because the only two that exist are by and for logicians rather than linguists. We went as far as hiring a good student to do a first pass translation of my first three lectures; she and we encountered a large number of terminology problems that bogged us down and we never reached a final translation even of those three lectures. Later we thought that because the terminology issues are so important, and the standard terminology is all in English, we should perhaps do a dual-language textbook instead. But by now so many of the Russian students know English so well that I am no longer sure there is even a need for such a thing. Perhaps we may still do it; I don't know. But all my lecture notes are online, and they are virtually a textbook (but in English, of course), and I am not sure there's a demand for a regular textbook in either language anymore.

I am not very big on drawing generalizations, but if I try to verbalize what I would conclude about teaching from my experience, it is that if you love your subject and you love teaching and you care about your students, it will probably work pretty well. Of course, pay some attention to feedback, but do not overdo it: you and some students are probably just incompatible. Happily the bulk of my experience has left me as much in love with teaching as I was back when I was ten and thought what I would love most was to be a fifth-grade teacher. I will bet that would have been fun, but at some point in graduate school I realized that if I was getting a PhD, I probably was going to be not a fifth-grade teacher but a college teacher. Luckily that has been great fun too.

References

Bach, E. 1989. *Informal lectures on formal semantics*. New York: State University of New York Press.

Chierchia, G. and S. McConnell-Ginet. 1990. *Meaning and grammar: An introduction to semantics*. Cambridge: MIT Press.

Dowty, D.R., R.E. Wall and S. Peters Jr. 1981. *Introduction to Montague semantics*. Dordrecht: Reidel.

Gamut, L.T.F. 1991. *Logic, language, and meaning*. Vol. 2: *Intensional logic and logical grammar*. Chicago: University of Chicago Press.

Heim, I. and A. Kratzer. 1998. *Semantics in generative grammar*. Oxford: Blackwell.

Larson, R. 1995. Semantics. In *An invitation to cognitive science*. Vol 1: *Language*, pp. 361-80, ed. L. Gleitman and M. Liberman. Cambridge, MA: The MIT Press.

Partee, B. 1975. 'Montague grammar and transformational grammar'. *Linguistic Inquiry* 6: 203-300.

Partee, B. 1995. 'Lexical semantics and compositionality'. In *An invitation to cognitive science*. Vol. 1: *Language*, 2nd edn, pp. 311-60, ed. L. Gleitman and M. Liberman. Cambridge: MIT Press.

Partee, B.H. 1979. *Fundamentals of mathematics for linguists*. Stamford, CT: Greylock Publishers. Reprinted Dordrecht: D. Reidel.

Partee, B.H. 2004. 'Reflections of a formal semanticist'. In *Compositionality in formal semantics: Selected papers by Barbara H. Partee*, pp. 1-25. Oxford: Blackwell Publishing.

Partee, B.H., A. ter Meulen and R. Wall. 1990. *Mathematical methods in linguistics*. Dordrecht: Kluwer.

Notes

* **Barbara Partee**

What got me into linguistics? I loved math and I loved languages, and for the longest time I thought I would have to choose. Early in my college career, I decided on math. I managed to put together a programme with a major in math and minors in Russian and philosophy; I didn't see any connection – they were just the three things I liked best. In my junior year, my uncle sent me the programme of a conference on mathematical linguistics. I wrote letters to a number of the contributors, asking for ideas of how I might use that summer (1960) to find out what linguistics was. Surprisingly many wrote thoughtful answers, including Chomsky. All the replies suggested inquiring at the University of Pennsylvania, and luckily it turned out that there was a seminar on structural linguistics at Penn that very summer for people with a background in mathematics, philosophy or psychology – perfect. It was about Harris-style transformational grammar, taught by Henry Hiż. And they knew that MIT was about to start a graduate programme in linguistics, led by Harris's student Chomsky. So since linguistics seemed indeed to be great fun for someone who liked math and languages, I applied to graduate school at MIT and Penn, went to MIT, and indeed loved it.

Where was I trained and who were the teachers who influenced me? I was in good public schools in Baltimore County, then Swarthmore for my BA, and MIT for my PhD. The biggest influences on my professional development were Noam Chomsky and Ed Klima for syntax and Morris Halle in general. Klima loved language puzzles first and theory second, while Chomsky was clearly the reverse, and it was interesting to listen to both of them and try to work out where I stood (closer to Klima in my heart, but I appreciated Chomsky's perspective.) The influences on my teaching were many and diverse. My fifth grade teacher, Mrs Shields, somehow encouraged us to see ourselves as potentially independent thinkers; it felt like some kind of awakening. In high school I adored the gruff geometry teacher, Mr Brandt, who inserted wonderful 'extra stuff' at the beginning of many classes, sneaking bits of number theory into geometry class. Swarthmore was amazing, because there we were expected to be critical – actually engaging in arguments with the people who wrote the books. MIT was more amazing, because suddenly we were supposed to become the people who wrote the books. One of my favourite teachers ever was the composer Vincent Persichetti, a Juilliard professor who taught a course on contemporary music at Swarthmore: he showed me that, even without a natural 'ear', I could learn a lot from writing ultra-short compositions using specific techniques (like chords made of piled-up fourths): once you have created it, suddenly you can 'hear' it. He was a big part of my inspiration in teaching math for linguists.

What happened after that? I'll make this part short, because I have an essay online, 'Reflections of a formal semanticist', that tells that story. Short version: I went to UCLA in 1965 as a Chomsky disciple and taught syntax, met the logician Richard Montague, got excited about his approach to semantics, and then took it as my mission to try to get Chomskyan syntax and Montague's semantics together. That effort, by no means single-handed, eventually led to the field of formal semantics. Chomsky remained totally sceptical about it, but I learned early on that you don't try to convert your teachers – you just do your best with your peers and your students. I have been at UMass Amherst in Linguistics and Philosophy since 1972, Emerita since 2004, dividing my time between Moscow and Amherst since 1996, still happily teaching part-time in both places.

7 Teaching pragmatics

Christopher Potts *

7.1 Controlling the discourse

In the fall of 2003, Lyn Frazier suggested that she and I co-teach an undergraduate course on pragmatics and human discourse processing, and I leapt at the opportunity. We soon began designing the syllabus and preparing materials, with the help of then-graduate students Helen Majewski and Florian Schwarz. Our goal was a curriculum that would satisfy the UMass Amherst interdisciplinary general education requirement by emphasizing psychological methods for understanding language, drawing also on ideas from philosophy and computer science. Other departments on campus were pulling in scores of students with flashy interdisciplinary titles. Needless to say, we thought linguistics could play that game well.

We wanted the course to be free of prerequisites, so the title 'Pragmatics and Discourse Processing' was going to miss its intended audience. 'The Linguistics of Discourse Structuring' and its variants were too drab. 'The Flow of Information' was too generic, but its variant 'The Control of Information' introduced a sense of agency and action. Riffing on 'Control', we ended up with 'Controlling the Discourse', which stuck, and which quickly had an impact on how we conceived of the course. The phrase 'Controlling the Discourse' is underspecified about who is in control, and it leaves open just what kind of discourse this might be. I find it vaguely ominous, suggesting high-stakes talk exchanges – courtroom dramas, interrogations, political debate. The title shaped our short catalogue description, which carved out a lasting path for us:

> The question 'Why did you commit the murder?' is likely to be met with a sustained objection if asked in a courtroom. Why? 'Who on earth would listen to polka?' sounds more like an assertion than a question. Why? Under what circumstances do speakers choose 'Bagels, I like' over 'I like bagels'? These are questions about how speakers use language to structure and control discourses. We'll look to current linguistic theory to find answers to them. Students will pick up skills that are vital to understanding how to structure effective arguments. They will discover why information structure can be a matter of life or death (politically, socially, liter-

> ally). Intuitional, corpus, and experimental data will be used to examine issues in pragmatics and discourse processing.

Trained eyes can probably make out the beginnings of a syllabus in this: presuppositions, speech acts, implicatures, information structuring. The fuller description gestured at ellipsis, anaphora and intonational meaning. Thus, the course was founded in the tried-and-true subject matter of pragmatics textbooks. Our basic conceit was to address each topic from both theoretical and experimental perspectives. Roughly speaking, I would set up a basic theoretical framework, and Lyn would assess the degree to which it was known to be wrong (right) using psycholinguistic evidence. Students would get a feel for the rhythm of hypothesis formulation, testing and reformulation, while also gaining some conscious awareness of the pragmatic calculations we all perform when interacting with other intentional agents.

More unusually, I think, the description emphasizes what students will learn to *do*, rather than what knowledge they will acquire. It highlights the ways in which they will be asked to apply the course's ideas to problems they confront outside of linguistics. We had even more of this in mind for the course itself: a hands-on introduction to running psycholinguistic experiments, live debates drawing material from landmark court cases, and assignments that asked students to sniff out their own interesting instances of pragmatic enrichment. Finally, taking a stab at a meta-application of the course's content, we aimed to get students to apply their knowledge of pragmatics to their own papers and those of their classmates.

Developing and teaching 'Controlling the Discourse' with Lyn profoundly affected my views of pragmatics. It opened my eyes to the many ways in which the lessons of pragmatic theory can be usefully applied to real-world situations, and it led me to a better understanding of the special challenges that surround generalizations and theoretical constructs in this area. The present chapter tells the story of some of these personal and pedagogical discoveries.

7.2 Getting started

The first opening for 'Controlling the Discourse' on the UMass Amherst schedule was spring 2005. As it happened, I first taught the course in the summer of 2004 as a solo effort, at the New York Institute for Cognitive and Cultural Studies, at St Petersburg State University in St Petersburg, Russia. That version had just a two-week, six-meeting run, so it was a sort of pilot study for the semester-long class we would teach in the next academic year. My St Petersburg version emphasized information structuring: passivization, scrambling, referential expressions. This made it easy to draw lots of examples from Russian morphosyntax. (It also helped avoid overlap with the introduction to pragmatics that I was teaching there simultaneously.) The emphasis on information structuring carried over to the first time Lyn and I taught the course together, in a 15-week format, but we eased up somewhat on that aspect of things in later years, largely because it ended up depending so much on the analysis of sentence structure, which most of our students were unfamiliar with.

By the spring 2009 semester, after two previous co-taught versions and one solo effort by me (fall 2007), the syllabus had evolved to have the following basic structure:

0. Overview; introductions to pragmatics and psycholinguistics
1. Gricean pragmatics
2. Information structuring
3. Presupposition and anaphora
4. Ellipsis and discourse coherence
5. Intonation
6. Framing

Students wrote short papers connected with each of these topics, and they did at least one experimental study of their own, usually a small questionnaire-based pilot at about unit 4 in the course flow. Some students also did a second study, elaborating on their first or starting from scratch, for the final project. At one time, the course finished with a week on 'Applied pragmatics', where we made connections between language and the law, language and the media, and so forth. This worked well, but we soon realized that the applied part could be woven into the fabric of the course itself. We simply needed to call on real examples when articulating concepts and motivating theoretical proposals. We did, though, successfully stage some courtroom-like debates at the semester's end, which emphasized the potential for applied aspects to the material.

As I said, the course had no prerequisites, and we succeeded in our attempts to draw in students from other departments with our catchy title and description. I still have the opening-day surveys for the fall 2007 and spring 2009 courses. Of the 53 students who took these surveys, 25 had never taken a linguistics course, and 8 had taken just one. There were 25 distinct majors represented, from all over campus. Conversely, the course attracted many linguistics majors; 10 of these 53 students had taken at least four linguistics courses before, and 13 of them had declared a linguistics major or minor. Groups with widely spread experience levels are always challenging; some could define a lot of the terms in our topics list, whereas others probably saw only a baffling hodgepodge of Greek, computer science and architectural terms. Students who finish day 1 feeling bored or overwhelmed are unlikely to return; having hooked them with our flashy title and active description, we needed to keep them.

Our opening surveys also asked, 'What is your understanding of the course's title "Controlling the Discourse"? (What do *you* think falls under this heading?)' and followed up with 'Provide an example of someone or something attempting to *control the discourse* in the sense that you understand that phrase'. The answers we got indicate that our students arrived with the right mindset. A lot of the answers were like this one: '"Controlling the discourse" to me refers to the different ways in which things are said to omit, tweak, or deliberately mislead people about the truth'. Students' examples mentioned devious politicians, job interviewers and interviewees, diplomatic situations, and the media, as well as things we had not thought of but that fit squarely under our rubric: code-switching as a conversational tactic, the power of dictionary makers, self-directed pep talks.

Thus, in general, the students were receptive to units 1–6 on the syllabus, whether they knew it or not, and we just had to capitalize on this. The overview and introductory lectures listed in unit 0 totalled about two and a half hours of class time, with the overview occupying the whole first meeting. Even before we started going through requirements, office hours and other syllabus details, we distributed a handout that consisted of just the headings in 1–6, a few sentences of explanation, and lots of live examples. For each example, the question was the same: 'What's going on here?'

For example, under a subheading 'The power of false presuppositions' we had the spam email subject-line 'Are you still looking for a job?' Drawing on student comments, we would assemble on the board general information about the context of email and the way spammers take advantage of it, the linguistic details of the examples – in technical terms, the indexical *you*, the particle *still*, the resulting bias – and variants of the example that would be pushy to a greater or lesser degree. Punchline: notice the power of presuppositions, and the ways in which these spammers leverage our natural impulses to be charitable when interpreting others. (Instructors are warned that, if the discussion is going well, this particular example will probably lead at least one student to suggest the similar spam subject-line 'Why be an average guy any longer?', which raises many of the same issues and which might or might not feel safe for your classroom.)

In spring 2009, we were in luck when it came to ellipsis examples. Newly elected US president Barack Obama had made 'Yes, we can' a campaign slogan. What is special about this example? Experienced linguistics students home in quickly on the site of the missing verb phrase; the non-linguists in the room need to be reassured that the terminology will come clear in a couple of months. What is important for now, we would say, is that *something is missing*. Why didn't the Obama campaign flesh out the missing part? How might it have worked to their advantage to leave the phrase underspecified?

And so on like this. What is unusual about the title 'There is no God and Dawkins is his prophet'? How is 'You're a Communist.' different from 'You're a Communist?' and 'Are you a Communist?' When, if ever, could you say, 'Bagels, I like' without being accused of sounding like Yoda? What exactly is right-wing political operative Frank Luntz doing to us when he brands political issues, and why might we react strongly to his efforts? How do his techniques compare with those of the political left? Humanities disciplines have a useful word for this: 'problematizing'. Our goal was just to make students aware that there is something noteworthy going on in all these seemingly mundane cases. In drawing exclusively on examples from the media, politics and their own experiences, we were trying to show them that the issues have immediate relevance to life outside the classroom. Now the rest of the course could be devoted to showing them how developing explicit hypotheses would make them savvier producers and consumers of utterances.

7.3 Selective viewing

In the linguistics classroom, we often teach specialized forms of selective viewing. In syntax, students must learn to see morphosyntactic structure, and only morphosyntatic structure, through the confusion of meaning, register and style that attaches to every example we give them. In phonology, they must grow adept at hearing only the sound patterns, whereas semantics requires them to look past the details of sound and structure to the underlying conventional content, all the while setting aside, as much as possible, the obvious fact that meaning arises from human interactions as well as lexical ones. Typically, if the lectures are interactive, beginning students spend a great deal of time probing your examples and offering new ones in an effort to acquire something like the same fuzzy sense you have for where these fuzzy boundaries between subfields lie.

All inquiry demands this sort of selective viewing, and students who cannot or will not engage in it tend to do poorly. We should acknowledge, though, that it is remote from people's everyday experiences with language. Part of the magic of language processing is that we so rapidly and accurately apprehend and assimilate a wide range of diverse information coming at us via a number of different streams. Thus, reluctance to focus on any one aspect of linguistic communication is sometimes a reluctance to sell the whole phenomenon short. We should remain aware also of the fact that perceptive students might find the boundaries we have erected artificial. Students who refuse to distinguish phonology from phonetics, morphology from phonology, syntax from semantics are in good company among our professional ranks.

Pragmatics is interestingly different in this regard. Pragmatics encourages us, and our students, to embrace the full complexity of our examples, to take them roughly as discourse participants would take them in context, and to work with them in their full richness – attentive to all information that might be lurking in the signal, inclusive of form, intonation, gesture, the background of the speaker, the speaker's assumptions about his audience, the audience's assumptions about the speaker, their respective socio-cultural backgrounds, and on and on. This makes teaching pragmatics a real pleasure. One can let students loose, encouraging them to gather evidence as they see fit, without having to nudge them back into the problem space.

This is what we did on day one of 'Controlling the Discourse'. We just let them loose on the examples, open to the idea that any and all information might be relevant to our understanding of the examples. This comes with its own dangers, of course. Students can get lost in the complexity of specific examples, unable to generalize to new cases. Sometimes the example has special emotional resonance for them, sometimes they have just invested a lot of time in it, and sometimes they lose sight of the fact that they will not make progress without some idealization and generalization. So, though the empirical domain is wide open, teaching pragmatics is still teaching a kind of selective viewing – pushing students to see the underlying structure of the examples and helping them identify those patterns in new cases. Thus, we return to the paradigm of selective viewing, as students learn to see past irrelevant distractors to the core of the underlying strategies for production and comprehension.

'Controlling the Discourse' was a constant battle for control over this point. Having acquired a taste for wild exploration on the first day, the students were often inclined to continue in that mode. So we had to push back, to get them to find abstractions in the data. To give one example, the following darkly comic example from Lawrence M. Solan and Peter M. Tiersma's wonderful book *Speaking of crime: The language of criminal justice* (University of Chicago Press, 2005) is always a hit:

(1)

John and Mary have recently started going together. Valentino is Mary's ex-boyfriend. One evening John asks Mary, 'Have you seen Valentino this week?' Mary answers, 'Valentino's been sick with mononucleosis for the past two weeks.' Valentino has in fact been sick with mononucleosis for the past two weeks, but it is also the case that Mary had a date with Valentino the night before. Did Mary lie?

Suppose you want students to focus on the nature of Mary's assertive response to John's polar interrogative, connecting this with Grice's maxims of relevance, quantity and quality, as well as the basic pragmatics of posing and addressing questions. There is so much in the example beyond this that one can sympathize with students who would prefer to take it as its own unique creature. Revelling in the complexity of the situation will not deepen our understanding of it, though. We must push for abstractions.

To this end, examples like (1) can be presented alongside similar cases like (2) and (3) (which are also from *Speaking of crime*), with the challenge being to find what threads run through all three.

(2)

Speakers A and B have the following conversation:

A: I lost a twenty dollar bill – do you know where it is?

B: I saw it on the floor somewhere.

Speaker A later discovers that B picked up A's $20 from the floor and had it in his pocket at the time of this conversation.

(3)

Bronston v. United States, decided by the U. S. Supreme Court in 1973. Bronston's company had petitioned for bankruptcy.

Q: Do you have any bank accounts in Swiss banks, Mr. Bronston?

A: No, sir.

Q: Have you ever?

A: The company had an account there for about six months, in Zurich.

The truth: Bronston also had a Swiss bank account in the past.

To meaningfully group these cases, one must set aside the dark comedy of kissing diseases that (1) makes salient, along with the contextually variable worth of $20, all questions about who is or is not friends with whom, whether Bronston was a good business man or a bad one, whether the lawyer was competent, and so on, and focus instead on how the person giving the response is exploiting basic pragmatic principles to deceive his/her audience. Crucially, one is not saying that this other information is not relevant to our pragmatic inferences, but rather that we need to move to a higher level of abstraction in order to identify new cases of deceptive pragmatics when they arrive on the lips of politicians and pundits.

7.4 Pragmatic hypotheses

In pragmatics, absolutes are rare. Linguists often worry about the ways in which judgments become fuzzy in phonology and syntax, but this is nothing compared to the seemingly hopeless muddle of intuitions people have about discourse well-formedness and speaker intentions. What is more, violating core generalizations of the theory tends not to result in a feeling of ill-formedness or incoherence, but rather a feeling that, well, something interesting has occurred. I try to accept this and use it to my advantage. I like, for example, to drive my students crazy the first time they ask (4) by replying with (a), (b) or (c).

(4)

When is our next quiz?

a. It's supposed to rain on Friday.

b. Are we in earthquake country?

c. Consider the lobster!

After the confused looks have rippled across the classroom, I jot my answer onto the chalkboard and then ask students what they think it means. A diverse cloud of extra, largely unjustified assumptions forms. Accepting any of them would turn my answer into one that partially resolved the original question, but, without such contextual support, I can and should be accused of violating the maxim of relevance. I then pose two questions: what compels us to work overtime to get (4) to cohere, and what is the nature of that coherence?

From here, we can start to probe slightly different examples involving different background assumptions. Suppose it is known that the person being addressed is uncooperative, as in (5) (from the TV show *Monk*), in which Stottlemeyer seeks to dodge the direct question by supplying true but partly irrelevant information, in an effort to avoid giving the commission a good reason to keep Monk off of the police force.

(5)

Commission member:	Is Mr. Monk ready to be put back on the force?
Stottlemeyer:	Mr. Monk has *excellent* instincts.
Commission member:	Yes, but is he ready to be reinstated?
Stottlemeyer:	He is an *excellent* investigator.
Commission member:	Captain, please…

Alternatively, suppose the person being addressed is cooperative but is known to have only partial information about how to resolve the issue. How do these scenarios differ from situations in which people seek to explicitly 'opt out' of cooperative behaviour, with remarks like 'No comment'? What information is conveyed by such utterances? And so forth. If I am lucky, it has now been so long since the tedious question (4) was posed that I do not have to answer it. Instead, we have achieved a deeper appreciation of the lengths to which people will go in order to bring others' verbal behaviour in line with the principles of cooperativeness.

Information-structuring principles follow a similar pattern, but here the situation is even trickier, since the basic grammaticality of specific clauses often does seem to be at stake. If one says, 'old information goes to the front' or 'people won't use a proper name where a pronoun will do' in front of a roomful of engaged undergraduates, they are sure to object. The trick is to shift the debate slightly. Get specific examples from them, and then study this new data set as a group, attempting to find ways in which it supports the original generalization. Do the new examples reveal that the speaker has an unusual perspective on the discourse? Or is the speaker deliberately trying to run up against your expectations, which are shaped by these principles?

I was slow to appreciate how challenging this situation is for students. Experienced researchers in linguistics are adept at holding specific assumptions constant and watching to see what happens when the variables under investigation change their values. If a journal article asserts that the combination of (4) and any of (a)–(c) results in incoherence, we know that this is a qualified sort of incoherence, one that implicitly restricts attention to contexts in which no special assumptions have crept in to save the dialogue. We deliberately suspend our normal charitable assumptions about cooperative agents in order to better understand why and how this discourse has gone off track. Our students might be unprepared to do this. That is what the cloud of special assumptions reveals. It is one of the deeply impressive things about how humans communicate, but it can get in the way of understanding what makes discourses like those in (4) pragmatically unusual.

These concerns are not unique to teaching pragmatics. In syntax, for instance, strings are marked as ill-formed only under specific assumptions about their internal structure, and students often have a hard time holding those assumptions constant. Similarly, semantic judgments are often about specific combinations of structure and compositional interpretation, both of which might be hard for students to keep a mental grip on. The problems are particularly acute in pragmatics, though, because the number of relevant factors is awesomely huge and even the 'ill-formed' cases often turn out to have some discourse utility.

Experimental data are invaluable for overcoming these conceptual hurdles. They force students to back off from their particular reactions to the particular examples under discussion, looking instead at a general pattern of responses. In 'Controlling the Discourse', Lyn presented most of the experimental studies, and it was always enlightening to watch her linger over an experimenter's background assumptions and their connections to the design, emphasizing how all of it connected (or failed to connect) with the theoretical ideas on the table. Not only did this help students grow accustomed to the abstractions discussed in section 7.3 above, but it also helped them sort out their own conflicting intuitions about felicity and discourse coherence, by highlighting the importance of keeping particular background assumptions fixed when probing their examples.

The students might have gained a sense for pragmatic inquiry by watching us develop and test others' hypotheses, but I think it was not until they had tried it out themselves that they truly appreciated the delicate nature of psycholinguistic work. Nothing drives home the importance of having a uniform set of examples and keeping tight control over the points of variation like a chaotic set of responses to one's own experimental stimuli.

In general, the most successful experimental projects in 'Controlling the Discourse' involved ellipsis or anaphora, which is why, in our own act of controlling the discourse, we introduced these topics alongside the basic mechanics of running a pilot questionnaire study. Ellipsis and anaphora are ideal for first pragmatics experiments because they involve all the complexity of discourse, but they provide plenty of room for constructing controlled experimental items in which it is easy to identify the variables. There is still plenty of room for methodological innovation. Our students did forced-choice grammaticality tasks, graded acceptability tasks, and fill-in-the-blank tasks, all aimed at getting at preferred interpretations and exploring the contours of these phenomena. Most used textual examples, but we saw successful experiments involving pictures, recordings and full-scale performances.

Ellipsis and anaphora hide a major challenge, though, for non-linguists. The following block of examples will look highly varied to specialists in ellipsis, but the budding young pragmaticist is likely to see a lot of basically identical cases:

(6)

Edna passed the test,

a. and Sam did too.

b. as did Sam.

c. and Sam too.

d. and Sam did that too.

e. and Sam did it too.

f. and Sam did so too.

g. which Sam can too.

Consider the student who runs a questionnaire-based study probing the extent to which the antecedent for the ellipsis case can be far from the ellipsis site in the discourse. The answer will be 'Very far' for (a) and (d)–(f), but 'Not far at all' for the others in this list. This student will *henceforth* appreciate the difference between these phenomena, but the experiment itself might have crashed, leaving the student distraught. So it is important to implement multiple checks on the materials. We had students workshop each other's examples, and we checked them carefully ourselves before anyone ran any subjects, correcting examples in various ways in order to better align materials and hypotheses. This kind of checking is crucial for any student experimental study, but the wide-open nature of pragmatic inquiry makes it all the more important. Student experimenters are unlikely to be sensitive to distinctions like those in (6), but, by the miracle of human language processing, their subjects probably will be.

7.5 Assignments

Our first assignment, generally distributed on the opening day, broke down into four parts and helped to establish the rhythm of our work schedule. Here is the first and most important part:

> Find an utterance that seems to be just the merest sketch of what the speaker actually intended with it. Intuitively, this will be a situation in which the speaker seems to 'mean more than she says'. Your utterance can come from anywhere: it can be something you overhear, something you read, something you encounter in the media, and so forth. It need not be an utterance in the traditional sense: signs, texts, rules and regulations – any language-based medium is a potential source of data.

At this point, they had heard the name Grice, but not much more than that, and if they had heard 'implicature' from us at all, it was probably a terminological slip on our part, a violation of our temporary ban on technical terms. All we had done in class was explore examples. This assignment was meant as a transition to meatier theoretical ideas, but we wanted them to continue exploring without being weighted down in that way. The above was followed by a note called 'Context is crucial', which emphasized that they needed to provide a full picture of the context of utterance along with their example. 'Part of the lesson here,' we said, 'is that utterances in isolation are almost meaningless. It's only once they are situated in context that we can see what they really mean.'

Personally, I am wary of defining pragmatics as 'the theory of language use' or as 'the theory of the relation between language and language users'. These phrases, though arguably accurate, convey very little about what there is to theorize about. In *Presumptive meanings* (MIT Press, 2000), Stephen C. Levinson comes closer to encapsulating the nature of pragmatic inquiry. He first observes that the phrases we utter are just a 'sketch' of what we actually convey when we use language with each other, and then he characterizes pragmatics as the study of the ways in which people systematically flesh our these sketches into full-fledged meanings. One can hear the echoes of this more specialized definition in the above introduction to assignment 1, which, in conjunction with our own illustrative examples, did reliably steer students to core problems of pragmatic theory. In response to it, we received examples involving implicit quantifier domain restrictions, scalar implicatures, metaphor, jokes and implicit speech-acts (as well as, admittedly, more unusual things that did not work at all – e.g. the pragmatics of meeting yourself while time-travelling, absurdly intricate passages from philosophy texts, children arguing with their parents).

Step 2 of the assignment was to write a description of the example with commentary about what they thought was happening in it. Step 3 was an in-class workshop of these descriptions. Before this workshop, we devoted a class period to the basic tenets of Gricean pragmatics: the cooperative principle, the maxims and their interactions, and a lot more illustrative examples. The immediate focus of the lecture, and the organizing principle of the workshop, was to address the following open question about their examples:

> Is Grice relevant? If the maxims seem not to be relevant to your example, that's important too, because it means that Grice's theory might not be as comprehensive as we would hope. In this case, explain why Gricean pragmatics doesn't suffice for your example.

Students love the sense that they might uncover a gap in the theoretical coverage, so they can be zealous about saying 'No', but generally the effect is good, and this kind of question engenders lively group discussion. That discussion fed into step 4, the final draft, which extended the (perhaps modified) description of the example with 'the Gricean connections (or lack thereof)' that emerged from the group discussion.

This sounds complicated, but we were with students every step of the way, and the overall effect was worth the students' constant questions about what they were supposed to do next. With this assignment, we established that the course's papers would not be one-off affairs, but rather layered, multi-step processes resembling the progression of a research project. (This is pretty heavy-duty for a general-education course. Our deal with the students was that we would devote large chunks of class time to writing, editing and revising in small groups.)

Over the course of 15 weeks, the students did four or five more assignments like this, in addition to weekly quizzes and other small assignments. In the information-structuring unit, we controlled the empirical basis a lot more, but then we opened it back up again for presuppositions and the later units, which tolerate a lot more variation in the nature of the examples.

Not all the group work that students did was connected directly with their assignments. We often used that forum to further develop course material and to explore new kinds of examples. There are always students who dislike group work, no matter what its design, but the majority opinion of our use of it was positive. In the fall of 2007, a mid-semester course evaluation by the UMass Amherst Center for Teaching revealed that students wanted more of it. They characterized it as 'very helpful' and 'clarifying', especially in that it gave them the chance to get 'ideas of what other students are doing/thinking' and, in a playfully meta-move, they passed on the comment that they benefitted from holding 'discourses on discourse'.

7.6 Meta-applications

Our short course description says, 'Students will pick up skills that are vital to understanding how to structure effective arguments.' We had in mind that students would begin to apply the lessons of the class to their own writing. For instance, by the end of unit 2 on the syllabus, students knew a lot about the discourse conditions that favour preposing over postposing in English-like languages, and this in turn governs passivization, topicalization, dislocation and other constructions that vary how information is structured. This could be applied, at the sentence-level, to crafting essays. Similarly, our in-depth look at the techniques of framing in the political realm provided a lot of information about what works and what doesn't work when it comes to persuading people of a particular position. This too could be used on the very assignments that we handed out.

A few students entered the course with the expectation that we would be helping them at this practical level. For example, responding to the question about what the course title meant to them, one student wrote, on day 1, 'I took it to mean that this course would elevate my ability to clearly and concisely express any point I was trying to get across to any given audience', and a few others mentioned things that sound vaguely prescriptive (e.g. the title as a gentler version of 'Talking Better'). A few hoped we could make them better con artists.

In practice, I think we did not see much evidence that students were applying the ideas of the class to their writing for the class. This is initially puzzling; we do have plenty of evidence that they understood the material. They even designed original experiments to probe sophisticated hypotheses inspired by the course material. So we were definitely getting through to them at an analytic level. We did not, though, see a real change in, for example, the artfulness with which students mapped out their basic ideas, nor did we find evidence of increased attention to the phrases they used to describe things in their assignments.

Perhaps it was just too meta, too inward looking. Most students were simultaneously getting an introduction to the ins and outs of linguistic theorizing as they tried to get a look at the outlines of pragmatic theory and the basic techniques of psycholinguistic experimentation. Implicitly asking them to apply those ideas right away might have been too much. In contrast, when we *explicitly* asked them to apply the ideas in their writing, they generally succeeded. For example, one lively in-class group work involved writing short advertisement-like descriptions for obviously faulty products and ideas: televisions with no volume control, shopping mall designs that would destroy their quaint New England town, real estate on fraternity row, and so forth. Here, they wielded their new expertise at presupposition, implicature and information structuring to quite good (or ill) effect. But when it came to the analytic essays for the course itself, they seemed to slip back into writing in their usual mode – at least as far as I could tell; I should add that the students generally did very well, which might mean that they were manipulating us rhetorically in ways too subtle for us to detect consciously.

7.7 What teaching pragmatics can teach us about the rest of linguistics

It is a common complaint among university instructors that students have become too career-oriented, that they do not appreciate the intrinsic value of a broad liberal arts education. I am sympathetic with this complaint, but I think the student perspective is less about pay cheques than it might seem. In my experience, students are concerned about what we will teach them to *do* – what skills they will acquire and what those skills will empower them to accomplish. They are quite sensibly thinking past their short college years to the much longer time that they will spend out in the professional world, where having a whole lot of knowledge is of little value if you do not know where and how to put it to use. We owe it to them to articulate how our classes will help them go on to greater (and, yes, more lucrative) things.

Teaching 'Controlling the Discourse' has helped me to see that pragmatic theory provides students with valuable, empowering skills. I am glad that students in the class learned who Grice is, where ellipsis can and cannot occur in English, what dependent and independent variables are, and so forth, but I am most proud of the fact that we made them more intelligent, sceptical consumers of others' utterances. The course title suggests, not unfairly, that discourse can be a struggle for control of important issues, and we taught our students how to navigate this mess intelligently and successfully.

It is all well and good to tell students this, but it was more valuable to let them experience it. That was the goal of the 'Great Debates' we held in the final class meetings.

In spring 2009, the great debate centred on the dialogue in (3) above, from *Bronston v. United States*. The question: Did Bronston perjure himself here? We provided just the basic context, the short piece of dialogue, and a passage outlining the basics of perjury. The debate would run like this: after an initial vote on the issue, the class would split into two teams. One team would be tasked with arguing for perjury, the other against. Each team would have 15 minutes to build its initial case and five minutes to present that case, with time for follow-up questions from the opposing team and from Lyn and me. The teams would then retreat to prepare one-minute closing statements. After those were presented, there would be a second vote, to assess what influence the debate had had. The winning team would be the one that converted the most votes to its side.

Both sides attacked both the dialogue and the definition of perjury, identifying places where pragmatic enrichment was required and seeking to exploit those, if not to support their position then at least to question our basic understanding of what happened in that courtroom. What does it mean to tell the whole truth? This is surely bounded by relevance. Can we determine what Bronston thought was relevant? Does it matter? Can we be sure that Bronston knew about all his personal accounts? Perhaps the maxim of quality prevented him from offering a direct answer. What background assumptions are we making about companies, their owners, and the relationships between them, and how might these assumptions have shaped the discourse? Not all indirect answers are misleading. Some are quite cooperative. How should we classify Bronston's?

Our initial vote on the question of whether Bronston had perjured himself resulted in a slight majority of 'yes' votes. The post-debate vote had roughly the same result. There was one thing they could agree on, though: *none of them* would be as naive as the lawyer was in this case. It now seemed inconceivable to them that Bronston's indirect answer slipped by without objection. I myself felt reassured that they now had the skills and confidence to keep control of their own discourses.

Acknowledgments

I owe a huge thanks to Lyn Frazier for suggesting that we co-teach 'Controlling the Discourse' together, and for teaching me so much about pragmatics and discourse processing along the way.

Notes

* **Christopher Potts**

Christopher Potts got his start in linguistics while an undergraduate at NYU. At first, it was just the odd introductory class here and there, but linguistics soon took over his schedule. By his senior year, he was immersed in syntax and semantics projects, under the sceptical, encouraging eye of Paul Postal. After NYU, Chris headed west, to UC Santa Cruz Linguistics, where undergraduate teaching is central to the entire intellectual life of the department. As a TA, he marvelled at how Sandy Chung and Geoff Pullum would seem to hand control of their lectures to their students, only to realize later that they had never relinquished control at all – that they were skilfully guiding the students' comments towards the truth. After UC Santa Cruz, Chris headed east again, to UMass Amherst, where his colleagues taught him the ins and outs of mentoring graduate students as they develop their own research projects, lead their own courses, and go on to become mentors themselves. In 2009, Chris moved west once again; he is currently Associate Professor of Linguistics at Stanford University.

8 Teaching historical linguistics: A personal memoir

Harold Koch *

8.1 Teaching the basic course in historical linguistics

8.1.1 Place in the curriculum

The ANU linguistics program has always had a course on historical linguistics. It was first called 'Introduction to Comparative Linguistics', but later its name was altered to 'Language Change and Linguistic Reconstruction'. It has been offered every year until 2007, after which it alternates with a course on the history of the English language. ANU's historical linguistics course has always had the phonetics (and phonology) course as a prerequisite. Thus it has been classified as a second/third year course. The reason is that ANU courses have emphasized the mastery of analytical methods. The principal methods to be mastered in historical linguistics involve phonetics and phonology. Therefore students must have command of the concepts and terminology of articulatory phonetics (places and manners of articulation, major classes of consonants and vowels, etc.) and phonology (contrast, allophony, distinctive features, phonological systems, etc.), since these are all involved in describing sound change and reconstructing phonological systems. Syntax, morphology and semantics have not been prerequisites, because there are typically few if any available assignments based on change in these domains of language.

8.1.2 Textbooks

A primary consideration with regard to teaching an introductory course is the selection of a textbook. I have found that students like a textbook, rather than reading just a collection of articles and book chapters. I had learned historical linguistics in the 1960s from Lehmann 1962b. When I first taught the course at ANU I used the newer textbook Anttila 1972, but students protested about its difficulty (its language is in fact very abstract). Anderson 1973 was also used, but not found by students as useful as others that were available to them such as Jeffers and Lehiste 1979. For a number of years we used (various editions of) Crowley's more practical textbook[1] (1981, 1987, 1992, 1997), supplemented by further readings. Since the late 1990s we have used either Trask's (Trask 1996; Millar 2007) or Campbell's (1998, 2004) textbook. The choice between them has been determined by availability, price, or the fact that Trask has two separate chapters on sound change (phonetic change vs change in phonological systems) corresponding to the single chapter on 'sound change' in Campbell's textbook. The other current strong candidates are Hock and Joseph 1996 and the latest revision of Crowley's book by Bowern (Crowley and Bowern 2010). Hock's textbook has always been strong on contact issues. Crowley and Bowern 2010 includes a section on recent computational phylogenetic methods that derive from evolutionary biology. An alternative strategy for textbook use would be a combination of a text on language change (McMahon 1994), which replaces the older Bynon 1977, and one on linguistic reconstruction (Fox 1995).

I have normally included in the course outlines a reference list of books on historical linguistic topics, many of which are available in one of the libraries. I include a statement such as: 'Many topics are discussed in a number of books. Students are advised to read from at least two sources for each topic.' The course outlines gave references to a number of textbooks for each topic. Textbooks other than those mentioned above are: Aitchison 1981; Anttila 1989; Arlotto 1972; Bloomfield 1933; Haas 1969; Hock 1986, 1991; Lehmann 1973, 1992a; Meillet 1967; Samuels 1972. Also indicated in the course materials are books containing useful readings: Baldi and Werth 1978; Durie and Ross 1996; Greenberg 1957; Jones 1993; Joseph and Janda 2003; Keiler 1972; Li 1977.

8.1.3 Order of topics

Historical linguistics being what it is, there are many ways that topics can be ordered for presentation. One could deal first with all aspects of phonology – change, internal reconstruction, comparative reconstruction – then do the same with morphology, syntax and semantics. Or one could first cover all kinds of change, then tackle reconstruction in each of the domains. To me it makes sense to describe change before reconstruction within each domain of language. (The first time I taught the course I taught the comparative method before sound change; I soon realized that this was a mistake.[2])

I eventually made another change in the order of presentation of topics. The comparative method for reconstructing phonology involves two variants, depending on whether subgrouping is involved or not. I normally assign two assessable assignments in reconstruction, the first of which does not involve subgrouping and the second which does. But I have found that it is better to introduce subgrouping apart from the comparative method, rather as part of the explanation of language relationships – along with family trees. So after students have done two assignments on describing the phonological changes between two chronologically separated stages of the same language, I give an assignment which requires them to describe the sound changes between one earlier language and three or four descendant languages, of which two form a subgroup. The goal of this exercise is to describe accurately all the phonological changes and to see which set of languages has undergone identical changes which took place before other changes that they each underwent separately and which therefore justify a subgroup. Then by the time they get to the later assignment on the comparative method with subgrouping – which requires them to establish correspondences, reconstruct a proto-system, describe the sound changes leading to each language, and discover the relevant subgroups – they will be confident about what is involved in the subgrouping part of the exercise.

Tutorials were used to practise the analytical methods and included sample problems of the kind that were given for the assignments. Tutorials may also discuss problems in methods that are not assessed, such as internal reconstruction, change and reconstruction in morphology, syntax and semantics, and lexicostatistics. I normally devote one tutorial to learning how to use etymological dictionaries.

8.1.4 Emphases

In accordance with the pedagogical philosophy of ANU's linguistics program, I have made it a central aim of my course to ensure that students learn how to apply the key methods of historical linguistics: describing phonological change, doing phonological reconstruction using the comparative method, and subgrouping on the basis of common innovations. At the same time I want them to understand the main kinds of and motivations for language change. Considerable attention is given to typologies of change – especially in phonology and morphology, with copious exemplification. Special attention is given to prevailingly unidirectional changes – such as assimilation and lenition in phonology, grammaticalization, and whole to part semantic shifts (see Wilkins 1996) – and their usefulness for reconstruction. A persistent challenge is to help students develop an understanding of what are plausible changes and to use this knowledge in their solutions to exercises. I like to emphasize the role of plausibility in informing both diachronic and synchronic typology, both of which should serve as checks on reconstruction hypotheses.

I have found it an interesting challenge to try to formulate the procedures to be followed in describing phonological changes, the comparative method (these were published in Koch 1996), and internal reconstruction (these are cited in Crowley and Bowern 2010, chapter 7). An attempt to provide similar procedures for morphological reconstruction was behind my paper on morphological reconstruction (Koch 1996). I had to conclude that for domains other than phonology such procedures were not feasible, but that we should content ourselves with understanding the types of change that can occur and posit plausible reconstructions consistent with the related forms and known kinds of change.

I have used guest lectures for topics for which there was available a colleague with special expertise. Recent expert presentations have been on tonogenesis by Phil Rose, lexicostatistics by Paul Sidwell, philological methods by Jennifer Hendriks, syntactic change by Cynthia Allen (on English) or Rachel Hendery (typologically), reconstruction of culture from language by Andrew Pawley, and, when contact was still part of the syllabus, grammatical borrowing (especially metatypy) by Malcolm Ross. Another aim of the guest lectures, in addition to allowing presentations by experts, was to communicate to students the range of expertise and research interests in historical linguistics that our university possesses.

8.1.5 Exercises

How many assignments should be given in a 13-week semester? The first few times I taught the course, beginning in 1975, I assigned nine. Throughout the 1980s I and other colleagues who taught the course, Bill Foley and Bob Dixon, assigned eight or nine problems. Eventually I reduced the number to six, then cut out the sixth assignment (on loanword analysis) when the weight of the course was reduced from eight to six credit points and the content on language contact was removed from the syllabus. The recent pattern has been: two assignments on phonological change, the first emphasizing types of phonetic change and the second introducing the phonological aspects of split, merger and chain shifts; the third has been sound change from one to three languages, with students being required to justify subgrouping found in the data; the fourth has been the comparative method – establishing correspondences, proposing proto-phonemes and describing the consequent changes – without subgrouping; the final problem is the same but involves subgrouping. The final examination involves a compact set of artificial data to which students must apply the comparative method with subgrouping. This provides coverage of the kinds of analytic skills one would want students to develop.

In recent years I have not assigned assessable problems using the method of internal reconstruction (IR). We do a number of practice problems in tutorials using the method, and many are available in textbooks. The reason I attribute a lower priority to this method is because I consider that it is often not safe to use the method. The method starts with morphophonemic alternations (different phonemes occurring in different allomorphs of the same morpheme – in the terminology of morphemics) and posits for an earlier stage of the language a single phoneme in the place of each set of alternating phonemes, plus sound changes. The problem is that much allomorphy results from morphological (analogical) changes, so the premise of IR that allomorphy results from phonological changes in a phonological environment is not justified in all cases. However, where clear phonological conditioning is apparent in the data, it may be safe to apply the method. At any rate, the method of IR is very similar to the synchronic method used in generative phonology (GP) to establish underlying forms for phonologically related surface phonemes (as pointed out by Lass 1977); students will learn this technique in a course in morphology or phonology. It is fun to call attention, nevertheless, to the different status of solutions in IR and GP. Take for example, the Palauan data of Table 1 in Appendix 8.1. The most economical solution for a synchronic analysis is to posit contrasting underlying vowels and two rules, one which reduces vowels to shwa in unstressed syllables, and another which deletes vowels word-finally. These are not likely to correspond to the actual historical changes, however. Rather, the most plausible diachronic change is that all vowels in unstressed syllables first reduced to shwa, then these shwa vowels disappeared from final syllables. Furthermore, in the GP solution the 1Sg suffix would be reconstructed as *-k*, with no final vowel, since there is no alternation that would require one; but the IR solution allows rather that the suffix may have ended in a vowel; which vowel is not determinable from the data, since any vowel would have been lost. This solution allows for a pre-Palauan phonotactics that involves word-final vowels. The stress rule for such a language state would involve regular penultimate stress placement.

A persistent issue for teachers is where to find problems. Some textbooks include practice exercises. This is true of the books by Crowley, Campbell and Trask. Lehmann's textbooks are accompanied by a workbook (see Lehmann 1962a, 1992b). Columbus 1974 and Cowan 1971 both contain problems in sound change, the comparative method and internal reconstruction. Cowan and Rakušan 1987 includes, among others, problems on sound change, comparative method (called 'reconstruction'), as well as a large number on 'phonemic alternations', which could be used for internal reconstruction. Schane and Bendixen 1978, a workbook which accompanies Schane 1973, a textbook in generative phonology, contains exercises on 'phonological processes', 'phonological rules', 'underlying representations' and 'ordered rules', which can be adapted for internal reconstruction.

An interesting aspect of teaching historical linguistics is the opportunity to make up problems of one's own. I made up one problem in historical phonology, which involves describing the sound changes between Proto-Ngayarda and Yindjibarndi, a language of Western Australia. I based this on O'Grady 1966, supplemented by further data from Wordick 1982. It involves an interesting chain shift: (non-apical) stops in intervocalic position lenite to glides and laterals undergo fortition to stops. Thus 'escape' *caca* becomes *caja* and 'rubbish' *caʎa* becomes *caca*. For examinations each year I make up a compact problem using artificial data and involving subgrouping. An example is given in Appendix 8.2. In subsequent years I have used a version of these as practice problems for sound change plus subgrouping, providing the proto-forms this time. I have also made up a problem for sound change plus subgrouping using real language data from Indo-Iranian. Without naming the languages, I provide the forms for Proto-Indo-Iranian words (which I have constructed from the relevant Indo-Europeanist literature) plus the reflexes in Sanskrit, Avestan and Old Persian. Students are to describe the sound changes and discover that the latter two belong to a subgroup on the basis of common innovations.

When loanword analysis was still part of the syllabus of the historical linguistics course, I used an excellent problem in sorting loanwords from cognates, which I adapted from one constructed by Calvert Watkins. It involves approximately equal numbers of compared forms from Armenian and Avestan (standing in for the Iranian languages). Students are informed that the languages are genetically related, that one of them has borrowed extensively from the other, and that sound changes may have taken place after the borrowing. They are to determine which pairs of compared words are cognates and which are borrowed (and in which direction), using the phonological criterion of rival sound correspondences, the morphological criterion of analysability in the source language, and the semantic criterion of basic versus cultural vocabulary.

I have also made up some problems on grammatical change. I constructed one problem that involved both sound change and analogical extension within paradigms, using data from Proto-Indo-European to classical Greek. An exercise in purely morphological change involving Scandinavian pronouns was constructed from data in Haugen 1976. I have also used a problem in the morphological reconstruction of personal pronouns in Western Australian languages that was constructed by Alan Dench (for the facts see Dench 1994). An open-ended exercise that I made up gives the Lord's Prayer in Old English – with words fully glossed – accompanied by later versions and asks the students on the basis of this data to make a list of grammatical changes that have taken place in the history of English.

A more controlled exercise in grammatical change was a set of artificial data I constructed to illustrate my favourite grammatical changes:

- grammaticalization of stance verbs to tense and aspect auxiliaries;
- development of postpositions from local nouns like 'front', 'back' and 'side';
- grammaticalization of third person pronouns to definite articles;
- change of alignment from ergative to nominative and consequent reinterpretation of case markers;
- absorption of third person possessor markers into the stem of bodypart nouns and that of first person possessors in kin nouns;
- expansion of a third person singular allomorph throughout a verbal paradigm by levelling;
- shift of the boundary between stems and suffixes as a result of final vowel loss;
- and so on.

I made up a set of sentences in 'language A', using a particular grammar and a limited vocabulary, applied a number of obvious phonological changes as well as grammatical changes to these sentences, then presented the 'language B' version of each sentence beside the language A version. Data like this is best used in a tutorial session, with small groups of students each working on particular domains (the grammar of verbs, nouns and adpositions respectively). A small portion of this exercise is presented in Appendix 8.3.

For semantic change, I once gave a set of definitions of words used in Shakespeare's English that now have a different sense and asked students to comment on semantic changes. This did not work very well; for example, what semantic change is to be deduced from the fact that *glass* has lost the senses of 'telescope' and 'mirror' but gained the senses of 'spectacles' and 'drinking vessel'? More interesting (as a tutorial exercise) is to offer a set of etymologically related forms and expressions and ask students to do some internal reconstruction of semantics. For example, given expressions like *quicken*, *quicksilver*, *cut to the quick*, *the quick of the matter*, *the quick and the dead*, what might be reconstructed as an earlier meaning of *quick* and how might the 'speedy' meaning have developed?

My assessment pattern always includes an essay on a choice of topics. In early years I allowed students to do data-based studies – on the identification of loanwords between two languages or a description of semantic or phonological changes between two stages of a language. The latter could have disastrous results: if a student tried to work out the sound changes between Latin and French from a sample of related words, they risked putting together as reflexes of a Latin form both words transmitted throughout the whole developmental period, such as *froid*, and later learned borrowings, such as *frigide* – both ultimately from *frigidus*. In recent years I have only given topics that require learning about more theoretical aspects of the subject, such as social factors in sound change, grammaticalization, semantic change, the Natural Morphology theory of change, the role of typology in reconstruction and distant genetic relations.

8.1.6 Examinations

A question worth considering is whether to require an end-of-semester exam – given that students will have been doing assignments during the term. I take the view that a main objective of the course is to train students in the methods of historical linguistics. They learn these by a combination of seeing them demonstrated in lectures, practising them in non-assessable problems in tutorials, and applying them in assessable problems. However, it seems unfair to me to base all of the assessment on their performance in what are still learning exercises. Rather, their achievement is best assessed at the end of the teaching period. Hence I give a final examination, and one component is a problem which involves comparative reconstruction, subgrouping and the description of sound changes. Given the time limitations of the final examination, such a problem must be compact. I find it easiest to provide data for such a problem by making up my own data set, consisting of 8 to 12 words in four languages, with at least one subgroup in the data. In recent years I have provided a worksheet to expedite their compilation of the facts and to ensure consistency in the format of their answers. (Appendix 8.2 gives a sample data set: when used as a problem in comparative method, the proto-form line is left blank.)

Another reason for requiring a final examination is to hold students accountable for the course content (available in lectures and readings) which is not tested in the term assignments. I want them to demonstrate their mastery of the main concepts of the sub-discipline. Half of the examination is normally devoted to this kind of question. If the examination involves no access to reading material, the exam can include a question asking for short explanations of a number of key terms. If it is an open-book exam or a take-home exam, this kind of question is not suitable, since the answers can quickly be supplied by consulting books or notes. With any kind of exam it is possible to ask for a short essay on topics such as: causes of change, comparing different kinds of change, directionality of change, comparing reconstruction methods, the basis for language classification, and so on.

Let me sound a warning about the wording of a question about the last issue. I once included an exam question that was meant to elicit a discussion of the grounds for establishing a genetic relationship between languages. The question read as follows:

> Suppose that you are a linguist studying a language spoken in a particular village in the highlands of New Guinea. This language and the language spoken in the nearest village, on the other side of the mountain, are mutually unintelligible. You suspect, however, that they are genetically related.
>
> How would you go about proving a genetic relationship? What kinds of evidence would you use? What relative importance would you attach to each kind of evidence used? Why?

One hapless student professed an inability to answer the question on the grounds that he or she didn't know anything about the languages of New Guinea!

8.2 A course on language contact

Topics on language contact were originally included in our course in historical linguistics, but around 2000 these were removed and put into a newly created course called 'Languages in Contact'.[3] Given the recent florescence of contact studies, there are enough contact-related topics to fill a whole semester course. Topics that can be discussed include: diglossia and societal multilingualism, borrowing and loanword analysis, structural borrowing (metatypy), linguistic areas, koineization, pidginization, creolization, hybrid languages, code-switching, language shift, language endangerment, language death, language maintenance.

Most of these topics include a diachronic component. But most also involve more social and sociolinguistic issues than are normally included in a historical linguistics course. Possible textbooks are Winford 2003 or Thomason 2001. Personally I have found Winford easier to use as a textbook.

One of the issues with such a course is that of prerequisites. Ideally students should have had courses in both historical linguistics and sociolinguistics. It is not realistic, however, to require either of these. One kind of skill that students should get experience in is loanword analysis. This has been one of the topics for which exercises have been provided in courses in historical linguistics. Campbell 2004, for example, has some good ones. A difficulty, however, is that students who have not done a course in historical linguistics will lack an understanding of correspondence sets. This does not matter for comparing loanwords between English and Japanese or Maori, but in situations where the borrowing languages may also be genetically related the existence of contrasting correspondences may be an important indicator of the presence of loanwords. So ideally students should be exposed to this application of the methodology.

8.3 Courses on a language family

Courses on a language family involve their own issues. One has to do with prerequisites. Should students have had a general course in historical linguistics? Should they have familiarity with at least one of the languages of the family? The answer partly depends on the aim of the course. For many years ANU offered a course on the Romance languages that had no linguistics prerequisite beyond the introductory course but expected a knowledge of French, Italian or Spanish. We have also offered courses on Indo-European, Austronesian and Australian comparative linguistics. The Indo-European course that I taught required historical linguistics as a prerequisite, but it was unrealistic to expect students to have studied one of the classical Indo-European languages such as Latin, Greek, Sanskrit, Gothic or Old Church Slavonic – as they may have done at Harvard in the 1960s. At best our students may have studied some French, German or Italian, which are so different structurally from the classic Indo-European languages that the comparative data normally discussed in an Indo-European course is as unfamiliar to them as Austronesian or Australian. At the request of students, I did for a few years spend the first few weeks teaching an inflecting language – but not Latin, Greek or Sanskrit, which were being taught elsewhere in the university. I used Lithuanian a few times, but it was then hard to integrate this individual language study into the comparative phonology and morphology presented in subsequent weeks. In the 1970s the courses on Austronesian and Australian comparative linguistics were year-long, so there was time to spend a third of the year on the structure of a particular language.

In 2006 I taught a course on Indo-European which was targeted primarily to classics students who had Greek and/or Latin but no linguistics; it was called 'The Indo-European Background to Greek and Latin'. This was facilitated considerably by the availability of a textbook containing exercises, Fortson 2004. In order to diversify the course somewhat from pure linguistics, my syllabus included topics on vocabulary, poetic language, mythology and the homeland question (which involves archaeology), and students were allowed to write essays on topics outside of comparative linguistics. In 2008 I coordinated a course on 'The Germanic language family', which was somewhat similar in conception. Most of the students had studied a Germanic language, and not all had a background in linguistics. Since the emphasis was on historical-comparative aspects of Germanic, some time was spent on learning the basics of two of the older Germanic languages, Gothic and Old Saxon – especially their inflectional and derivational morphology systems, which differ considerably from those of the modern languages. The course also included lectures (by colleagues) on: the main early Germanic sound changes, syntactic change in English, Icelandic dative subjects, the Scandinavian languages, standardization issues illustrated by the history of Dutch. Each student did a report on a particular language, in addition to what they studied in common, and there was wide latitude in essay topics. Useful sources of readings were Harbert 2007, König and van der Auwera 1994, and Robinson 1992. An interesting assignment I made up (but it was labour-intensive) involved what might be called comparative textology. I took versions of Bible translations of the same passage in various languages (several are provided in Prokosch 1939 as 'specimen texts'), along with the Greek and Latin (Vulgate) originals with interlinear glosses, and asked the students to make observations on syntactic differences between the languages (especially in word order) and try to determine to what extent these were influenced by the original language from which they were translated.

For the last ten years ANU has regularly offered a course called 'Study of a Language Family'. (We no longer offer regular courses on Romance, Indo-European, Comparative Australian and Austronesian: the student numbers do not justify it.) The choice of language varies. We have offered courses in: Sub-Saharan African languages, Austronesian, Australian or Pama Nyungan, Mon-Khmer, Tai-Kadai, Chinese, Papuan, Germanic, and expect to offer Japonic. (We can do this only by using staff from outside of our linguistics program (i.e. from the Faculty of Asian Studies, Research School of Pacific and Asian Studies, as well as visiting fellows). Typically students have no background in any of the languages of the family but do know historical linguistics. These courses necessarily involve presenting a considerable amount of information of a typological nature. A pattern that I have used for Australian (especially the Pama-Nyungan family) is to discuss subdomains of language (phonology, nominal inflection, personal pronouns, verb inflection) from three perspectives:

- synchronic typology: what are the available patterns?
- shallow diachrony: what are obvious changes (e.g. visible as dialectal variants)?
- reconstruction: what are the main correspondences and the proto-systems and changes that can be reconstructed from them?

We have tried to offer this course every year if possible, as part of the educational thrust of the language change emphasis of our (virtual) Centre for Research on Language Change (see http://crlc.anu.edu.au).

8.4 Supervision of theses

An important kind of teaching is the supervision of theses, which involves facilitating our students to do actual research in our discipline. I have not done as much supervision in historical linguistics as in the grammatical description of languages. It is in fact rather difficult for students to do historical-comparative linguistics research topics, since this typically presupposes knowledge of several languages. One relatively restricted topic that I have found feasible is to do some comparison and reconstruction within a particular subgroup of an Australian language. Theses by Brammall (1991), Bowern (1998), Laffan (2003) and Barrett (2005) were of this type. Evans 1995 involved morphological reconstruction of a small set of forms across a large number of related languages. Toulmin 2006 (cf. Toulmin 2009) gathered new data and attempted to articulate a method for linguistic and sociolinguistic reconstruction in a dialect continuum situation. Grammaticalization within a single language was pursued in honours theses by Bullen (1995 on English) and Slater (2000 on Thai). Two theses that I helped to supervise involved grammatical change, in Romance (Daniliuc 2003) and in general (Hendery 2007). Language contact was the subject of two dissertations that I helped to supervise, by Amuzu (2004) (cf. Amuzu 2010) and Love (2006). One thesis involved archaeology and historical linguistics (Miceli 1993). I am currently supervising two PhD theses that involve reconstituting Aboriginal languages of New South Wales from earlier and incomplete documentation, as an aid to language revitalization.

8.5 Teaching and research

My university likes to brand itself as a research-intensive university and emphasizes links between teaching and research. It should be relatively easy for most of us academics to demonstrate how our own research informs our teaching. In my case, the results of my study of the historical phonology of the Arandic languages (Koch

1997b) have featured in a course on comparative Australian linguistics at the ANU, as well as in a short course that I taught, with Patrick McConvell, at the Australian Linguistic Institute held at Macquarie University in July 2004. It is more unusual to find examples of our research being led by our teaching. I would like to mention one clear example, however.

In the area of morphological change and reconstruction I felt that the textbooks present an inadequate picture. One of the new ideas regarding morphological change, which was popular at Harvard University during my student days, was a phenomenon popularly called 'Watkins' Law' (Watkins 1962: chs. 13-14; Arlotto 1972: 156; Collinge 1985: 239-40). This was a principle of paradigm restructuring that involved the pivotal role of the third person singular in analogical transformations of a verbal paradigm, based on the semantically 'unmarked' value of the third person singular and its potential to have a zero marker (according to synchronic principles later described as 'iconicity').

Obviously I wanted to teach my students this principle enunciated by my own mentor; but I had a suspicion that as a recurrent process of paradigm change it could be described in more general terms. My attempt to generalize the Watkins' Law principle led to a research project which extended over several years in the 1980s. The results of this search for the more general principles behind Watkins' Law – motivated initially by my need to know what to teach students in this regard – were eventually presented at the 1993 International Conference on Historical Linguistics in Los Angeles, and published as Koch 1995, where I rephrased the principle in the following terms: 'A word-form which expresses by means of a non-zero marker a property which is typologically expected to be coded by zero is liable to be reanalysed as containing a zero marker' (Koch 1995: 64).

8.6 Teaching through conference presentations and publications

One of the themes of my teaching career has been bringing my methodological training in Indo-European historical linguistics to bear on the comparative study of language families (especially Australian) that were being studied by linguists working in Australia. This was reflected not only in my research, but in conference presentations and publications. This involved me in articulating the methods that were practised in the longer-studied language families and communicating them to a wider audience.[4] Presentations and (often resulting) publications that had an instructional purpose include the domains of: overview of reconstruction methods for archaeologists (Koch 1997a), etymology[5] (Koch 1983; Koch and Hercus forthcoming), morphological change (Koch 1995, 1996, 2010), morphological reconstruction (Koch 1996, 2000, 2003, 2009a), subgrouping (see next paragraph), and 'reconstituting' linguistic forms (including place names) from incomplete and phonologically inaccurate records (Koch 2009b). This reconstitution methodology is not taught in my courses on historical linguistics, but I have included it as an exercise in my course 'Language in Indigenous Australia'. The typology of morphological change that is included in Koch 1996 has formed the framework of my lectures on this topic since I compiled the research.[6]

Probably my most instructional contribution to a conference involves the issue of subgrouping. For a 'Workshop on Reconstruction and Subgrouping in Australian Languages', held at the 2001 International Conference on Historical Linguistics in Melbourne (see Bowern and Koch 2004a), my co-organizer Claire Bowern and I provided a set of instructions to participants, emphasizing the common innovation methodology that each was to use in supporting the subgroups they discussed (cf. Bowern and Koch 2004b). My own contribution, Koch 2004b, applied the criteria to the Arandic subgroup. To contextualize our work for non-Australianist readers and to justify the need for our studies, I added to the resulting volume a chapter (Koch 2004a) that critically discussed the various methodological approaches that had previously been applied in the classification of Australian languages.

8.7 Au revoir

Challenges to teachers of historical linguistics include how to fit language change into the curriculum, how to attract students into this fascinating sub-discipline, and how to equip them to practise this craft successfully. In my experience, students bring to the subject a natural curiosity about the origin and change of words (i.e. etymology). How can we best build on this interest to produce informed and expert practitioners of our sub-discipline? I hope this sharing of my experience will inspire other teachers to find their own ways of communicating their knowledge and enthusiasm to new generations of linguists.

Appendix 8.1 Internal reconstruction vs generative phonology

Table 8.1 Partial Palauan internal reconstruction problem (Schane and Bendixen 1978: 72)

	1	2	3	pre-Palauan suffix
Gloss	'ashes'	'question'	'skill'	
Unpossessed	ʔáb	kér	dúʔ	
1Sg Possessor	ʔəbúk	kəríк	dəʔák	
pre-Palauan stem				

GP solution:
Underlying forms: ʔábu, ʔabúk, kéri, kerík, dúʔa, duʔák
Underlying stems: ʔábu, kéri, dúʔa

Underlying suffix: -k
Stress assignment: final syllable if closed, otherwise penultimate
Phonological rules (unordered):
V → ə/ unstressed
V → ø/ _#

IR solution:
Earlier forms: ʔábu, ʔabúkV, kéri, keríkV, dúʔa, duʔákV
Earlier stress assignment: penultimate syllable
(Ordered) phonological changes:
1. V → ə/ unstressed
2. ə → ø/ _#

Appendix 8.2 Comparative reconstruction and subgrouping

Table 8.2 Artificial data for comparative reconstruction (without the pNan forms) or for sound change with subgrouping (with pNan forms provided)

	1	2	3	4
gloss	'house'	'grain'	'stone'	'dog'
pNan	ˈpitik	ˈpukut	ˈtapak	ˈkaput
San	pʰiˈtek	pʰuˈkot	tʰaˈpak	kʰaˈpot
Han	ˈpiðiʔ	ˈpuɣuʔ	ˈtaβaʔ	ˈkoβuʔ
Bab	ˈbisk	ˈbuxt	ˈdavək	ˈgoft
Beb	fəˈtiʔ	fəˈkuk	θəˈpaʔ	xəˈpuk

	5	6	7	8	9
gloss	'chicken'	'cow'	'tree'	'brother'	'water'
pNan	ˈtakip	ˈkitap	ˈpukat	ˈtutip	ˈkipuk
San	tʰaˈkep	kʰiˈtap	pʰuˈkat	tʰuˈtep	kʰiˈpok
Han	ˈteɣiʔ	ˈkiðaʔ	ˈpuɣaʔ	ˈtuðiʔ	ˈkiβuʔ
Bab	ˈdexp	ˈgizəp	ˈbuɣət	ˈdusp	ˈgifk
Beb	θəˈkip	xəˈtap	fəˈkak	θəˈtip	xəˈpuʔ

Appendix 8.3 Grammatical change with artificial data (portion only)

1. He is standing beside the house.

A	*Tis*	*buki-lu*	*nawo-na*	*kas-i.*
	he:ABS	house-GEN	side-LOC	PRES:stand-3SG

B	*Tizn*	*tis*	*budž-in*	*navon*	*kaž-on*	*kaž.*
	he:NOM	the	house-LOC	beside	stand-PPL	be:3SG

2. You stood behind a tree.

A	*Zag*	*simpu-lu*	*faso-na*	*no-kas-en.*
	you:ABS	tree-GEN	back-LOC	PAST-stand-2SG

B	*Zagn*	*šimb-un*	*hazon*	*no-gaž-en.*
	you:NOM	tree-LOC	behind	PAST-stand-2SG

3. I will stand by the horse.

A	*Boz*	*sarma-na*	*wi-kas-ar.*
	I:ABS	horse-LOC	FUT-stand-1SG

B	*Bozn*	*tis*	*sarm-an*	*kaž-ar*	*gum-ar.*
	I:NOM	the	horse-LOC	stand-INF	will-1SG

References

Aitchison, J. 1981. *Language change: Progress or decay?* Bungay, Suffolk: Fontana Paperbacks.

Amuzu, E. 2004. 'Ewe-English code-switching: A case of composite rather than classic codeswitching'. PhD thesis, School of Language Studies, Australian National University.

Amuzu, E.K. 2010. *Composite codeswitching in West Africa: The case of Ewe-English codeswitching*. Saarbrucken: Lambert Academic Publishing.

Anderson, J.M. 1973. *Structural aspects of language change*. Harlow, Essex: Longman.

Anttila, R. 1972. *An introduction to historical and comparative linguistics*. New York: Macmillan.

Anttila, R. 1989. *Historical and comparative linguistics.* 2nd edn, revised; Amsterdam and Philadelphia: John Benjamins.

Arlotto, A. 1972. *Introduction to historical linguistics*. Boston: Houghton Mifflin.

Baldi, P. and R.N. Werth (eds.) 1978. *Readings in historical phonology: Chapters in the theory of sound change*. University Park and London: Pennsylvania State University Press.

Barrett, B. 2005. 'Historical reconstruction of the Maric languages of central Queensland'. Master of Linguistics sub-thesis, School of Language Studies, Australian National University.

Bloomfield, L. 1933. *Language*. London: Allen and Unwin.

Bowern, C.L. 1998. 'The case of Proto-Karnic: Morphological change and reconstruction in the nominal and pronominal system of Proto-Karnic (Lake Eyre Basin)'. BA (Hons) sub-thesis, Department of Linguistics, Australian National University.

Bowern, C.L., B. Evans and L. Miceli (eds.) 2008. *Morphology and language history: In honour of Harold Koch*. Current Issues in Linguistic Theory 298. Amsterdam and Philadelphia: John Benjamins.

Bowern, C.L. and H. Koch (eds.) 2004a. *Australian languages: Classification and the comparative method*. Current Issues in Linguistic Theory 249. Amsterdam and Philadelphia: John Benjamins.

Bowern, C.L. and H. Koch. 2004b. Introduction: Subgrouping methods in historical linguistics. In *Australian languages: Classification and the comparative method*, pp. 1-15, ed. C. Bowern and H. Koch. Amsterdam and Philadelphia: John Benjamins.

Brammall, D. 1991. 'A comparative grammar of Warluwaric'. BA(Hons) sub-thesis, Department of Linguistics, Australian National University.

Bullen, J. 1995. 'The histories of English connectives: A study of the paths and processes by which words have acquired connective uses in Middle and Modern English'. BA(Hons) sub-thesis, Department of Linguistics, Australian National University.

Bynon, T. 1977. *Historical linguistics*. Cambridge: Cambridge University Press.

Campbell, L. 1998. *Historical linguistics: An introduction*. Edinburgh: Edinburgh University Press.

Campbell, L. 2004. *Historical linguistics: An introduction*. 2nd edn; Edinburgh: Edinburgh University Press.

Collinge, N.E. 1985. *The laws of Indo-European*. Amsterdam and Philadelphia: John Benjamins.

Columbus, F. 1974. *Introductory workbook in historical phonology*. Cambridge, MA: Slavica Publishers.

Cowan, W. 1971. *Workbook in comparative reconstruction*. New York: Holt, Rinehart and Winston.

Cowan, W. and J. Rakušan. 1987. *Sourcebook for linguistics*. Philadelphia and Amsterdam: John Benjamins.

Crowley, T. 1981. *An introduction to historical linguistics*. Port Moresby: University of Papua New Guinea.

Crowley, T. 1987. *An introduction to historical linguistics*. Port Moresby: University of Papua New Guinea Press; Suva, Fiji: University of the South Pacific.

Crowley, T. 1992. *An introduction to historical linguistics*. 2nd edn; Auckland: Oxford University Press.

Crowley, T. 1997. *An introduction to historical linguistics*. 3rd edn; Auckland: Oxford University Press.

Crowley, T. and C.L. Bowern. 2010. *An introduction to historical linguistics*. 4th edn; Oxford and New York: Oxford University Press.

Daniliuc, L.A. 2003. 'Auxiliary selection in the Romance languages: Synchrony and diachrony'. PhD thesis, School of Language Studies, Australian National University.

Dench, A. 1994. 'The historical development of pronoun paradigms in the Pilbara region of Western Australia'. *Australian Journal of Linguistics* 14: 155-91.

Durie, M. and M. Ross (eds.) 1996. *The comparative method reviewed: Regularity and irregularity in language change*. New York: Oxford University Press.

Evans, B. 1995. 'Reconstructing object markers in Oceanic languages'. BA(Hons) sub-thesis, Department of Linguistics, Australian National University.

Fortson, B.W., IV. 2004. *Indo-European language and culture: An introduction*. Malden, MA and Oxford: Blackwell.

Fox, A. 1995. *Linguistic reconstruction: An introduction to theory and method*. Oxford: Oxford University Press.

Greenberg, J.H. 1957. *Essays in linguistics*. Chicago: University of Chicago Press.

Haas, M.R. 1969. *The prehistory of languages*. The Hague: Mouton.

Harbert, W. 2007. *The Germanic languages*. Cambridge: Cambridge University Press.

Haugen, E. 1976. *The Scandinavian languages: An introduction to their history*. London: Faber and Faber.

Hendery, R. 2007. 'The diachronic typology of relative clauses'. PhD thesis, School of Language Studies, Australian National University.

Hock, H.H. 1986. *Principles of historical linguistics*. Berlin: Mouton de Gruyter.

Hock, H.H. 1991. *Principles of historical linguistics*. 2nd edn; Berlin: Mouton de Gruyter.

Hock, H.H. and B.D. Joseph. 1996. *Language history, language change, and language relationship: An introduction to historical and comparative linguistics*. Berlin and New York: Mouton de Gruyter.

Jeffers, R. and I. Lehiste. 1979. *Principles and methods for historical linguistics*. Cambridge, MA: MIT Press.

Jones, C. (ed.) 1993. *Historical linguistics: Problems and perspectives*. Harlow, Essex: Longman.

Joseph, B.D. and R.D Janda (eds.) 2003. *The handbook of historical linguistics*. Malden, MA: Blackwell.

Keiler, A.R. 1972. *A reader in historical and comparative linguistics*. New York: Holt, Rinehart and Winston.

Koch, H. 1983. 'Etymology and dictionary-making for Australian languages (with examples from Kaytej)'. In *Papers in Australian linguistics No. 15: Australian*

Aboriginal lexicography, pp. 149-73, ed. P. Austin. Canberra: Pacific Linguistics.

Koch, H. 1995. 'The creation of morphological zeroes'. In *Yearbook of Morphology 1994*, pp. 31-71, ed. G. Booij and J. van Marle. Dordrecht: Kluwer Academic.

Koch, H. 1996. 'Reconstruction in morphology'. In *The comparative method reviewed: Regularity and irregularity in language change*, pp. 218-63, ed. M. Durie and M. Ross. New York: Oxford University Press.

Koch, H. 1997a. 'Comparative linguistics and Australian prehistory'. In *Archaeology and linguistics: Aboriginal Australia in global perspective*, pp. 27-43, ed. P. McConvell and N. Evans. Melbourne: Oxford University Press.

Koch, H. 1997b. 'Pama-Nyungan reflexes in the Arandic languages'. In *Boundary rider: Essays in honour of Geoffrey O'Grady*, pp. 271-302, ed. D. Tryon and M. Walsh. Canberra: Pacific Linguistics.

Koch, H. 2000. 'Order and disorder in the reconstruction of the ablaut pattern of athematic verbs in Proto-Indo-European'. In *Proceedings of the eleventh annual UCLA Indo-European conference, Los Angeles June 4–6, 1999*, pp. 251-66, ed. K. Jones-Bley, M.E. Huld and A. Della Volpe. Washington, DC: Institute for the Study of Man.

Koch, H. 2003. 'Morphological reconstruction as an etymological method'. In *Historical linguistics 2001: Selected papers from the 15th International Conference on Historical Linguistics, Melbourne, 13–17 August 2001*, pp. 271-91, ed. B.J. Blake and K. Burridge. Amsterdam and Philadelphia: John Benjamins.

Koch, H. 2004a. 'A methodological history of Australian linguistic classification'. In *Australian languages: Classification and the comparative method*, pp. 17-60, ed. C.L. Bowern and H. Koch. Amsterdam and Philadelphia: John Benjamins.

Koch, H. 2004b. 'The Arandic subgroup of Australian languages'. In *Australian languages: Classification and the comparative method*, pp. 127-50, ed. C. Bowern and H. Koch. Amsterdam and Philadelphia: John Benjamins.

Koch, H. 2009a. 'On reconstructing pronominal proto-paradigms: Methodological considerations from the Pama-Nyungan language family of Australia'. In *Discovering history through language: Papers in honour of Malcolm Ross*, pp. 317-44, ed. B. Evans. Canberra: Pacific Linguistics.

Koch, H. 2009b. 'The reconstruction of Aboriginal placenames: Methodology and application to the Canberra region'. In *Aboriginal placenames: Naming and re-naming the Australian landscape*, pp. 115-71, ed. H. Koch and L. Hercus. Canberra: Aboriginal History Inc and ANU E Press.

Koch, H. 2010. 'Morphological change'. In *The Cambridge encyclopedia of the language sciences*, pp. 514-15, ed. P. Hogan. Cambridge: Cambridge University Press.

Koch, H. and L. Hercus. forthcoming. 'Obscure vs. transparent cognates in linguistic reconstruction'. In *Sprung from a common source? Studies on structural and lexical etymology*, ed. R. Mailhammer. Canberra: Pacific Linguistics.

König, E. and J. van der Auwera (eds.) 1994. *The Germanic languages*. London and New York: Routledge.

Laffan, K. 2003. 'Reconstruction of the Wakka-Kabi languages of south-eastern Queensland'. BA(Hons) sub-thesis, School of Language Studies, Australian National University.

Lass, R. 1977. 'Internal reconstruction and generative phonology'. *Transactions of the Philological Society* (1975): 1-26.

Lehmann, W.P. 1962a. *Exercises to accompany Historical linguistics: An introduction*. New York: Holt, Rinehart and Winston.

Lehmann, W.P. 1962b. *Historical linguistics: An introduction*. New York: Holt, Rinehart and Winston.

Lehmann, W.P. 1973. *Historical linguistics: An introduction*. 2nd edn; New York: Holt, Rinehart and Winston.

Lehmann, W.P. 1992a. *Historical linguistics: An introduction*. 3rd edn; London and New York: Routledge.

Lehmann, W.P. 1992b. *Workbook for historical linguistics*. Dallas, TX: Summer Institute of Linguistics.

Li, C.N. (ed.) 1977. *Mechanisms of syntactic change*. Austin and London: University of Texas Press.

Love, S.B. 2006. 'Tahitian French: The vernacular French of the Society Islands, French Polynesia: A study in language contact and variation'. PhD thesis, Department of Linguistics, RSPAS, Australian National University.

McMahon, A.M.S. 1994. *Understanding language change*. Cambridge: Cambridge University Press.

Meillet, A. 1967. *The comparative method in historical linguistics*. Trans. Gordon B. Ford, Jr. Paris: Champion.

Miceli, L. 1993. 'Archeology, linguistics and the prehistoric Celts'. BA(Hons), Departments of Linguistics and Archeology & Anthropology, Australian National University.

Millar, R. McColl. 2007. *Trask's historical linguistics*. 2nd edn; London: Hodder Arnold.

O'Grady, G.N. 1966. 'Proto-Ngayarda phonology'. *Oceanic Linguistics* 5: 71-130.

Prokosch, E. 1939. *A comparative Germanic grammar*. Baltimore: Linguistic Society of America.

Robinson, O.W. 1992. *Old English and its closest relatives: A survey of the earliest Germanic dialects*. Stanford, CA: Stanford University Press.

Samuels, M.L. 1972. *Linguistic evolution: With special reference to English*. Cambridge: Cambridge University Press.

Schane, S.A. 1973. *Generative phonology*. Englewood Cliffs, NJ: Prentice-Hall.

Schane, S.A. and B. Bendixen. 1978. *Workbook in generative phonology*. Englewood Cliffs, NJ: Prentice-Hall.

Slater, R. 2000. 'The Thai irrealis marker *ca*^{2}: A critical description with reference to grammaticalisation'. BA(Hons) sub-thesis, Department of Linguistics, Australian National University.

Thomason, S.G. 2001. *Language contact: An introduction*. Edinburgh: Edinburgh University Press.

Toulmin, M. 2006. 'Reconstructing linguistic history in a dialect continuum: The Kamta, Rajbanshi, and Northern Deshi Bangla subgroup of Indo-Aryan'. PhD thesis, School of Language Studies, Australian National University.

Toulmin, M. 2009. *From linguistic to sociolinguistic reconstruction: The Kamta historical subgroup of Indo-Aryan*. Canberra: Pacific Linguistics.

Trask, R.L. 1996. *Historical linguistics*. London and New York: Arnold.

Watkins, C. 1962. *Indo-European origins of the Celtic verb, 1. The sigmatic aorist*. Dublin: Dublin Institute for Advanced Studies.

Wilkins, D. 1996. 'Natural tendencies of semantic change and the search for cognates'. In *The comparative method reviewed: Regularity and irregularity in language change*, pp. 264-304, ed. M. Durie and M. Ross. New York: Oxford University Press.

Winford, D. 2003. *An introduction to contact linguistics*. Malden, MA and Oxford: Blackwell.

Wordick, F.J.F. 1982. *The Yindjibarndi language*. Canberra: Pacific Linguistics.

Notes

* **Harold Koch**

In my professional life I have defined myself primarily as a historical linguist, although my teaching and research have extended considerably beyond this sub-discipline.

My training in historical linguistics was primarily in Indo-European studies. After studying French and Latin for my BA (Hons) at Waterloo Lutheran University (later renamed Wilfrid Laurier University) in Canada and doing a course-work MA in Classics – which included a considerable amount of linguistics as well – at the University of Washington in Seattle, I undertook a PhD at Harvard University. Indo-European linguistics, as taught at that time by Professor Calvert Watkins, focused on morphological issues. This was before phonological issues were reconsidered; later students pursued topics in syntactic change and reconstruction, and Watkins' own focus later changed to the reconstruction of poetic terminology. My thesis involved reconstruction of a particular aspect of derivational morphology, and included to some extent the study of etymology.

My whole subsequent academic career has been based at the Australian National University, where I was on the staff from 1974 until my retirement in July 2009 – in the Department of Linguistics, which was absorbed into the School of Language Studies in about 2000. I continue my research work as a Visiting Fellow in the School of Language Studies. With my appointment to the ANU, my research focus changed to Australian Aboriginal languages. This involved descriptive work on the Kaytetye language of

Central Australia, supervision of descriptive theses on Australian languages, as well as (more incidental) work on land claims and on Aboriginal English, but my primary interest has been in contributing to the solution of historical-comparative problems concerning Australian languages.

My teaching in the field of historical linguistics included formal university courses, short courses at Australian Linguistic Institutes, presentation at seminars, conferences, and workshops, the supervision of theses, and elements of my publications.

1 This book was written as a text for the course he taught at the University of Papua New Guinea, and was reproduced by the university's printery. Terry explained his motivation in a letter to colleagues on 5 April 1982, when he was considering revising it as a proper publication. 'My original motivation in writing the textbook was to help students specifically at this institution who were taking our course Comparative Linguistics. I could find no textbook that was even remotely suitable. Textbooks were either too basic, with not enough problems for practice, or too "erudite" (i.e. using vocabulary and constructions that made it difficult or impossible for most of our students to understand, given that for most, English is a third or fourth language). An additional problem was that students were often assumed to have certain kinds of background knowledge, which would be automatically provided in a European, Australian or North American socialisation, but not in Melanesia. Problems for analysis also seldom dealt with languages in this region. I therefore deliberately set out to simplify the language used to explain concepts (without simplifying the concepts themselves), to use examples that students in this region are familiar with to illustrate points, and to construct problems for analysis using languages of this area.'

2 Lehmann's textbook presents reconstruction methods before language change.

3 This followed from a restructuring of the BA degree, with later-year courses being reduced from eight credit points (equivalent to one-third of a full-time enrolment load) to six credit points (equivalent to one-fourth of a workload).

4 My role in codifying the methods of historical linguistics, especially in morphology, is referred to in the introduction to my Festschrift (Bowern *et al.* 2008).

5 These studies have informed my lectures on etymology.

6 A summary of these is given in chapter 10 of Crowley and Bowern (2010).

9 Teaching sociolinguistics

Miriam Meyerhoff[*]

9.1 Introduction

I have taught sociolinguistics with many different kinds of audiences. High school students, undergraduate majors in linguistics degrees, undergraduate non-majors learning through the medium of a second language, undeclared undergraduate majors, qualified teachers looking for continuing professional development, adult learners of English, (post-)graduate students in search of a PhD topic, law students who want to know about language use, education inspectors, training and development officers in the public service. I have even been asked to do a critique of language used in Question Time at the Scottish Parliament for the in-house magazine, but since they never invited me back, we would have to say that that foray into communicating sociolinguistics to an interdisciplinary audience was of limited success.

Most people in sociolinguistics would be able to list a range of similar audiences. It is partly a testimony to the social relevance of the linguistic issues we deal with in the field, partly a testimony to the breadth of methods and problems the field engages with, and partly a testimony to the ease with which technically forbidding content (such as potentially unfamiliar scripts (IPA) or familiarity with particular software and hardware) can be stripped away from sociolinguistics, without completely denaturing the methods and theory that we use to describe and generalize from language in use. It would be pointless, therefore, to attempt a survey of all the different ways in which you can teach sociolinguistics. Instead, I will focus this chapter on outlining in some detail the structure and goals and aims of a five-week, intensive unit that introduces second-year undergraduates to the practicalities of analysing language variation.

I had the very great good fortune to inherit this unit from a colleague at the University of Edinburgh, and I am enormously indebted to Ellen Gurman Bard, who is responsible for the overall structure of the unit. The relative balance between teacher-/tutor-led activities and student-led activities is key to the popularity and pedagogical success of this component of the course, and it was Ellen who came up with the right recipe. I have tinkered with the content to turn it into a hands-on introduction to theory and methods of variationist sociolinguistics, but in principle, the structure could be adapted to any sub-field as long as there is some messy, un-Bowdlerized data for students to analyse.

The guiding principles are that (a) students learn best by doing, and (b) they are smart, resourceful people who will respond to the professional challenges presented by facing real data.

I outline first the background, goals and objectives of the course (both skills and content knowledge); I then break down the structure of the unit into its different activity and learning modes.

9.2 Ellen Gurman's hands-on approach to teaching (socio)linguistics

9.2.1 Context and background

While the structure of the unit is extremely flexible, it helps to understand the context in which it is taught. Most of the first-year students in linguistics at Edinburgh are not majors. They are taking linguistics as an 'outside' subject, usually because it has been recommended as a complement to their principal degree subject (mostly modern languages, social anthropology, computer science, psychology). In the first year, they have been given 12 hours of lectures in what I would call macro-sociolinguistics (language attitudes, language vitality, multilingualism) and basic methods for discourse analysis (spoken and written).

By the time students are doing second-year linguistics, the proportion of people taking the class as an outside subject has dropped, but remains significant: half are not going to complete a degree solely majoring in linguistics. So a sociolinguistics unit that focuses simultaneously on the development of transferable skills – and the transmission of information – is very important. This dual focus is important for all the usual reasons transferable skills are lauded in universities, but it is also important because of the very local needs of our audience. Some students will never go on to take any more sociolinguistics classes at all. Aspiring psycholinguists, syntacticians and phoneticians in the department find the practical orientation of the second-year sociolinguistic unit as rewarding as budding sociolinguists.

In addition, for reasons peculiar to Edinburgh's degree structure, students doing a joint major in any modern language and linguistics have to spend their third year abroad. During this time they have to write their final undergraduate dissertation in linguistics. For these students, having a second-year unit that focuses on skills is essential preparation for their dissertation the next year. As a lot of them become interested in the linguistic variation they observe around them during their year of study abroad, a focus on methods and core readings/theory in variationist sociolinguistics is of direct, practical benefit.

The sociolinguistics unit unfolds over the last five weeks of the final semester. As well as needing to serve our students' particular needs as described above, it is also the last chance we have to 'convert' people to switch into a linguistics major. Consequently, the department has a major incentive to make it an enjoyable and challenging experience.

9.2.2 The task

A clear analytic task is established from the outset. Students are introduced to the variable they will be working on – in recent years, we have been looking at the alternation between alveolar and velar nasals in polysyllabic English words ending in <ing>. We also explain from the outset what kinds of linguistic and non-linguistic factors they will be expected to take into consideration in their analysis. These include: grammatical category of the word, following segment, speaker and genre/style.

9.2.3 Activity types and modes of learning

The unit consists of four types of activity. The way these are interleaved through the five week unit is shown in detail in Figure 9.1. In this section, I discuss how the different group activities serve different learning goals.

Lectures take the (usual) form of a single speaker at the front of a lecture hall, talking to handouts and/or PowerPoint. Lectures introduce theory and classic readings. As the course goes on, they are increasingly a forum for students to compare notes about problems they have encountered in workshops, and they provide a forum for brainstorming treatments and solutions for those problems.

Lectures have three forms of support:

Tutorials. Exercises are provided for students to work through with the help of a tutor. There is one tutorial a week. The course co-ordinator provides the exercises. The exercises are intended to establish a baseline of knowledge and practical experience which students can draw on for their independent work. They rehearse some of the skills or background information students need in order to analyse their own data.

Workshops. Tutorial groups meet once a week alone without the tutor present. An important task for students in the first workshop is to organize themselves as a work group. At a practical level, they have to be responsible for collecting and returning equipment, and they have to decide who will take notes and report back in lectures. They also have to establish constructive and cooperative work patterns on their own, work patterns that will see them through this part of the course. The workshops are the place where students jointly negotiate the identification, coding and analysis of data in spontaneous speech.

Students are provided with recorded data for the course. Ideally, we might have time for the students to get some experience in making recordings of spontaneous speech (thereby experiencing all the difficulties and rewards associated with that), but this is not practical within a compressed five-week time frame. In the last few years, our students have been working from excerpts of Scots English, and they use this as the basis for analysis of style effects on the single consonantal variable (ing). The recordings include two short pieces of football commentary and three recordings of Scots teenagers in conversation with a chosen friend or friends. Given the now widespread availability of various regional components of the ICE (International Corpus of English), and corpora available commercially through the Linguistic Data Consortium at the University of Pennsylvania, there is no reason why instructors working in English-speaking communities could not access sound files and carefully checked transcripts for varieties similar to their students'.

We provide a full transcription of the teenagers' conversations. This is essential because quite a few of our students are not speakers of Scots English and because the recordings were made outside the lab (so there is the inevitable background noise and frequent overlapping speech). Hence, many students would find it hard to understand the materials without a transcript. However, the transcription is fairly free: it generally conforms to Standard English spelling (but includes some standard representations of Scots, e.g. *dae* 'do', *wi* 'with', *wizna(e)* 'wasn't'), so we stress the importance of *listening* to how the speakers say a given word – that is, not relying on how a word is transcribed or what students might expect to hear in the varieties of English they are more familiar with. Crucially, the variable we are analysing – (ing) – is almost always transcribed with the Standard English <ing>, so students quickly perceive the need to forget about the transcript and to listen and transcribe the variable phonemically where it occurs.

There is not a full transcript of the sports commentary as these are much cleaner and more standard-like recordings, but students are provided with a pre-prepared coding sheet on which each token of words ending in <ing> has been listed in order of occurrence on the tape.

Each week, the workshop has specific set tasks for students to work through. These progress through identifying and extracting tokens, through to coding tokens and simple quantitative methods for testing for significance (chi-square tests).

The current data set consists of recordings of spontaneous broadcast and conversational speech; in the past, the course has also used recordings of people doing the Map Task (Anderson *et al.* 1991). The object of investigation was not stylistic variation then, but rather the linguistic realization of given and new referring expressions. This demonstrates two things: first, the flexibility of the overall course structure, and second, the potential in recordings of naturally occurring speech for teaching a range of linguistic concepts.

In the final week of the unit, the tutorial and workshop periods are used to work on presentation of the final assignment. Many of the students are not very confident in writing social science-style research reports at this stage in their university career, and the course organizers provide resources that directly support this (as well as providing more individualized advice where students require it).

Workshop-plus. Once a week, the day after the students have workshopped data alone, the tutor joins each group. This gives students an opportunity to discuss issues and/or questions that have arisen during the workshop session and draw on the tutor's sociolinguistic experience.

We emphasize that the tutor is not there necessarily to provide 'answers'. Tutors' role in the workshop-plus is to guide students in making (socio)linguistically well-motivated decisions, and to help students apply their decisions systematically to all the data they encounter. Tutors can also provide useful practical help with managing record-keeping.

We have found that it is a good idea to ensure the tutors have a similar skills base to draw on. This means that students in every tutorial can draw on a certain level of practical expertise. It also helps to provide a relatively consistent set of expectations for drawing up a marking schedule for grading the final assignment.

Staffing implications

The course requires a somewhat heavier load than many others in terms of departmental allocations of tutoring moneys and a greater time commitment from the postgraduate students we employ as tutors, since tutors are available to their groups twice a week (instead of our usual once a week roster for tutorials). However, since the workshop-plus requires no direct preparation on the tutor's part, and since the exercises in the weekly tutorials are designed and ready for the tutors to take off the shelf, the time commitment has not been an issue. The implication of having a slightly higher dedicated budget for tutors on this unit is one that needs to be considered in advance.

Special-needs students

Students are given access to the recordings via the closed course webpage. (This is on the express understanding that the recordings of the teenagers' conversations are not for further dissemination or reproduction. The football commentary is in the public domain.) This arrangement allows students more time or better listening conditions than a tutorial room for working on the materials independently.

One potential challenge lies in actively involving students with hearing problems. If a particular student has a hearing impairment that makes it difficult for them to actively participate in the workshop tasks, and if the student does not choose to disclose this problem to their tutorial, there can be some friction within tutorials towards the end of the course. This is because the notes each tutorial has taken during their discovery process constitute the basis for the final assignment. Some students may feel reluctant to work closely with another student who (mistakenly or not) they believe to be coasting.

In practice, if a student has not participated actively in tutorials, simply having the figures will not enable them to write a good final assignment, because they do not understand the decision-making processes that went into the extraction and coding of tokens. As a result, there is a qualitative difference in the assignment which, for instance, a hearing-impaired student who has faithfully attended tutorials can write and the assignment written by someone who has blown off the entire unit and showed up in the last week for the 'results'.

I do not know if there is a uniform way of heading off this sort of problem (or misunderstanding). We try to explain that there are clear qualitative differences in final assignments between those who have actively participated (whether as leaders or as quiet support) in the analysis and decision-making, and those who have failed to take part in any of the hard work. We could perhaps be more open about our grading criteria from the outset of the unit.

Ultimately, we have to encourage students (a) to think the best of each other and (b) to be open with each other. Thinking the best of each other requires them to consider that different people may have different learning styles, and that people can be active participants without necessarily leading the discussion or analysis. Being open with each other requires them to trust each other, and to try and talk about problems as they begin to surface, rather than leaving them to grow unchecked.

These are both good principles for life in general (more transferrable skills!), but since we do not always follow them to the letter in life, maybe it is not surprising that they do not always get followed in class.

Aims and objectives of the sociolinguistics unit

We explain to students that by the end of the unit we hope they will be more aware of variation in language and, specifically, that they will be able to:

- describe in precise terms how linguistic variation is realized (answer questions like *What is a variable? What are variants of a variable?*);
- give examples of different kinds of quantitative methods that can be used to study variation in spontaneous language;
- say how patterns of variation in the group and the individual relate to broader sociolinguistic generalizations;
- explain what makes a study reliable;
- apply this knowledge in their own study of variation.

Arguably, this knowledge – on top of the 12 hours of macro-sociolinguistics and skills in discourse analysis taught in Year 1 – is the bare minimum all linguists need to know in order to understand how research in other sub-fields of linguistics informs, or can be informed by, sociolinguistics.

In other linguistics programmes, for example, where there is more direct training in research and experimental methods, it might well be appropriate to de-emphasize the quantitative training in our plan. As I have noted, given the structure of our third and fourth year (especially for joint-degree majors), there are good reasons why we need to get basic quantitative methods into the second year.

9.2.4 Topics covered in the five-week unit

The lectures progress through the following topics, with the principal medium(s) of learning shown in square brackets. Each of the topics is annotated to indicate what skills and key concepts are covered.

9.2.4.1 How sociolinguists identify what is varying in language and how they have shown that 'free variation' is not as 'free' as it looks. [lecture; tutorial]

Quantitative methods and the study of variation

Quantitative methods are central to this unit, and the importance of relative frequencies of a variant in different (groups of) speakers is introduced very early. Some connections are made with the principles of regional dialectology, and the ways in which these initially were echoed in the research agenda of social dialectology are discussed, for example, the importance of relative frequencies of variants in deciding where to draw isoglosses.

9.2.4.2 What methods sociolinguists use for gathering data and why you cannot just ask people about variation. [lecture; tutorial; workshop]

Becoming aware of variation

Students conduct small-scale surveys as homework in Week 1. Their task is to collect self-report data on one frequent phonological and one frequent syntactic variable. Respondents are asked

'Do you say:

lib'ry or *library*?'

'Do you say:

The problem is that we simply don't know enough

OR

The problem is is that we simply don't know enough?'

Respondents inevitably offer commentary on the variables, sometimes relating to the importance of self-styling, attention to an audience, or rate of speech. So this exercise allows them to get a small taste of handling and grouping data, as well as foreshadowing issues that are developed further in the next month.

Students then use the Internet as an independent source of data on the same variables. This highlights both the strengths and limitations of self-report data, and the strengths and limitations of collecting data on variation from the Internet.

9.2.4.3 How linguistic and social factors constrain variation: word classes, style; age and sex of speaker. [lectures; tutorials; workshops]

Extracting and coding variants

The core of the unit involves practical experience in identifying, extracting and coding variants of (ing). Students are provided with datasheets that are pre-formatted and which they will complete in their workshops.

A lecture discusses previous findings on (ing) in other speech communities and introduces the linguistic factors that have been shown to be the most important constraints on the variation: grammatical class of the word; following segment. Divergent findings on, for example, the importance of stress patterns and preceding segment are discussed. These all become open questions for coding and investigation in workshops and an introductory tutorial.

In addition, potentially relevant non-linguistic factors are discussed. Since the sound corpus includes recordings from at least two distinct speech styles/genres (commentary and conversation) students also have to decide how to classify subroutines in discourse and how to code variants in each of these styles according to non-linguistic (social) factors. Groups differ in how they decide to handle non-linguistic factors. They may decide to code for individual speakers, or they might decide to group all speakers together by genre, or according to key within a genre – the sports commentary includes colour and action commentary; the conversations include joking, animating other people's speech, complaints.

The students also have to decide how they will handle dialectal (Scots) and/or invariant forms. For example, *mingin(g)* and *fuckin(g)* never occur with the velar nasal, and *daen* can be analysed as an (ing) token with a final alveolar, or excluded as an invariant Scots form. In grading the assignments we are less concerned with what they decide to do with such cases than we are with *how* they motivate their decisions.

9.2.4.4 The effect that the social networks (or more local practice-based communities) have on the way we talk. [lecture; workshop]

Network membership and communities of practice

The Scots teenagers are all members of a local social organization, so they can be sub-divided according to their friendship networks and/or their depth of commitment to the social organization. In other data sets, these theoretical and analytical constructs might not be so relevant.

9.2.4.5 How variation may relate to language change (but does not have to). [lecture; tutorial]

Stable variables vs changes in progress

This important distinction between different patterns of variation is discussed very briefly. There is not time to get into the growing literature on the relationship between individual (lifespan) change and community change/stability. The goal is to ensure that the class is familiar with the inferences sociolinguists draw from the relative distribution of variants over apparent time (different generations in one sample). Unlike most of the sociolinguistic variables that current research focuses on, the (ing) variable is relatively stable, even though different varieties of English have different input frequencies.

I personally feel that it is a good idea to look at a stable variable because I think it is important that the fundamental importance of linguistic constraints on even socially stratified variation is fully understood. I suspect that it is easier to extract systematic linguistic constraints on a stable variable from even a small database (such as the one we are working on) than it is for a change in progress.

9.2.4.6 How to write up a small study of language variation. [lecture; tutorial]

A lot of the students in this unit will not have written a social-science style research report before. We provide detailed instructions on the typical structure of such reports and the kinds of questions they should be asking themselves and answering for the reader in each of the different sections.

Testing patterns for significance

Most of the data presented in the lectures is shown as frequency counts or percentages. In the last week, as students are pulling together their final assignments, we also introduce the notion of statistical significance, and show how chi-square tests can be employed as simple measures of statistical significance. The lecture is supported with some hands-on exercises, and web-based resources that students can explore themselves.

9.3 Assessment of the unit

The assessment for this unit is entirely based on a written assignment which contributes 30 percent to students' final mark for the entire semester. There are institutional blocks that prevent us having attendance and/or participation in tutorials contribute to students' final grades. I would prefer to have attendance at tutorials and workshops contribute a small amount towards individuals' final grade for the course. This is mainly to forestall some of the complaints there can be about members of a tutorial not pulling their weight in analysing the data.

Tutors mark assignments done by members of their tutorial. In order to make sure there is consistency across groups, before marking starts, the tutors and course coordinator meet to agree on a marking schedule that everyone will use. The starting point for this is the university's publicized Common Marking Guide, but the descriptors for different grades in the CMG need to be anchored against specific content and skills that are appropriate to what we have covered in the course and to what students have discussed and dealt with in workshops. The course coordinator moderates the tutors' marking.

9.4 Summary

The overall format of the unit (at a glance) is shown in Table 9.1.

Table 9.1 Unit outline showing pacing of lectures and student-led activities, also content of lectures and guided development of skills in tutorials and workshops. Readings associated with different activities or lectures are shown in plain text (recommended readings in parentheses).

Week	Monday	Tuesday	Wednesday	Thursday	Friday
1	**Lecture** *Overview and Introduction to social dialectology* Meyerhoff 2006: chs. 1-2 (Scherre 2006)	**Tutorial (1)** *Identifying variables*	**Workshop (1)** *Awareness of variables*	**Workshop Plus**	**Lecture** *Variationist methods; key concepts* Meyerhoff 2006: Ch.2; Hazen 2006
2	**Tutorial (2)** *Football commentaries: Identifying variants of (ing)*	**Workshop (2)** *Fife teenagers: Identifying variants of (ing)*	**Lecture** *Style-shifting: Individual variation* Meyerhoff 2006: ch. 3 (Fought 2006)	**Workshop Plus**	**Lecture** *Stable variables and changes in progress* Meyerhoff 2006: ch. 7; Sankoff 2006 (Labov 1989)

3	**Tutorial (3)** *Variation across individuals*	**Workshop (3)** *Coding for part of speech*	**Lecture** *Social class* Meyerhoff 2006: ch. 8 (Macaulay 2006)	**Workshop Plus**	**Lecture** *Social networks* Meyerhoff 2006: ch. 9
4	**Tutorial (4)** *Changes in progress; Social class* Meyerhoff 2006:ch. 7; ch.8 p. 175	**Workshop (4)** *Coding other factors*	**Lecture** *Testing for significance* Bayley 2002	**Workshop Plus**	**Lecture** Incl. *Writing a research report*
5	**Tutorial (5)** *Pulling things together*	No class; writing up	**Lecture** *Tutorial reports and synthesis*	No class; writing up	Hand in assignment, 10.00am

Acknowledgments

My thanks go first and foremost to Ellen Gurman Bard who designed the interactive module for teaching quantitative methods for analysing language and who gave her blessing to my writing it up like this. I also thank Jennifer Smith, with whom I have spent many very happy hours sharing ideas about problems and successes in teaching hands-on sociolinguistics.

References

Anderson, A., M. Bader, E. Bard, E. Boyle, G.M. Dougherty, S. Garrod, S. Isard, J. Kowtko, J. McAllister, J. Miller, C. Sotillo, H.S. Thompson and R. Weinert. 1991. 'The HCRC map task corpus'. *Language and Speech* 34: 351-66

Bayley, R. 2002. 'The quantitative paradigm'. In *Handbook of language variation and change*, pp. 117-141, ed. J.C. Chambers, P. Trudgill and N. Schilling-Estes. Oxford: Blackwell.

Hazen, K. 2006. 'IN/ING variable'. In *Encyclopedia of language and linguistics*. Vol. 12, pp. 581-84, ed. K. Brown. Oxford: Elsevier.

Fought, C. 2006. 'Style and style-shifting'. In *Encyclopedia of language and linguistics*. Vol. 12, pp. 210-12, ed. K. Brown. Oxford: Elsevier.

Labov, W. 1989. 'The child as linguistic historian'. *Language Variation and Change* 1: 85-97.

Macauley, R. 2006. 'Sociolects/Social class'. In *Encyclopedia of language and linguistics*. Vol. 12, pp. 484-89, ed. K. Brown. Oxford: Elsevier.

Meyerhoff, M. 2006. *Introducing sociolinguistics*. London: Routledge.

Sankoff, G. 2006. 'Age: Apparent time and real time'. In *Encyclopedia of language*

and linguistics. Vol. 12, pp. 110-16, ed. K. Brown. Oxford: Elsevier.
Scherre, M. 2006 'Speech community'. In *Encyclopedia of language and linguistics*. Vol. 12, pp. 716-22, ed. K. Brown. Oxford: Elsevier.

Notes

* **Miriam Meyerhoff**

Miriam Meyerhoff found linguistics entirely by accident, as a second-year student after having started a degree in comparative literature at Victoria University of Wellington. Winifred Bauer tutored her introductory course, and she was initially captivated by the clarity and aesthetic pleasure of Winifred's analyses of even the simplest linguistic problems. Later, as a PhD student at the University of Pennsylvania, she had the extraordinary experience of being taught by William Labov, who made every class an empirical challenge and always seemed to be teaching something he was working on *right now*, and Ellen Prince, whose classes were like beautiful 14-week long jazz sessions. She continues to take lessons on how to combine research and supervision with something approximating a normal life from Janet Holmes and Gillian Sankoff. After completing her PhD at Penn, she taught sociolinguistics and creole languages at the University of Hawai'i at Mānoa, before moving to the University of Edinburgh and then the University of Auckland. She has had visiting teaching positions at Cornell University, Michigan State University, Victoria University of Wellington and New York University.

10 Psycholinguistics for linguists

Paul Warren[*]

10.1 Introduction

The first use of the term *psycholinguistics* to refer to the study of the psychology of language appears to have been in the 1920s, although a seminar at Cornell University in 1951 is often claimed to be the birthplace for psycholinguistics as a field of study. Interestingly, the report of that seminar was published as an annex both to a linguistics journal (Osgood and Sebeok 1954a) and to a psychological one (Osgood and Sebeok 1954b). Such double-dipping would probably get academics into trouble nowadays, but it is nevertheless an acknowledgment that the field was (as it still is) influenced by research and teaching practices and methodologies in both psychology and linguistics. Psycholinguistics is still taught in both those disciplines, as well as in multidisciplinary cognitive science units throughout the world, though the particular emphases in what is taught and how it is taught tend to vary depending on the disciplinary backgrounds of teachers and their students.

In this chapter I present a personal view of the teaching of psycholinguistics, a view which will inevitably be influenced by how I currently teach the subject, as well as by my personal history as a researcher and teacher working predominantly in linguistics, but with forays as a post-doctoral researcher into psychology, forays that were particularly instructive for my understanding of experimental methodology and data analysis. My approach centres on experimental psycholinguistics, involving the presentation and discussion of empirical evidence for the structures, representations and processes involved in language production and comprehension. In my psycholinguistics courses I devote relatively little time to developmental aspects of language (which are introduced to students in courses on language learning and teaching) or to language impairment (which my colleagues in the School of Psychology make a much better job of teaching, and aspects of which they kindly summarize for my students in guest appearances in my courses). My primary focus, then, is on so-called 'normal' adult language production and comprehension, and on what studying this can tell us about what language is and how we use it.

10.2 Goals/objectives

There are a number of both general and specific goals or objectives that I think are important factors in the teaching of this subject area. On the general side, in addition to imparting enthusiasm for the subject (which must be one of the most crucial motivating factors in teaching anything), I think it is important that we help students see the relevance of psycholinguistics. This might be the relevance it has to their other studies, to their intended vocations, to their interactions with others, but also of course to their understanding of both psychology (if this is one of their majors) and of linguistics (which tends to be the major of most of my students). It is impractical if not impossible to tailor a psycholinguistics course to the disparate interests and vocational needs of a whole class, but one of the great appeals of much of the psycholinguistic data is that it can be found in everyday language use, and even the experimental data can generally be related to language experience outside of the laboratory. The challenge, then, is to link this experience back to the potentially dry theoretical positions propounded in the psycholinguistic literature.

More specifically, by the time they have completed a course in psycholinguistics, students should be able to understand some of the basic psychological processes of language production and comprehension and some of the claims made about the mental representation of language; they should be able to apply such understanding to the analysis of data; they should be able to evaluate the role of linguistic theory in the psychological examination of language production and comprehension and also the theoretical positions taken in psycholinguistic research; and they should understand and be able to evaluate a range of experimental approaches, as well as being able to apply experimental and analytical tools in completing their own assignments and exercises.

10.3 Subject matter and methods

As indicated in the Introduction, the focus here is on psycholinguistics as the study of 'normal' adult language use. Indeed, the focus is more specifically on adult monolingual speakers, though the relevance of many of the claims and much of the research extends to bilingual speakers as well. In the context of the communicative act, we can see such language use as involving a speaker and a listener. (Note that this could equally be a writer and a reader. The selection of speaker and listener betrays another of the biases in my own teaching of the subject, reflecting my research interests in speech production and comprehension. This bias does not mean that issues involving written language – and indeed other non-spoken forms of language such as sign language – do not form part of what is and should be taught in a course on psycholinguistics.) Taking an interaction between a speaker and a listener as a starting point, we can divide the subject matter of psycholinguistics into two main areas: the development of a spoken output from an underlying intention (production), and the retrieval of an interpretation from a heard input (comprehension). Using an appropriately developed modular course, this subject matter can be taught in two main orders: production then comprehension, or vice versa, depending on the overall emphasis of the course, as well as perhaps on constraints imposed by covering particular material before project work is started. In addition, material can be included in a module that deals with issues such as the overall architecture of the language-processing system, the relationship of production and comprehension, and the links between language and other cognitive skills (covering issues such as modularity of mind, etc.). Along the way, students get to consider what kinds of things language users might carry around in their heads as part of their linguistic knowledge (what information we store for words, what rule systems we have for generating word and sentence structures, and so forth), and what resemblance this stored knowledge bears to the structures and rules propounded in theoretical linguistics.

For teaching purposes, each of the larger subject areas of language production and language comprehension can usefully be broken down into stages of the production or comprehension process (putting together sentences, finding words, producing articulatory schema, etc.), or they can be considered from the point of view of the relevant levels of linguistic analysis (syntax, morphology, phonology, etc.). To an extent these may coincide, but an important lesson for students is that the levels of linguistic analysis do not overlap neatly with stages of processing. Therefore, as students investigate these levels and processes, they also explore the interactions between them.

10.3.1 Production

A starting point for the study of language production is that a speaker needs to find linguistic expression for an idea. So we pose a general research question, concerning the evidence for how the speaker goes about this task, and look for evidence for this from a combination of observation and experiment. Using observational data as the first source of evidence has the advantage that students can monitor what is going on around them and gain an appreciation for the processes involved in speaking, without becoming bogged down in experimental control and other methodological issues. This may be a compelling reason for teaching production before comprehension, since the evidence for the processes of comprehension is much less tangible and generally emerges best with experimental intervention.

The two main areas of observational evidence for speech production are hesitation phenomena (pauses, repetitions, false starts) and speech errors. Students learn that hesitations – in particular filled and empty pauses – can reflect planning processes, as well as indicating sentence structure to the listener. Choices need to be made about content and form, but these choices take time and may interfere with the actual process of production, resulting in hesitation. Students typically come to understand this better by looking at a transcribed and annotated sample of spontaneous speech (and listening to this if possible), and comparing this with a tidied-up written-language version of the same sample. This general overview prepares students for looking at more detailed studies that manipulate task type (prepared vs unprepared exposition, for instance) and which investigate consequent differences in the number and distribution of hesitations. An assignment task that I have used to help students in their appreciation of this is one that is based on two different spoken texts from the same speaker, for example a reading of a story and a retelling of that story, together with orthographic transcripts of those texts. The students mark on the transcripts where the pauses and other hesitations occur, then tabulate their occurrence relative to different grammatical features (e.g. within or between clauses or phrases, before content or function words, etc.), and compare pause patterns in the two texts.

However, perhaps one of the most entertaining sources of evidence for language planning processes, and therefore one that frequently and understandably gets exploited in the teaching of psycholinguistics, is the speech error. Most students are aware of speech errors, and can bring their own illustrative examples to classes. Tutorial sessions can be devoted to discussion of what these errors, and other examples provided by the teacher, might show. Almost inevitably students will not previously have noticed the ways in which errors form patterns, and that these patterns can inform us about the processes of selecting and ordering linguistic material during speech production. Most likely, students' interest will also have been in the underlying causes of speech errors (including 'Freudian' interpretations of errors), rather than in what really concerns the psycholinguist, namely the mechanisms by which errors occur. A joke attributed to American comedian Henny Youngman goes something like this: a passenger checking in at an airport notices that the female check-in clerk is particularly well endowed, and to his shame he finds himself asking for a 'picket to Titsburgh'. When the passenger relates this episode later to a colleague, the latter explains that this is known as a Freudian slip, and that everyone does this. 'Why,' he says, 'just the other day I was having coffee with my wife and I meant to ask her to pass me the sugar, and instead I said "you bitch, you've ruined my life!"' We point out to our students that rather than the underlying causes of errors, what interests psycholinguists is that this kind of error (*ticket to Pittsburgh* → *picket to Titsburgh*), involving the exchange of syllable-initial consonants, is fairly common and tells us something about planning frames involved in speech production. Students will undoubtedly be able to recount their own examples of slips of the tongue in which the initial consonants or consonant clusters of two words in the same sentence get exchanged. They may even know that this particular error type is typically referred to as a spoonerism (after the

Reverend William A. Spooner, 1844–1930, Dean and Warden of New College, Oxford). But they will rarely have reflected on why the initial consonants of one word exchange with the initial consonants of another, rather than – for instance – with the final consonants of that other word (which happens, but is a vanishingly rare occurrence). Such patterns can be made sense of in the context of particular theories of language production, in this case a slots-and-fillers model, which argues that the speaker selects a set of words to express the intended idea in a sentence. As these words join the queue of words waiting to be uttered, structural information about them becomes available, such as which are the initial consonants of the words. An articulatory plan is generated for the production of the queued-up words, but then consonants with the right general properties but from the wrong word in the queue are inserted into that plan.

Students can also be asked to focus on other error patterns which should reveal different aspects of the speech production process, such as the tendency for word blends to involve words of similar meaning (such as *smever* for *smart* and *clever*). It is not difficult for them to realize that for such errors to occur it is likely that in the process of planning an utterance more than one candidate word is often available for expressing the same meaning, and that if the speaker is unable to select between these candidates then they both get produced, in a blend.

Once sufficient examples of errors have been discussed in class, the patterning of errors, and how this patterning can inform our understanding of speech production processes, can be reinforced through appropriate assessment material. For example, a dataset such as that in Table 10.1 can be provided, with instructions firstly to classify the errors in terms of the domain of the error (i.e. whether it involves sounds, words or phrases) and the mechanism of the error (an error of anticipation, exchange, blend, substitution, etc.); secondly to comment on any additional factors that might be involved (such as errors tending to produce real words rather than nonsense); and thirdly to discuss what the errors – as a group – tell us about the language-production process.

Incidentally, one of the most difficult things to achieve in lecturing on speech errors is to totally avoid making any yourself. But then it is always good practice to illustrate the phenomena being discussed.

Data from hesitation studies and speech error studies in fact allow the psycholinguistics teacher to cover most major issues in speech production, including: the planning of sentence structure; the selection of words and their insertion into sentence frames; the question of whether morphologically regular forms are generated from the lexicon or by rule; the development and execution of a plan for articulation; the nature of the production lexicon, including its internal structure and the types of information associated with the representations of words. These data sources can be supplemented by other observational and experimental data, including the tip-of-the-tongue phenomenon (looking at what we can remember about a word that we can't quite recall), speaker performance in tongue twisters (which can also be tried out by students in tutorials) and in other experimentally induced speech errors, as well as a range of other laboratory tasks, such as picture naming, picture–word matching and so on, each of which may be looking in more detail at particular aspects of the production process.

Table 10.1 Error data
(all examples are listed as intended utterance → actual utterance; / indicates competing words)

1	sure/certainly	→	shertainly
2	...Amos Mansdorf from Tel Aviv, Israel	→	...Amos Mansdorf from Tel Aviv, Italy
3	Bronwen brought back the tea chest	→	Bronwen brought brack the tea chest
4	and now that I'm finishing I want to thank all the speakers	→	and now that I'm finishing I want to spank all the thinkers
5	I didn't get a cover with my copy	→	I didn't get a copy with my cover
6	a fine first half	→	a first fine half
7	as long as the air pressure is high enough to keep the water out, you'll have air at the right pressure to breathe	→	as long as the air pressure is high enough to keep the water out, you'll have air at the right pressure to drink
8	it's hard to measure the level	→	it's hard to measure the leisure
9	don't you know why he's going?	→	do you know why he's not going?
10	I have to get a tank of gas	→	I have to get a gas of tank
11	I just think they probably didn't have them in the Greek mountains then.	→	I just don't think they probably had them in the Greek mountains then.
12	It looks like Dante's Hell...	→	It looks like Hell's Dante...
13	It [Arab oil embargo] was the catalyst/cataclysm that brought it on [economic decline]	→	It was the cataclyst that brought it on
14	a separate pay plan	→	a separate play plan
15	They are having their day in the sun	→	They are having their night in the sun
16	the whole planning process, as you know	→	the whole planning process, as you knew...know
17	they are so ˌconfronˈtational	→	they are so conˈfronˌtational
18	weather permitting	→	weather preventing
19	I just came across some unpaid bills	→	I just came across some unpilled bays
20	it goes to show	→	it shows to go

10.3.2 Comprehension

Because the outcomes of comprehension processes are not as easily observable (except perhaps the overall outcome of seeing that someone has understood the message), the psycholinguistics of language comprehension has to be taught more indirectly. However, excessive reference to experimental data on the one hand or the overuse of abstract illustrations of theories and models of the comprehension process on the other can leave students rather too distanced from the subject matter. One successful strategy has been to intersperse lecture sessions on language comprehension with laboratory sessions in which students can experience the types of methodology that are used in the investigation of comprehension, and further classes (e.g. small group tutorials) in which the outcomes of these laboratory sessions are discussed. This works well for experimental tasks and designs that produce reliable and replicable outcomes – uncertainty in the outcomes can make these sessions less useful, except perhaps as a mechanism to get more advanced students thinking about shortcomings in experimental design and methodology, or to think about alternative explanations.

Using such a combination of lecture-based presentation of psycholinguistic theory and laboratory-based demonstration tasks, teachers can trace the course of language comprehension from a listener's/reader's first exposure to the input signal through to their arrival at an interpretation. Since words are typically (though perhaps naively) perceived to be the basic building blocks of language, a good starting point is to explore the processes of word recognition. This should deal with both the spoken and visual domains, and lends itself to discussion of issues to do with pre-lexical analysis and the role in such analysis of linguistic units such as letters and phonemes, and the relationship between spelling and pronunciation. For instance, a task that works well in the laboratory is visual lexical decision, where participants see letter strings and decide for each one whether or not it is a word of their language. As an example of its use to promote discussion, consider how for English, the string BRANE should receive a 'no' response, since it is not an existing word. However, because the probable pronunciation of that nonword is identical to that of the real word BRAIN, there are typically many 'yes' responses and the 'no' responses tend to be delayed, when compared with those to a string like BRAPE. This so-called pseudohomophone effect leads to interesting class discussion of models of reading and of lexical access, and the use of spelling-to-sound rules during visual word processing.

A neat theoretical framework for exploring spoken-word recognition, not least because it makes testable claims that can be explored in laboratory sessions, is the Cohort Theory put forward in various places over the years by William Marslen-Wilson and his colleagues (e.g. Marslen-Wilson 1987). In essence, this theory claims that spoken words are activated on the basis of the acoustic-phonetic input, following which access can be made to information about these words in the mental lexicon (such as meaning, grammatical information, etc.). This information is matched against the developing interpretation of the utterance, allowing the selection and recognition of the most appropriate word. This model opens up issues to do with the nature of the processing of the input signal, the role of phoneme-type representations in word recognition, the idea that there is competition between rival word candidates, the role of lexical frequency in the activation of these candidates, the nature of the information that is accessed when a word is activated, the interaction of word-level and sentence-level information in processing, and so on.

Cohort-related activities that students can engage in during classes or as part of the assessment schedule for a course in psycholinguistics might include determining the recognition point of words in isolation and in sentence contexts. The recognition point is the sound at which, on the basis of a left-to-right analysis (i.e. reflecting the linear arrival of the sounds of the word), a word becomes distinct from all its competitors. For example, using their knowledge of English as well as dictionaries and online databases (e.g. the MRC Psycholinguistic database available at the University of Western Australia), students determine the recognition points for the underlined words in the passage below. They might conclude that the recognition point for *zebra*, in isolation, is at the /b/, since this distinguishes it from *zest*, *zeppelin* and so on. In the context of the passage, and taking into account semantic constraints to do with watching animals in the zoo, and the like, the recognition point might be much earlier, perhaps as early as the /z/.

> The trip to the <u>zoo</u> was a great success. All the children loved watching the long-tailed <u>monkey</u> as it started to <u>swing</u> through the trees. We had to stand and look for a long time before we picked out the <u>light</u> and dark stripes of the <u>zebra</u> against the <u>dappled</u> shade of the trees.

Exploration of the recognition of morphologically complex forms is also important, and connects the student to questions such as the distinction between inflection and derivation, whether morphologically complex forms are recognized on the basis of a holistic stored representation or via a rule system, the role in processing of morphological productivity, and so forth.

Another key area is sentence parsing, the construction of a sentence structure (and interpretation) based on the words the listener or reader has encountered. Generally, this requires a certain understanding of phrase-structure grammar and of tree-building operations, but most relevant issues in sentence processing can be investigated without presupposing more advanced understanding of complex syntactic theory. The relationship between word recognition and sentence parsing can in turn lead to discussion of bottom-up (signal driven) and top-down (concept driven) processing. When spoken-language processing is included, then the role of intonation and prosody can be explored in the disambiguation of potentially ambiguous sentences (such as prepositional phrase ambiguities like *The man saw the spy with the binoculars*).

10.3.3 Demonstration of experimental techniques

A number of resources are available for use in the demonstration of experimental techniques, including freely downloadable psycholinguistic software. These resources are somewhat variable with respect to the programming experience and expertise required to tailor them to specific teaching needs, but for basic experimental techniques there are often examples available on websites that can be downloaded and adapted to suit the course being taught. Examples of such software packages are the DMASTR system developed by Ken and Jonathan Forster at the University of Arizona and the commercially available E-Prime package from Psychology Software Tools, Inc. (Schneider *et al.* 2002). Both of these packages have an active community of researchers and teachers who are developing routines and scripts that can be used to run both basic and more sophisticated experiments, including close replications of published experiments. Other resources can be found via the Psychology of Language page of links maintained by Roger Kreuz at the University of Memphis.

On the whole, it is advisable to use fairly simple experimental techniques to illustrate some of the more reliable basic phenomena in language processing. For instance, either of the packages mentioned above can be easily configured to present sequences of letter strings that correspond either to existing words or to non-words (e.g. DOG and HIG respectively) for a timed lexical decision response (i.e. pressing one of two keyboard keys to indicate whether or not the string forms a word of English). One of the most robust findings in psycholinguistic research is the frequency effect – the finding that high-frequency words are recognized more rapidly than low-frequency words. Controlling for other factors such as word length (since longer words take longer to read), and using as a source one of the published sets of frequency norms (available again via the Psychology of Language link, but including the MRC Psycholinguistic Database), the teacher can make appropriate selections of high- and low-frequency words (DOG vs BOG, for instance) for presentation in a lexical decision task. The software routines can be set up to provide individual feedback to students as the demonstration unfolds, or to save response times to disk for the teacher to collate and discuss in a subsequent class.

10.4 Assessment

An unavoidable aspect of university teaching is assessment. Like many areas of linguistics, psycholinguistics lends itself to assignment topics with a practical, data-oriented component. So, for instance, we have seen above how assessment of students' understanding of issues in language production can involve them in measuring, cataloguing and interpreting hesitation phenomena, using recordings provided from existing corpora or to be collected by the students themselves. Alternatively, they can be asked to provide interpretations of speech errors and the patterns they demonstrate, using materials taken from error corpora. Or they might use recordings of speakers giving spatial descriptions such as route directions, in order to investigate the processes of repair or the sequencing of instructions.

Practical comprehension tasks are somewhat more difficult to include in assignments, since most involve an understanding of how to write scripts for the experimental software. It is possible, however, to guide students in running simple listening tasks with a pool of their friends or fellow students (preferably from other courses), such as judging the well-formedness of a sentence, or determining whether a recording of *The man saw the spy with the binoculars* is best interpreted as indicating that the man had the binoculars or the spy had the binoculars. The general idea is to involve students in the research process. One alternative is to provide them with data already collected in a comprehension or listening experiment, but in my experience this is less satisfying for most students, and provides a less enriching learning experience, although such material might be suitable as part of an exam question.

One issue to be aware of in getting students to do assignments with a research component is that most will have little experience with statistical analysis of results. While some students, especially those with a psychology background, will have completed at least an introductory course in statistics, for the majority of students taking a linguistics major, this will not be the case. It is therefore important to emphasize that an undergraduate linguistics research project, worth perhaps 15-25 percent of the course marks for a psycholinguistics paper, should not require detailed statistical analysis – often averages or percentage counts of the dependent variable are enough to illustrate the pattern that can be found in the data. Appropriately designed tests for significance should be accepted by the teacher but not required.

10.5 Conclusion

This chapter has given a somewhat personal and biased view of the teaching of psycholinguistics. There will be many areas that other teachers will choose not to cover, and further areas that they would include but that I have not. There is no fixed menu for teaching in this field. There are few essentials that simply must be covered otherwise a course cannot be held up as an example of psycholinguistics. What is key, I believe, is to engage students in considering the relevance of linguistic analysis and constructs to the observable and testable phenomena of language production and comprehension, but above all to cause them to marvel at the intricacies of language processing and the sheer power of the human language faculty.

References

DMASTR. http://www.u.arizona.edu/~kforster/dmastr/dmastr.htm (accessed 29 September 2009).

Marslen-Wilson, W.D. 1987. 'Functional parallelism in spoken word recognition'. *Cognition* 25: 71-102.

MRC Psycholinguistic database. http://www.psy.uwa.edu.au/mrcdatabase/uwa_mrc.htm (accessed 29 September 2009).

Osgood, C.E. and T.A. Sebeok (eds.) 1954a. *Psycholinguistics: A survey of theory and research problems.* Indiana University Publications in Anthropology and Linguistics, Memoir 10 of *International Journal of American Linguistics.* Bloomington: Indiana University Press.

Osgood, C. E. and T.A. Sebeok (eds.) 1954b. *Psycholinguistics: A survey of theory and research problems.* Supplement to *Journal of Abnormal and Social Psychology* 49: 1-203.

Psychology of Language web pages. http://www.psyc.memphis.edu:88/POL/POL.htm (accessed 29 September 2009)

Schneider, W., A. Eschman and A. Zuccolotto. 2002. *E-Prime user's guide.* Pittsburgh: Psychology Software Tools Inc.

Notes

* **Paul Warren**

Paul Warren is Associate Professor in the School of Linguistics and Applied Language Studies at Victoria University of Wellington, New Zealand. Paul's primary research interests are in psycholinguistics, in particular spoken-word recognition and the use of intonation in sentence processing. Since moving to New Zealand in 1994, he has combined these interests with a growing fascination in the development of New Zealand English. Paul's entry into linguistics was as part of a BA in Modern and Mediaeval Languages at Cambridge. His PhD research at the same university was supervised by Francis Nolan and Peter Matthews. As a postdoctoral researcher Paul was heavily influenced by working on a research project together with psychologists William Marslen-Wilson and Lorraine Tyler.

11 Teaching *Linguistic Approaches to Nonliteral Language* or We really knew how to have fun

Diana Van Lancker Sidtis[*]

11.1 Introduction

In fall 1997, I was ready for a change in the life of work, when an advertised position as visiting guest professor at a small, liberal arts college 2,100 miles away from Los Angeles, where I lived, began to appear and reappear in my email. At first it seemed an unlikely prospect. The job description was to teach four courses in the newly formed linguistics programme from February to June at this institution, sometimes called the 'Harvard of the Midwest'. For some time, as a faculty member in a department of neurology of a medical school, teaching had been the least of my activities, and I was acutely aware that I missed teaching. I had been earning my keep performing clinical service as a speech pathologist in a Veterans Administration outpatient clinic and at the University Hospital, as well as submitting a continuous stream of grant proposals to fund our 'Neurolinguistics and Speech Science'[1] research laboratory. Of the academic triad – clinical service, research and teaching – my energies were well captured by the first two. In the clinic and research lab, the teacher in me enjoyed working with student interns and research assistants, but the thrill of developing a syllabus and pursuing a semester-long set of ideas in class week after week, chalk in hand, was not to be.

The research laboratory had the benefit of unlimited patient visits to the rehabilitation facility and extraordinary referrals to the tertiary care university hospital. A rich variety of disorders was represented: aphasia,[2] motor speech and voice impairments, right hemisphere disease, and an exotic sampling of neurobehavioural cases: agnosias, apraxias and other cognitive disabilities. We had only to obtain permission from the human subjects protection committee to pursue research topics of interest. A consistent observation reappeared in a variety of guises across all kinds of speech and language disorders, whether mild, moderate or severe: 'automatic speech' is preserved.

Automatic speech is the older term, popularized by the nineteenth-century neurologist, J. Hughlings Jackson (1874a, b), for overlearned, stored and memorized, familiar and known expressions, or, more generally, any speech that is not newly created using linguistic rules. Most people observing aphasia have identified this preserved ability (Bay 1962, 1964a, b; Critchley 1970; Pick 1973; Head 1926; Luria 1966, 1970; Goodglass and Mayer 1958[3]). It is striking to see a severely language-disabled individual counting fluently from one to ten and enunciating the days of the week with normal articulation and prosody.[4] In addition to the universally present serial speech, the majority of aphasic patients retain a set of formulaic expressions that they use: *Hello, how are you, thank you, well, ya know, that's about all, I guess so.* Recitation of nursery rhymes, poems and prayers, different ones for different people, is usually intact. Most patients swear and emit interjections, such as *gee, oh, dear, godsakes, gosh* and *wow.* The repertory in any language of such expressions is quite large,[5] such that each patient has a unique set. Singing familiar tunes – 'Happy Birthday' and 'Jingle Bells' – is often impressive. In the nonfluent speaker, the contrast in competency between halting, effortful, distorted novel utterances and fluent, normal-sounding, well-articulated formulaic expressions is dramatic. In fluent aphasic speakers, identifiable idioms and speech formulas appear among the otherwise incomprehensible neologisms[6] and jargon.

My interest in this phenomenon, beginning in graduate school, had spilled over into several studies through the years (Van Lancker 1973, 1987, 1990; Van Lancker and Bella 1996; Van Lancker and Canter 1981; Van Lancker and Kempler 1987). During the 1990s, Daniel Kempler and I developed a clinical protocol for evaluation of idiom recognition (Kempler and Van Lancker 1996). The notion of 'automatic speech' had expanded to include conversational speech formulas, idioms, proverbs, conventional expressions and so on. These have in common that they are not newly generated and they ordinarily do not subscribe to usual grammatical and lexical semantic processes,[7] and are thus often characterized as 'nonliteral'. So when the director of the linguistics programmme at Carleton College, Professor Michael Flynn, hired me as 'Benedict Distinguished Visiting Professor' and asked me to choose a course title and content, my response was immediate (see Figure 11.1).

In the 1990s, generative grammar (Chomsky 1965; Pinker 1995[8]) was dominant in linguistics, so that studies of holistic, unitary expressions making up formulaic language, however ubiquitous and vital in everyday language use, were far from mainstream. There was no accepted term for these expressions, further handicapping progress in establishing a field of study. Nonetheless, fragments of evidence that normal language competence includes a separate facility for commonly shared

Nonliteral Language: Linguistic Perspectives
Professor Diana Van Lancker
Carleton College
Winter Term, 1998

Figure 11.1. Flier for new course offering

fixed expressions had emerged in psychology, sociology, second-language learning, child development, literary criticism, corpus studies, journalism and the media, old-fashioned phraseology and, given the observations mentioned above, behavioural neurology. I had been scouting these outcroppings over many years, and now saw the opportunity to stitch them together into an official course. It seemed like this just might be almost more fun than humanly possible. I listed the topics (Table 11.1) on the syllabus and prepared to begin. As will be seen, due to the vibrant nature of formulaic language as a dynamic aspect of linguistic competence, many other topics and themes arose in the course of the semester.

Table 11.1 Proposed topics for the course

1	Typology of nonliteral expressions
2	Popular examples in everyday life
3	History of nonliteral language studies
4	Structure of nonliteral expressions
5	Linguistic modelling
6	Second language studies
7	Cognitive theory underlying study of nonliteral expressions
8	Psycholinguistic studies
9	Neurolinguistic studies
10	Right hemisphere role
11	Laterality versus the cortical/subcortical axis
12	Integrating cerebral function and linguistic structure

The class began with definitions and properties of formulaic expressions discussing, as the syllabus indicated, 'The typology of nonliteral expressions'. Having tested experimental subjects on various idiom protocols, I had discovered that people are quick to recognize these kinds of language. Give them a few examples of speech formulas (*Better luck next time*), idioms (*He kept a stiff upper lip*) or proverbs (*While the cat's away, the mice will play*) and they are nodding and smiling with appreciation of the genre. We noted that, without linguistic training, speakers easily recognize something about the role of these expressions. Insights centred on the need for mastery of these expressions to get by in social situations and to sound like a native speaker (Fillmore 1979; Pawley and Syder 1983). Jack Olson's journalistic study of female clerical workers quoted one as saying:

> Most of my life had been spent completely alone, and I knew none of the code responses of young people. I didn't know what to *say*. Like when somebody comes up to you and says, 'How you doing, kid?' you're supposed to say something back, you're supposed to know a code answer. But I didn't make the proper responses because I didn't know them. I would have given anything to know them! (Olson 1972: 145).

11.2 Ubiquity of formulaic expressions

In the first week, our goal was to acknowledge the large presence of familiar nonliteral expressions in social settings (Tannen 1989). In order to become acquainted with the topic, students brought in utterance samples heard in the dormitories and around campus. Going over student submissions provided the class with instant entertainment, which seemed to arise from awareness of their common knowledge of the expressions. Each new contribution was met with vocal assent and interjections of appreciation, and, in some cases, hoots and hollers. The sharing of formulaic expressions seemed to breed a special solidarity among the students. On the other hand, lively amusement arose whenever the 'over thirty' instructor did not know an expression. Interestingly, the students did not expect me to know certain ones, such as *phat with ph*, meaning *cool* or (as we used to say) *hip*, which had just begun to make the rounds. The list of formulaic expressions gathered by class members at Carleton College in the winter of 1998 is presented in Table 11.2.

Table 11.2 Formulaic expressions contributed by students as heard in daily communicative interactions

(blank) has to do with (blank)	Are you going to eat that?
A few fries short of a happy meal.	Are you okay?
A few screws loose.	As sick as a dog
A long day.	At any rate
A picture's worth a thousand words.	Bats in the belfry
A red-letter day.	Biggest toad in the puddle
A stitch in time saves nine.	Black sheep
A watched pot never boils.	Break a leg.
All smooth sailing from there.	Can I come in?
Are they still an item?	Can you pass the napkins?

Cat's in the bag!
Cat's pyjamas
Caught red handed
Cold feet
Cool it.
Cut-cheese and blow-nose
DBSD
Dip
Do you have your keys?
Dog eat dog
Don't bite the hand that feeds you.
Don't count your chickens before they hatch.
Don't cry over spilled milk.
Don't have a cow.
Don't let the bedbugs bite.
Don't put all your eggs in one basket.
Don't shit in the nest.
Drive safe.
Eat shit and die.
Even monkeys fall from trees. (Japanese)
Fish out of water
Flex (to leave)
Flip the patty.
Fools go where angels fear to tread.
Fuck you!
Get a little of your own back.
Get your swerve/freak on.
Gets your goat.
Go figure.
Go for the whole kielbasa.
Go postal
Go to hell.
Green with envy
Hang on.
Have a butchers (look – Cockney)
Have a granny (look – Cockney)
Have you ever had...?
Having a full day
He has got a snowball's chance in hell.
He hates my guts
He knows how to push my buttons.
He ripped me off.
He was born with a silver spoon in his mouth.
He's gone round the bend.
He's in the doghouse.
He's interested in her.
He/she/that kicks ass!
Heart of gold
Heaven help us.
Hit the head
How are you doing?
How are your classes going?
How does that grab you?
How was break?
How's it going?
How's it hanging?
How's life?
Hurt like a bitch
I booked it across the parking lot.
I do.
I have to piss like a racehorse.
I was like '...'
I was out of pocket at the time.
I'll be there with bells on.
I'll give you a piece of my mind.
I'm at the end of my rope.
I'm cooking with gas.
I'm not crazy about it.
I'm on cloud nine.
I'm sorry.
I'm there.
I've been running around all day.
I've been running in circles all day.
I've got you wrapped around my finger.
I've had it up to here with that kind of thing.
If the shoe fits, wear it.
If wishes were horses then beggars could ride.
In a nutshell.
In the bag
Is that you?
It just isn't me.
It's all fun and games until someone loses an eye.
It's all good.
It's dark over here.
It's Greek to me.
It's like pulling teeth.

It's raining buckets.
It's raining cats and dogs.
It's really pissing down. (raining hard)
It's the tail wagging the dog.
It's way over my head.
Just in the nick of time.
Keep plugging away.
Keep your eyes peeled.
Knock on wood.
Knowing is half the battle.
Left and right
Let sleeping dogs lie.
Life's a bitch and then you die.
Like
Like three peas in a pod.
Look before you leap.
Mind your p's and q's.
My virgin ears
Never eat the seed corn.
Nice one.
Now you see it...
Off the hook
Oh boy oh boy!
Oh well.
Peace out dog.
Phat
Plates of meat (feet – Cockney)
Pull the rug out from under us
Quit cold turkey.
Red herring
Rejecting the mold
Roll with it.
Rome wasn't built in a day.
Same shit, different day.
Same shit, different shovel.
Scary!
Screw the pooch.
See ya later!
She likes to burst my bubble.
She screwed me over.
She was hanging around the house.
She went ape-shit.
Shit happens.
Shit.
Shoot for the stars.
Shoot the shit.
Shut your cakehole.
Sleep with one eye open
Snapping dogs off lampposts (it's cold out)
Snug as a bug in a rug
Sour grapes
Sweet tooth
Sweet!
Swingin'!
Take it with a grain of salt
That bites.
That's a blast.
That's going to need some elbow grease.
The buck stops here.
The cat's out of the bag.
The early bird catches the worm.
The flip side of the coin
The needle becomes a stick. (Japanese)
They don't go in for that much.
They put two and two together.
They [jalapenos] make my head pop off.
Think outside the box
This city is hopping.
This sucks!
This vacuums.
Throw in the towel
Time flies when you're having fun.
To come full circle
Underdog
Unhh...
Up the old ballet dancers. (go upstairs to bed – Cockney)
We don't need any comments from the peanut gallery.
What does that have to do with the price of eggs in China?
What goes around, comes around.

What's up?	You can say that and hold one foot in the fire!
Whatever trips your tree.	You look blue.
Whatever.	You lucky dog
Where have you been all my life?	You're a fag.
Yeah, you're really fishing around here.	You're going to catch your death of cold.
You betcha.	You're playing with fire.

11.3 Origin and other matters

We posed questions about formulaic expressions. How are they learned? How are they comprehended in distinction to literally intended utterances, especially when both meanings are plausible? The notion that the listener first considers a possible literal interpretation, finds it not to match the current context and moves to a look-up list was discussed. How do speakers know to produce these utterances exactly correctly (as they must be), including using a certain intonation? Students quickly grasped the role of sociolinguistic features of register (formality, politeness, etc.), cohort, and other parameters determining where and when these utterances can occur.

We discussed the provenance of fixed expressions. Indeed, we reflected, they all come from somewhere. The idea arose that the students could invent some expressions, or borrow items not yet current in the American Midwest from other geographical locations, and attempt to ignite their use around the campus. Candidates were proposed: *Smaller than a moth's ear*, *I'm colder than an Eskimo without a coat*, for which the meanings were more or less clear. We preferred to select a candidate with a nonobvious meaning. Thinking about launching fresh, new formulaic expressions onto the campus, we prepared a table glossing the proper meaning or usage of our invented formulas (Table 11.3).

Table 11.3 Invented formulaic expressions

Invented term	*Example or meaning*
Sexcellent	That girl/boy is excellent.
Could you spell that for me?	What?
It's a ticker tape parade out there.	It's snowing really hard.
A monkey's bum	'It's hot/cold enough in here to boil/freeze…'
That's flat, man.	Harsh, cold, cruel, evil – 'A pop quiz? That was so flat!'

Shiva	Holy Shiva (Hindu god of destruction) or Holy Kali
B.C.	Initials of current president (Bill Clinton) – 'I B.C.'d my way out of it.' 'I pulled some B.C. and nobody noticed.'
Flash	Leave/go – 'Are you ready to flash?' 'Let's flash.'
Green	Set or ready – 'We're green.'
Hit the snooze.	Catch oneself from falling asleep – 'That class was so boring, I must have hit the snooze 20 x.'
PMS	Post-Marriott sickness
Da da da	Say when there's a quiet moment in conversation.
I'm not going to eat any more Marriott fish.	I'm not going to take it any more.
Get/look spanky	To dress to be sexually appealing
She's apples.	Australian response to 'How's it going?'
Fresh! Badd!	Terms from the 1980s
He's fruit and cake.	West Coast saying
Flex	Leave – 'She had to flex.'
She/he's so 7-11	A promiscuous person
I can't tell if it's God's gold or Satan's scribble	It's Greek to me.
Can I have the time?	Instead of 'Do you have the time?'

The class voted on which expressions to adopt for the dissemination ruse. Figure 11.2 shows numbers of students voting for 8 expressions chosen from the list. The winner was B.C., with 'Get/look spanky' and 'That's flat' as close second choices.

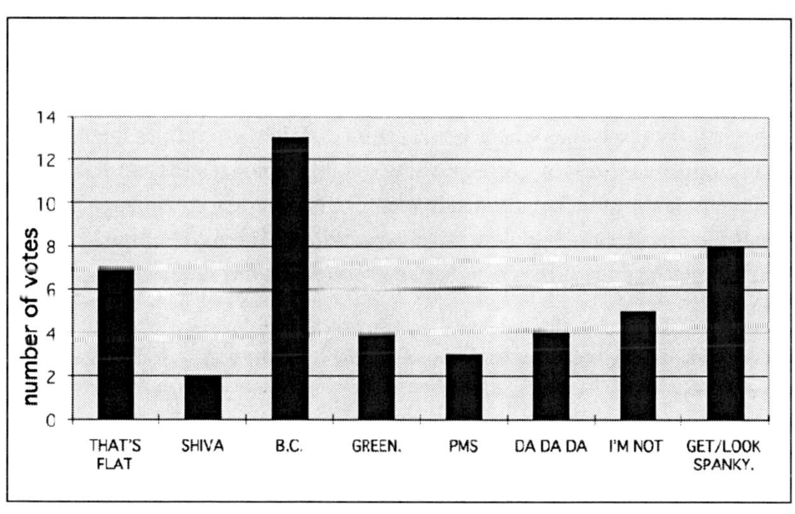

Figure 11.2 Numbers of votes (on ordinate) for proposed invented expressions

Students agreed to use the expression 'B.C.' in appropriate contexts during regular conversation, and at the end of the semester the class would assess the success of artificial formulaic propagation.

11.4 Previous literature on formulaic language

We surveyed linguistic mention about any type of utterance that was not strictly newly created. Most of these early comments had been lost to current thought about language structure. In his one-time popular *Introduction to theoretical linguistics*, John Lyons (1968) recommended separate analysis of 'ready-made utterances', which he described as being learned as a whole and passed on from one generation to the next. These were distinguished from newly created expressions, he stated, and are 'not profitably regarded as sentences... Their internal structure...is not accounted for by means of (grammatical) rules' (p. 177). Otto Jesperson in his 1933 text *Essentials of English grammar* described the 'important distinction between formulas or formular units and free expressions' that 'pervades all parts of the grammar' (p. 18). He proposed that formulas are 'felt and handled as a unit' and that they therefore may involve different kinds of mental activity (pp. 19-21). We looked in many places for perspectives on our topic. In a chapter called 'Collocation and commonplace knowledge', Tyler (1978) discusses certain kinds of speech occurring 'as whole units which we do not, on every occasion of their use, assemble from their component words' (p. 230). Tyler goes on to say that the usual meanings of the words are not used to process an idiom. The class read about irreversible binomial expressions such as 'pepper and salt', and trinomials such as 'red, white and blue' (Malkiel 1959; Cooper and Ross 1975) and about the currently popular discussions of indirect speech acts; conventionalized utterances were seen to routinely communicate a different – a nonliteral – meaning (Searle 1975, 1985; Sadock 1974; Lewis 1969).

We considered passages where writers from different disciplines mentioned two types of language processes, corresponding roughly to novel and formulaic. The linguist Dwight Bolinger often alluded to memorial processes in language use (1976, 1977) as distinct from newly generated expressions. The psychologist Lounsbury (1963) had outlined the differences between novel and formulaic expressions quite succinctly:

> Of two constructions made according to the same pattern, one may be an *ad hoc* construction of the moment and the other may be a repetition or use of one coined long ago, often heard, and much employed as a whole unit, e.g., as an idiom, a cliché... It is apparent that as behavioral events they are quite different and that in some sense their psychological statuses and in the actual speaking behaviour may be quite different (1963: 561).

11.5 Properties and typology

Table 11.4 presents characteristics which are unique to formulaic expressions, or occur in greater degree than seen in literal expressions.

Table 11.4 Properties and characteristics of formulaic expressions

- Cohesion, unitary structure, holistic, strong coherence of items
- Stereotyped form, including prosody
- Conventional meaning
- Flexibility of form, leading to flexibility of meaning
- Schemata, with slot-filler format
- Incomplete parts sufficient to cue the entire expression
- Portions of utterances serve to keep speech fluent
- Introductory parts to begin utterances[9]
- Literal *or* figurative meanings (figurative meaning not required)
- Often highly context-bound (social and linguistic context)
- If ditropic[10] meanings, literal use is less likely or common
- Affective and attitudinal content usually present
- Evaluative (approval, disapproval) content often present.
- Require heavy inferencing[11]
- Involve pragmatic factors such as conversational postulates (Grice 1875, 1978)
- Carry innuendo of group membership, social commitment revealed
- Establish register or 'formality' index
- Contain archaic or extremely rare lexical items[12]
- Words used in nonstandard ways[13]
- Archaic or odd grammatical forms[14]
- Indefinite reference[15]

Formulaic expressions can be classified according to structure, usage, content, context, function and/or type. Idioms, for example, are relatively context free and utilize lexical items nonliterally. Proverbs are generally in the present tense and point toward a generalized meaning. Many conversational speech formulas are just that – phrases that occur in conversation, are highly situation-bound, and can be either literal or nonliteral in meaning (Goodwin 1981; Schegloff 1998; Tannen 1980). The difficulty of having rigid categories became clear.

11.6 Incidence question: How many in a day?

At this time, studies of actual speech examined as texts and in naturalistic corpora were underway (Halliday and Hasan 1976; Svartvik and Quirk 1980) and certain estimates of recurrent combinations of words, indirectly indexing different kinds of formulaic expressions, were in print (Altenberg 1998; Sinclair 1987; Strässler 1982; Moon 1998a, b; Cowie 1992). Students had brought in samples of formulaic expressions continuously through the first half of the quarter, bearing witness to a subjective sense of their magnitude in everyday language use (Table 11.2). Questions arose amongst us about actual incidence. How many formulaic expressions did a given student use or hear each day? Was the number something like 10? Or was it nearer to 200? We entertained various suggestions for making objective measures: a few students volunteered to 'wear a wire' throughout the day, for example, and to audio-record and transcribe all conversations. The legal, logistical, and practical implications of this were daunting, if not prohibitive.

Somehow we hit upon the idea to count the number of formulaic expressions used in a film. The class agreed to select a date for 'Movie Night'. A film on videotape would be projected over the digital projector system and the entire class would write down every formula heard in the dialogue. We would then collate these responses and determine the number of formulas per minute of film action. A hearty debate arose around which film to select. I had not heard of most of the films on the list (see Table 11.5), and some of the titles worried me a bit, given thoughts about the instructor's position as implicit moral authority and explicit role model.

Table 11.5 Films from which to choose for a group project

Films
Clueless
Wayne's World
Beavis and Butthead Do America
Swingers
The Princess Bride
Monty Python and the Quest for the Holy Grail
Ferris Bueller's Day Off
Clerks
The Breakfast Club
Austin Powers
Some Like It Hot

Lack of class consensus led to a rating exercise. Students rank ordered their first, second and third preferences (Figure 11.3).

As can be seen in Figure 11.3, *Swingers* and *Austin Powers* gained the most votes. I previewed the Austin Powers movie in the privacy of my own home, and although the star's frequent outburst of 'Yeah, Baby!' provided an outstanding example of unique intonation and voice on the formulaic utterance (features we had discussed), I judged the overall ambience as too raucous. I cannot remember why I

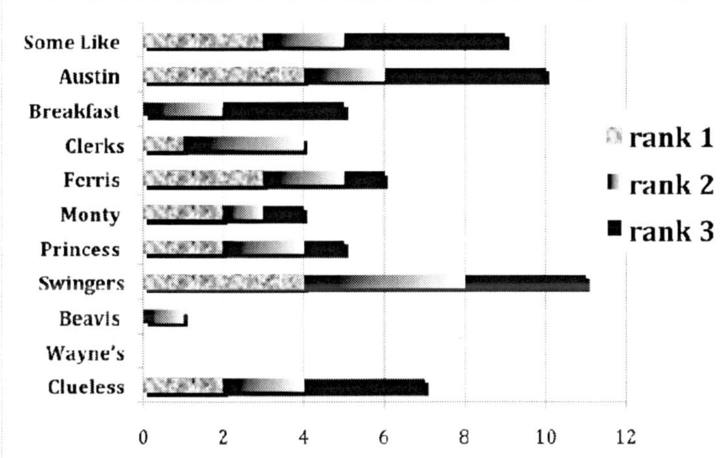

Figure 11.3 Student votes for 11 proposed films to use in class project

rejected *Swingers*. I settled on the third class pick, *Some Like it Hot*, and several students assured me that it was a classic film and very humorous.

I reserved a classroom with a digital projector and screen for an evening time slot, and Movie Night was scheduled. As incentive to appear, a listing of preferred snacks was obtained, later annotated with special preferences by those with strong opinions on the topic. Most students attended Movie Night. Writing tablets and utensils were provided and we rolled the film. Everyone watched intently and wrote down formulaic expressions as they emerged in the dialogue. The lists were handed in at the end of the evening and collated for discussion the next day. In class, we did our best to categorize the expressions in terms of how many students identified each item and its classification as formula, idiom or proverb. This method did not allow us to account for repetitions of utterances; we tabulated unique instances only. The total count was 276 formulaic expressions in a film lasting 122 minutes, resulting in an average of 2.3 formulaic expressions per minute.

11.7 Linguistic and psycholinguistic modelling

It became apparent that the standard generative theory in linguistics of constituent structure and transformational rules did not accommodate idioms and other formulaic expressions very well. The few attempts to enfold idioms into the generative model were unconvincing. Weinreich (1969) had called idioms 'an unfashionable topic' and a 'basic theoretical stumbling block' (1969: 23) within current linguistic approaches. Chafe (1968) viewed idioms as anomalous, suggesting that other descriptive methods were required for them. Katz (1973) identified 'idiomaticity' as a property of language distinct from 'compositionality', a notion carried forward by

Bolinger (1977) and by Fillmore, Kay and O'Connor (1988) in their treatment of the persistent idiomaticity of the expression 'let alone'.

Treatments of alleged degrees of frozenness in idioms, as an inroad into a structural description, proliferated (Gibbs, Nayak and Cutting 1989). While Fraser (1970) proposed that relative fixedness of idioms was related to which transformations they could undergo, Cutler (1982) suggested that the proposed frozenness parameter may actually reflect the age of the expression. But the notion of degrees of frozenness itself, if it were to be seen as any stable metric, was severely challenged by contradictory reports arising from linguistic analyses and psycholinguistic performance measures. Linguistics studies blended into psycholinguistics studies, as questions about native speaker competence were cast into measures of performance. Numerous experiments by Gibbs and his colleagues (1980, 1994; Nayak and Gibbs 1990) and others strove to uncover mental processing for idioms and their constituents (Cutting and Bock 1997; Titone and Connine 1994; Cacciari and Tabossi 1993). Extensive analyses of idioms and their semantic processes appeared, each proposing criteria for degrees of compositionality and semantic transparency (Burgess and Chiarello 1996; Nunberg, Sag and Wasow 1994; Cacciari and Tabossi 1988, 1993; Estill and Kemper 1982; Gibbs and Gonzales 1985) as well as determining the effects of context and familiarity on listeners' judgments (Bobrow and Bell 1973; Schweigert 1986). Some classified the idiom as a fixed lexical item (Heringer 1976; Swinney and Cutler 1979) while others disagreed (Burt 1992; Gibbs 1994). The results of subject testing were inconsistent and discrepant, which likely arose from varying task demands in metalinguistic procedures, so that a definitive model of idiom structural properties did not emerge (see review in Van Lancker Sidtis 2006).

While structural descriptions within the large set of idioms remained controversial, psychological studies revealed reliable, gross performance differences between formulaic and novel exemplars (Horowitz and Manelis 1973; Osgood and Housain 1974; Swinney and Cutler 1979; Pickens and Pollio 1979). In these studies, subjects could recall individual words from novel expressions more successfully than the same words presented in formulaic expressions. Simon's (1974) article outlining memory processes gave credence to the concept of 'chunks' as units of processing containing different numbers of elements. Simon (1974) demonstrated that when people are asked to remember and recall a list of items, the number of recallable items – or chunks – is nearly the same for syllables, words, compound words and idiomatic phrases.

A few hints had emerged to suggest that motor speech and prosodic processes differ for the two types of language. Lieberman (1963) demonstrated that individual words matched in novel and formulaic expressions yield different articulatory sequelae. The word 'nine' in a sentence like 'I say the number nine' is spoken differently from the word 'nine' in a proverb such as 'A stitch in time saves nine.'

Early studies by Van Lancker and Canter (1981) demonstrated that listeners could distinguish literal from idiomatic meanings of ditropic sentences (those with balanced ambiguity between literal and idiomatic meanings, such as 'It broke the ice') from auditory presentation alone, without benefit of other context, and later studies indicated that pitch contours, pausing and word length were significantly involved in distinguishing the meanings (Van Lancker, Canter and Terbeek 1981).

Studies of child language describe two interactive processes underlying acquisition: holistic and analytic, bringing in again a viable chunking process alongside an unfolding of analytic grammatical rules for the language (Peters 1977, 1983; Wong Fillmore 1979; Vihman 1982; Kempler, Van Lancker, Marchman and Bates 1999). These insights supported the picture of two essentially different modes that unfold, seemingly in parallel, during child language acquisition and continue to be operative throughout language competence.

11.8 Neurolinguistic perspectives

Coming around full circle to the original observations stimulated by J. Hughlings Jackson, we viewed videotapes of aphasic persons who demonstrated a dissociation between novel and formulaic expressions. Most striking to the students were otherwise nonfluent patients who could emit a range of swearwords fluently and with normal articulation and prosody. Further, students heard the recorded speech of persons with Tourette's syndrome, with the frequent emission of taboo phrases occurring in the regular stream of talk (Friedhoff and Chase 1982; Shapiro, Shapiro, Bruun and Sweet 1983). This led to interest in the phenomenon of expletives, a topic that can readily stimulate a classroom of undergraduates. We found a scattered literature of books and papers (Hughes 1991; Jay 1992, 1996; Montagu 1967; Foote and Woodward 1973) as well as a creative field study by Gallahorn (1971), who documented use of swearwords by clinical personnel in hospital team meetings. Class enthusiasm inspired a review article on the neurology of expletives, which was completed during my sojourn at Carleton College (Van Lancker and Cummings 1999).

Other types of 'automatic' speech were often described in many kinds of aphasic disorders: preserved counting, conversational speech formulas, and a variety of other conventional expressions. These had been anecdotal, clinical reports. The first scientific surveys of preserved automatic speech had appeared (Blanken 1991; Code 1982, 1989), identifying the categories – formulaic expressions, sentence stems, interjections and proper nouns – that remain fluent in severe aphasia. Lum and Ellis (1994) performed a controlled study showing that automatic speech was relatively preserved in aphasia in most tasks, except for repetition, which was replicated by Van Lancker and Bella (1996). We viewed video footage of a fluent aphasic patient with transcortical sensory aphasia, who spoke nearly exclusively in speech formulas; similar other cases had appeared (Nakagawa *et al.* 1993; Whitaker 1976).

The aphasic patients had in common that their right hemispheres are intact, and so we explored evidence for a right hemispheric site of these preserved utterances. Several studies had attributed residual speech in aphasia to right hemisphere functionality (Czopf 1981; Kinsbourne 1971); indeed, such residual speech was observed in a normally developed, right-handed adult who had undergone removal of the left hemisphere for treatment of malignancy (Smith 1966). Interesting to us at the time were measurements of mouth asymmetries in stroke patients by Graves and Landis (1985). This study revealed that counting (a type of 'automatic speech') was spoken with greater left-sided mouth opening, implicating control by the right hemisphere, while spoken words were generated with asymmetrically larger opening on the right side of the mouth, suggesting left hemisphere control. These and other studies drew on a large body of information contrasting types of behaviours attributed to left- or right-hemisphere specialization, or the horizontal axis. Holistic processing had often been associated with the right hemisphere abilities (Bever 1975; Bogen 1969; Martin 1979; Bradshaw and Nettleton 1983), for which a different kind of language processing, involving rich contextual cues, had been also reported (Drews 1987; Sidtis, Volpe, Holtzman, Wilson and Gazzaniga 1981; Brownell, Gardner, Prather and Martino 1995).

Related ideas arose from the contemporary rise in interest in pragmatic topics, and their association with right-hemisphere function. At this time, the new field of pragmatic studies was burgeoning. Naturalistic texts were subjected to meticulous analyses. Comprehension studies using the test of Formulaic and Novel Language Comprehension (FANL-C; Kempler and Van Lancker 1996) and other approaches had revealed that persons with right-hemisphere damage were impaired in recognizing idiomatic meanings (Winner and Gardner 1977; Van Lancker and Kempler 1987). Other studies of communicative disorders in right-hemisphere damage revealed the role that social and linguistic context plays in language comprehension, and in what ways this communicative ability is diminished in right-hemisphere damage (Brownell, Simpson, Bihrle, Potter and Gardner 1990; Gardner, Brownell, Wapner and Michelow 1983; Joanette and Brownell 1990). These insights provided a bridge to our thinking about cerebral representation of formulaic expressions, which have as a main feature that proper use is contingent on appropriate social context.

Next we considered the vertical axis of the cerebrum, whereby cortical and subcortical structures (which include the basal ganglia, the site of motor output, and the limbic system, seat of the emotions) stand in a certain relation to each other with respect to types of behaviour. One study up to that time had implicated portions of the basal ganglia in modulation of formulaic expressions. This was a description of a 75-year-old right-handed man, who, following a stroke in the right basal ganglia, had impaired prayer recitation and other formulaic performance (Speedie, Wertman,

Ta'ir and Heilman 1993). Other papers had drawn increasing attention to basal ganglia nuclei as important modulators of motor initiation, monitoring and control (Marsden 1982). Whereas previously the cortex was identified as representing all language behaviours, an important role of subcortical structures in speech and language functions was proposed (Lieberman 1963; Robinson 1976). Some of these proposals included two types of processing on the vertical axis of the brain – with habits and routinization associated with subcortical structures as popularly outlined by Koestler (1967) and presented in other contexts by neurologists (Mishkin, Malamut and Bachevalier 1984), while voluntary, controlled action was cortically modulated. When formulaic utterances are viewed in their capacity as overlearned motor gestures, it is easy to imagine that the basal ganglia may play a major role in production of formulaic expressions.

Understanding of the speech of Alzheimer's disease was in its early stages; anecdotal clinical observations told of preserved formulaic expressions in persons with severe dementia affecting language and cognition. In contrast, it had been shown that auditory recognition of formulaic expressions was impaired even in mild Alzheimer's disease, those with a definitive diagnosis based on biopsy results (Kempler, Van Lancker and Read 1988). These and other studies suggested that cortical damage impairs comprehension of the nonliteral meanings of formulaic expressions, while intact basal ganglia, the site of motor initiation and management in the brain, allow for facile output of formulaic expressions, which are overlearned and behave like motor gestures in the individual with cortical dementia. It is known that the basal ganglia are preserved quite late into the progression of Alzheimer's disease.

In summary, our review of the neurolinguistic studies of the time suggested that, for production, a right-hemisphere subcortical circuit might be involved in modulating formulaic expressions, and that the right hemisphere played an important role in comprehending the holistic meanings of these expressions.

11.9 Student papers

Students' research projects explored formulaic language into a dizzying range of domains at a time when little knowledge of the topic existed. Formulaic language, with all its intrinsic interest, unleashed a fresh, dynamic creativity. Table 11.6 provides a list of student topics on 'FEs' (Formulaic Expressions).

Table 11.6 Topics for research projects involving formulaic expressions (FEs)

1	Survey of origins and familiarity ratings of FEs
2	FEs in old and new Russia
3	Translations into German of FEs in *Calvin and Hobbes*

4	Phonology versus lexicology in idiom recognition
5	Use of FEs compared in TV vs radio transmission
6	Grammaticality judgments of transformed idiomatic expressions
7	How geographic location affects speech patterns: FEs
8	Online processing differences in propositional and formulaic sentences
9	Preserved automatic speech in transcortical sensory aphasia
10	Differences in perception of spoken vs written sarcasm
11	Advertising and nonliteral language: use and recognition studies
12	Role of popularity in FE usage in comic strips
13	Minnesotan FEs by natives and others
14	Idiom decomposability reconsidered
15	The role of FEs in rap music: the language of rap
16	FEs as used in taboo topics
17	FEs in presidential addresses from a historical perspective
18	Gender differences in FE usage in pop TV shows
19	FEs in ME Chaucer and Modern English translations
20	FEs in chat rooms: role of experience and topic
21	Comparing nonliteral language in sports and news
22	Nonliteral language in James Bond movies: use and alterations
23	FEs in speeches vs interviews of B. Clinton and R. Reagan
24	FEs in the media
25	FEs in *Rolling Stone* vs *New Yorker* magazines: usage differences
26	The gendering of familiar phrases
27	Role of FEs in ratings of movie dialogues, good vs bad

A survey[16] (Paper 1) drew out information about recognition and usage of an array of formulaic expressions in relationship to geographical background and other sociolinguistic factors. One of the students had visited Russia twice, once as the former Soviet Union and a second time after the collapse of that government (Paper 2). She noted how during the interim, sayings on billboards and public spaces had undergone a radical change. She documented and described these changes in her research project entitled ‘Formulaic expressions in old and new Russia’. A delightful study on cartoon translation was based on the correct assumption that many esoteric formulaic expressions, including onomatopoeia, expletives and exclamations, arise from cartoon characters (Paper 3). This student found published German translations of *Calvin and Hobbes* (designed by Bill Watterson, appearing from 1985 to 1995). Paper 9 analysed the videotapes of speech-therapy sessions from the previously mentioned aphasic patient, diagnosed with transcortical sensory aphasia. This patient spoke fluently and almost exclusively in fixed expressions. The student transcribed selected portions of the spoken material and classified expressions into speech formulas, idioms and proverbs, and compared their incidence with novel expressions. With the help of Professor Ohnesorge on the psychology faculty at Carleton College, another of our students tested reaction times in a computerized design to matching of idiomatic and literal expressions to response drawings derived from the Formulaic and Novel Language Comprehension Test (Kempler and Van Lancker 1996) (Paper 8). The result corresponded to those reported in previous studies (Ortony, Schallert, Reynolds and Antos 1978; Swinney and Cutler 1979) suggesting that formulaic expressions are processed holistically and independently from novel expressions. Two tales from Chaucer's *Canterbury Tales* were studied, comparing specific formulaic expressions in Middle English with Modern English editions (Paper 19). The student noted the effect of adherence to rhyme and metre, compared to free form translations, on the translated results. Shorter utterances were more likely to retain their original formulaic shape. In Paper 27, eight categories of formulaic expressions were identified in movies with allegedly bad dialogue (*Speed 2* and *Robocop 3*) and those judged to have good dialogue (*Pulp Fiction* and *Glengarry Glen Ross*). Slightly more idioms were counted in the better-written movies, but all the movies contained a lion's share of expletives and other speech formulas. Many of these projects were so well done that I recommended just a little more effort to prepare the papers for publication. But these undergraduate students had other goals and other miles to go, and none accepted my suggestion at the time. As they say: so many topics, so little time. Perhaps some day the chickens will come home to roost – hope springs eternal.

11.10 Concluding remarks

Because of time restrictions in the course, some topics received only brief mention, such as the place of formulaic expressions in second-language learning (Wray 1999a, b) and literary uses (Kiparsky 1976; Tannen 1980). Our major class project, capturing fixed expressions in real time in the movie *Some Like it Hot*, and collating the results from the whole class, provided a count of expressions-per-minute that was close to the number obtained in a later, systematic analysis using the written screenplay (Van Lancker and Rallon 2004).

Our secondary class project – to cause expressions invented by students to be taken up and carried forth by the college constituency – did not bear measurable results. Students were unable to report any independent usages of these invented expressions. It was interesting to find that we could not demonstrably conquer the originating processes underlying formulaic expressions. We concluded that it requires some mysterious feature manifest by the *Zeitgeist* to generate a proper energy for social acceptance and further diffusion of formulaic phrases into the language community.

A surge of understanding of formulaic language has occurred in the ten years since these materials were patched together to form an academic course at Carleton College. The importance of formulaic language in language competence has enjoyed increasing recognition (Wray 2002; Kuiper 2009; Van Lancker Sidtis 2004, 2009) and other courses on the topic have appeared. While it is clear that there is much more to be revealed, formulaic language has become a strong player in the academic scene, offering endless domains of challenge. And we also know how to keep it fun.

References

Altenberg, B. 1998. 'On the phraseology of spoken English: The evidence of recurrent word-combinations'. In *Phraseology: Theory, analysis and applications*, pp. 101-24, ed. A.P. Cowie. Oxford: Clarendon Press.

Bay, E. 1962. 'Aphasia and nonverbal disorders of language'. *Brain* 85: 411-26.

Bay, E. 1964a. 'The history of aphasia and the principles of cerebral localization'. In *Cerebral localization and organization*, pp. 44-52, ed. G. Schaltenbrand and C. Woolsey. Madison: University of Wisconsin Press.

Bay, E. 1964b. 'Principles of classification and their influence on our concepts of aphasia'. In *Disorders of language: CIBA Symposium*, pp. 122-39, ed. A.V.S. De Reuck and M. O'Connor. London: J. and A. Churchill.

Bever, T.G. 1975. 'Cerebral asymmetries in humans are due to the differentiation of two incompatible processes: Holistic and analytic'. *Annals of the New York Academy of Science* 263: 251-62.

Blanken, G. 1991. 'The functional basis of speech automatisms (recurring utterances)'. *Aphasiology* 5: 103-27.

Bobrow, S.A. and S.M. Bell. 1973. 'On catching on to idiomatic expressions'. *Memory and Cognition* 1: 343-46.

Bogen, J.E. 1969. 'The other side of the brain II: An appositional mind'. *Bulletin of the Los Angeles Neurological Societies* 324: 191-219.

Bolinger, D. 1976. 'Meaning and memory'. *Forum Linguisticum* 1: 1-14.

Bolinger, D. 1977. 'Idioms have relations'. *Forum Linguisticum* 2: 157-69.

Bradshaw, J.L. and N.C. Nettleton. 1983. *Human cerebral asymmetry*. Englewood Cliffs, NJ: Prentice Hall.

Brownell, H.H., H. Gardner, P. Prather and G. Martino. 1995. 'Language, communication, and the right hemisphere'. In *Handbook of Neurological Speech and Language Disorders*. Vol. 33, pp. 325-49, ed. H.S. Kirshner. New York: Marcel Dekker.

Brownell, H.H., T.L. Simpson, A.M. Bihrle, H.H. Potter and H. Gardner. 1990. 'Appreciation of metaphoric alternative word meanings by left and right brain-damaged patients'. *Neuropsychologia* 28: 375-83.

Burgess, C. and C. Chiarello. 1996. 'Neurocognitive mechanisms underlying metaphor comprehension and other figurative language'. *Metaphor and Symbolic Activity* 11: 67-84.

Burt, J.S. 1992. 'Against the lexical representation of idioms'. *Canadian Journal of Psychology* 46: 582-605.

Cacciari, C. and P. Tabossi. 1988. 'The comprehension of idioms'. *Journal of Memory and Language* 27: 668-83.

Cacciari, C. and P. Tabossi. 1993. *Idioms: Processing, structure, and interpretation.* Hillsdale, NJ: Lawrence Erlbaum Associates.

Chafe, W. 1968. 'Idiomaticity as an anomaly in the Chomskyan paradigm'. *Foundations of Language* 4: 109-27.

Chomsky, N. 1965. *Aspects of a theory of syntax*. Cambridge, MA: The MIT Press.

Code, C. 1982. 'Neurolinguistic analysis of recurrent utterance in aphasia'. *Cortex* 18: 141-52.

Code, C. 1989. *The characteristics of aphasia*. London: Taylor and Francis.

Cooper, W.E. and J.R. Ross 1975. 'World order'. In *Papers from the parasession in functionalism*, pp. 63-111, ed. R.E. Grossman. Chicago: Chicago Linguistic Society.

Cowie, A.P. 1992. 'Multiword lexical units and communicative language teaching'. In *Vocabulary and applied linguistics*, pp. 1-12, ed. P. Arnaud and H. Bejoint. London: Macmillan.

Critchley, M. 1970. *Aphasiology and other aspects of language*. London: Edward Arnold.

Cutler, A. 1982. 'Idioms: The colder the older'. *Linguistic Inquiry* 13: 3178-320.

Cutting, J.C. and K. Bock. 1997. 'That's the way the cookie bounces: Syntactic and semantic components of experimentally elicited idiom blends'. *Memory and Cognition* 25: 57-71.

Czopf, J. 1981. 'Über die Rolle der nicht dominanten Hemisphäre in der Restitution der Sprache der Aphasischen' (On the role of the nondominant hemisphere in the recovery of language in aphasic speakers). *Archiven Psychiatrischer Nervenkrankenheiten* 216: 162-71.

Drews, E. 1987. 'Quantitatively different organization structure of lexical knowledge in the left and right hemisphere'. *Neuropsychologia* 25: 419-27.

Estill, R.B. and S. Kemper. 1982. 'Interpreting idioms'. *Journal of Psycholinguistic Research* 11: 559-69.

Fillmore, C. 1979. 'On fluency'. In *Individual differences in language ability and language behavior*, pp. 85-102, ed. C.J. Fillmore, D. Kempler and W.S.-Y. Wang. London: Academic Press.

Fillmore, C., P. Kay and M. O'Connor. 1988. 'Regularity and idiomaticity in grammatical constructions: The case of "let alone"'. *Language* 64: 501-38.

Foote, R. and J. Woodward. 1973. 'A preliminary investigation of obscene language'. *Journal of Psychology* 83: 263-75.

Fraser, B. 1970. 'Idioms within a transformation grammar'. *Foundations of Language* 6: 22-42.

Friedhoff, A.J. and T.N. Chase (eds.) 1982. *Advances in neurology*. Vol 35: *Gilles de la Tourette syndrome*. New York: Raven Press.

Gallahorn, G.E. 1971. 'The use of taboo words by psychiatric ward personnel'. *Psychiatry* 34: 309-21.

Gardner, H., H.H. Brownell, W. Wapner and D. Michelow. 1983. 'Missing the point: The role of the right hemisphere in the processing of complex linguistic materials'. In *Cognitive processing in the right hemisphere*, pp. 169-92, ed. E. Perecman. New York: Academic Press.

Gibbs, R.W., Jr. 1980. 'Spilling the beans on understanding and memory for idioms in conversation'. *Memory and Cognition* 8: 149-56.

Gibbs, R.W., Jr. 1994. 'Figurative thought and figurative language'. In *Handbook of Psycholinguistics*, pp. 411-46, ed. M.A. Gernsbacher. San Diego, CA: Academic Press.

Gibbs, R.W., Jr. and G.P. Gonzales. 1985. 'Syntactic frozenness in processing and remembering idioms'. *Cognition* 20: 243-59.

Gibbs, R.W., Jr., N.P. Nayak and C. Cutting. 1989. 'How to kick the bucket and not decompose: Analyzability and idiom processing'. *Journal of Memory and Language* 28: 576-93.

Graves, R. and T. Landis. 1985. 'Hemispheric control of speech expression in aphasia'. *Archives of Neurology* 42: 249-51.

Goodglass, H. and J. Mayer. 1958. 'Agrammatism in aphasia'. *Journal of Speech and Hearing Disorders* 23: 99-111.

Goodwin, C. 1981. *Conversational organization: Interaction between speakers and hearers*. New York: Academic Press.

Grice, P. 1975. 'Logic and conversation'. In *Syntax and semantics*, Vol. 3, pp. 41-58, ed. P. Cole and J.L. Morgan. New York: Academic Press.

Grice, P. 1978. 'Further notes on logic and conversation'. In *Syntax and semantics*, Vol. 9, pp. 281-97, ed. P. Cole. New York: Academic Press.

Halliday, M. and R. Hasan. 1976. *Cohesion in English*. London: Longman.

Head, H. 1926. *Aphasia and kindred disorders of speech*. Cambridge: The University Press, and 1962. New York: The MacMillan Co.

Heringer, J.T. 1976. 'Idioms and lexicalization in English'. In *Syntax and semantics*, Vol. 6, pp. 205-16, ed. M. Shibetani. New York: Academic Press.

Horowitz, L.M. and L. Manelis. 1973. Recognition and cued recall of idioms and phrases. *Journal of Experimental Psychology* 100: 291-96.

Hughes, G. 1991. *Swearing: A social history of foul language, oaths, and profanity in English*. Oxford: Blackwell.

Hughlings Jackson, J. 1874a. 'On the nature of the duality of the brain'. In *Selected writings of John Hughlings Jackson*. Vol. 2: *1878–9/1932*, pp. 129-45, ed. J. Taylor. London: Hodder and Stoughton, 1932.

Hughlings Jackson, J. 1874b. 'On affections of speech from disease of the brain'. In

Selected writings of John Hughlings Jackson. Vol. 2: *1878–9/1932*, pp. 155-204, ed. J. Taylor. London: Hodder and Stoughton, 1932. Originally in *Brain* 1 (1878/79): 304-30; *Brain* 2 (1879/80): 203-22 and 323-56; also reprinted in *Brain* 38 (1915).

Jay, T.B. 1992. *Cursing in America*. Philadelphia: John Benjamins.

Jay, T.B. 1996. 'Cursing: A damned persistent lexicon'. In *Basic and applied memory: Research on practical aspects of memory*, Vol. 2, pp. 301-13, ed. D. Hermann, M. Johnson, C. McEvoy, C. Hertzog and P. Hertel. Hillsdale, NJ: Erlbaum.

Jesperson, O. 1933. *Essentials of English grammar*. London: George Allen and Unwin.

Joanette, Y. and H. Brownell (eds.) 1990. *Discourse ability and brain damage: Theoretical and empirical perspectives*. New York: Springer-Verlag.

Katz, J.J. 1973. 'Compositionality, idiomaticity, and lexical substitution'. In *Festschrift for Morris Halle*, pp. 357-76, ed. S. Anderson. New York: Holt, Rinehart and Winston.

Kempler, D. and D. Van Lancker. 1996. 'The formulaic and novel language comprehension test (FANL-C)'. http://blog.emerson.edu/daniel_kemplerfanlc .html

Kempler, D., D. Van Lancker and S. Read. 1988. Proverb and idiom comprehension in Alzheimer disease. *Alzheimer Disease and Associated Disorders* 2, 38-49.

Kempler, D., D. Van Lancker, V. Marchman and E. Bates. 1999. 'Idiom comprehension in children and adults with unilateral brain damage'. *Developmental Neuropsychology* 15: 327-49.

Kinsbourne, M. 1971. 'The minor cerebral hemisphere as a source of aphasic speech'. *Transactions of the American Neurological Association* 96: 141-45.

Kiparsky, P. 1976. 'Oral poetry: Some linguistic and typological considerations'. In *Oral literature and the formula*, pp. 73-106, ed. B. Stolz and R. Shannon. Ann Arbor: Center for the Coordination of Ancient and Modern Studies.

Koestler, A. 1967. *The ghost in the machine*. Chicago: Gateway.

Kuiper, K. 2009. *Formulaic genres*. Basingstoke: Palgrave Macmillan.

Lenneberg, E. 1967. *Biological foundations of language*. New York: Wiley.

Lewis, D. 1969. *Convention*. Cambridge, MA: Harvard University Press.

Lieberman, P. 1963. Some effects of semantic and grammatical context on the production and perception of speech. *Language and Speech* 6: 172-87.

Lounsbury, F.G. 1963. 'Linguistics and psychology'. In *Psychology: A study of a science*, pp. 552-82, ed. S. Koch. New York: McGraw-Hill.

Lum, C.C. and A.W. Ellis. 1994. 'Is "nonpropositional" speech preserved in aphasia?' *Brain and Language* 46: 368-91.

Luria, A.R. 1966. *Higher cortical functions in man*. New York: Basic Books.

Luria, A.R. 1970. 'The functional organization of the brain'. *Scientific American* 222(3): 66-78.

Lyons, J. 1968. *Introduction to theoretical linguistics*. Cambridge: Cambridge University Press.

Malkiel, Y. 1959. 'Studies in irreversible binomials'. *Lingua* 8: 113-60.

Marsden, C.D. 1982. 'The mysterious motor function of the basal ganglia: The Robert Wartenberg lecture'. *Neurology* 32: 514-39.

Martin, M. 1979. 'Hemispheric specialization for local and global processing'. *Neuropsychologia* 17: 33-40.

Mishkin, M., B. Malamut and J. Bachevalier. 1984. 'Memories and habits: Two neural systems'. In *Neurobiology of Learning and Memory*, pp. 65-77, ed. G. Lynch, J.L. McGaugh and N.M. Weinberger. New York: The Guilford Press.

Montagu, A. 1967. *The anatomy of swearing*. London: Rapp and Whiting.

Moon, R.E. 1998a. *Fixed expressions and text: A study of the distribution and textual behaviour of fixed expressions in English*. Oxford: Clarendon Press.

Moon, R.E. 1998b. 'Frequencies and forms of phrasal lexemes in English'. In *Phraseology: Theory, analysis, and applications*, pp. 79-100, ed. A.P. Cowie. Oxford: Clarendon Press.

Nakagawa, Y., H. Tanabe, M. Ikeda, H. Kazui *et al.* 1993. 'Completion phenomenon in transcortical sensory aphasia'. *Behavioural Neurology* 6: 135-42.

Nayak, N. and R. Gibbs. 1990. 'Conceptual knowledge in the interpretation of idioms'. *Journal of Experimental Psychology: General* 119: 315-30.

Nunberg, G., I.A. Sag and T. Wasow. 1994. 'Idioms'. *Language* 70: 491-538.

Olson, J. 1972. *Girls in the office*. New York: Simon & Schuster.

Ortony, A., D. Schallert, R. Reynolds and S. Antos. 1978. 'Interpreting metaphors and idioms: Some effects of context on comprehension'. *Journal of Verbal Learning and Verbal Behavior* 17: 465-78.

Osgood, C.E. and R. Housain. 1974. Salience of the word as a unit in the perception of language. *Perception and Psychophysics* 15: 168-92.

Pawley, A. and F.H. Syder. 1983. 'Two puzzles for linguistic theory: Nativelike selection and nativelike fluency'. In *Language and Communication*, pp. 191-226, ed. J.C. Richards and R. Schmidt. London: Longman.

Peters, A. 1977. 'Language learning strategies: Does the whole equal the sum of the parts?' *Language* 55: 560-73.

Peters, A. 1983. *The units of language*. Cambridge: Cambridge University Press.

Pick, A. 1973. *Aphasia*. Spring, IL: Charles C. Thomas. English translation by Jason Brown, from 1931. *Handbuch der normalen und pathologischen Physiologie*, Vol. 15, pp. 1416-1524.

Pickens, J.D. and H.R. Pollio. 1979. 'Patterns of figurative language competence in adult speakers'. *Psychological Research* 40: 299-313.

Pinker, S. 1995. *The language instinct*. New York: Harper Collins.

Robinson, B.W. 1976. 'Limbic influences on human speech'. *Annals of the New York Academy of Sciences* 280: 761-71.

Sadock, J.M. 1974. *Toward a linguistic theory of speech acts*. New York: Academic Press.

Schegloff, E.A. 1998. 'Reflections on studying prosody in talk-in-interaction'. *Language and Speech* 41: 235-63.

Schweigert, W.A. 1986. 'The comparison of familiar and less familiar idioms'. *Journal of Psycholinguistic Research* 15: 33-45.

Searle, J.R. 1975. 'Indirect speech acts'. In *Syntax and Semantics*. Vol. 3: *Speech acts*, pp. 59-82, ed. P. Cole and J.L. Morgan. New York: Academic Press.

Searle, J.R. 1985. *Expression and meaning: Studies in the theory of speech acts*. Cambridge: Cambridge University Press.

Shapiro, A., E. Shapiro, R.D. Bruun and K.D. Sweet (eds.) 1983. *Gilles de la Tourette syndrome*. New York: Raven Press.

Sidtis, J., B. Volpe, J. Holtzman, D. Wilson and M. Gazzaniga. 1981. 'Cognitive interaction after staged callosal section: Evidence for transfer of semantic activation'. *Science* 212: 344-46.

Simon, H.A. 1974. 'How big is a chunk?' *Science* 183: 482-88.

Sinclair, J.M. 1987. 'Collocation: A progress report'. In *Language topics: Essays in honor of Michael Halliday*, Vol. 2, pp. 319-31, ed. R. Steele and T. Threadgold. Amsterdam: John Benjamins,

Smith, A. 1966. 'Speech and other functions after left (dominant) hemispherectomy'. *Journal of Neurology, Neurosurgery and Psychiatry* 29: 467-71.

Speedie, L.J., E. Wertman, J. Ta'ir and K.M. Heilman. 1993. 'Disruption of automatic speech following a right basal ganglia lesion'. *Neurology* 43: 1768-74.

Strässler, J. 1982. *Idioms in English: A pragmatic analysis*. Tübingen: Gunter Narr.

Svartik, J. and R. Quirk. 1980. *A corpus of English conversation*. Lund: CWK Gleerup.

Swinney, D. and A. Cutler. 1979. 'The access and processing of idiomatic expressions'. *Journal of Verbal Learning and Verbal Behavior* 18: 523-34.

Tannen, D. 1980. 'Implications of the oral/literate continuum for cross-cultural communication'. In *Current issues in bilingualism: Georgetown University Round Table on Languages and Linguistics*, pp. 326-47, ed. J.E. Alatis Washington, DC: Georgetown University Press.

Tannen, D. 1989. *Talking voices: Repetition, dialogue, and imagery in conversational discourse*. Cambridge: Cambridge University Press.

Titone, D.A. and C.M. Connine. 1994. 'Comprehension of idiomatic expressions: Effects of predictability and literality'. *Journal of Experimental Psychology: Learning, Memory, and Cognition* 20: 1126-38.

Tyler, S. 1978. *The said and the unsaid: Mind, meaning and culture*. New York: Academic Press.

Van Lancker, D. 1973. 'Language lateralization and grammars'. In *Studies in Syntax and Semantics*, Vol. 2, pp. 197-204, ed. J. Kimball. New York: Academic Press.

Van Lancker, D. 1987. 'Nonpropositional speech: Neurolinguistic studies'. In *Progress in the psychology of language*, Vol. 3, pp. 49-118, ed. A.E. Ellis. Hillsdale, NJ: Lawrence Erlbaum Associates.

Van Lancker, D. 1990. 'The neurology of proverbs'. *Behavioural Neurology* 3: 169-87.

Van Lancker, D. and R. Bella. 1996. 'The relative roles of repetition and sentence completion tasks in revealing superior speech abilities in patients with nonfluent aphasia'. *Journal of the International Neuropsychological Society* 2: 6.

Van Lancker, D. and J. Canter. 1981. 'Idiomatic versus literal interpretations of ditropically ambiguous sentences'. *Journal of Speech and Hearing Research* 46: 64-69.

Van Lancker, D., J. Canter and D. Terbeek. 1981. 'Disambiguation of ditropic sentences: Acoustic and phonetic cues'. *Journal of Speech and Hearing Research* 24: 330-35.

Van Lancker, D. and J. Cummings. 1999. 'Expletives: Neurolinguistic and neuro-behavioral perspectives on swearing'. *Brain Research Reviews* 31: 83-104.

Van Lancker, D. and D. Kempler. 1987. 'Comprehension of familiar phrases by left- but not by right-hemisphere damaged patients'. *Brain and Language* 32: 265-77.

Van Lancker, D. and G. Rallon. 2004. 'Tracking the incidence of formulaic expressions in everyday speech: Methods for classification and verification'. *Language and Communication* 24: 207-40.

Van Lancker Sidtis, D. 2004. 'When novel sentences spoken or heard for the first time in the history of the universe are not enough: Toward a dual-process model of language'. *International Journal of Language and Communication Disorders* 39: 1-44.

Van Lancker Sidtis, D. 2006. 'Where in the brain is nonliteral language?' *Metaphor and Symbol* 21: 213-44.

Van Lancker Sidtis, D. 2009. 'Formulaic and novel language in a "dual process" model of language competence: Evidence from surveys, speech samples, and schemata'. In *Formulaic language*. Vol. 2: *Acquisition, loss, psychological reality, functional applications*, pp. 151-76, ed. R.L. Corrigan, E.A. Moravcsik, H. Ouali and K.M. Wheatley. Amsterdam: Benjamins.

Vihman, M.M. 1982. 'Formulas in first and second language acquisition'. In *Exceptional language and linguistics*, pp. 261-84, ed. L.K. Obler and L. Menn. New York: Academic Press,

Weinreich, V. 1969. 'Problems in the analysis of idioms'. In *Substance and structure of language*, pp. 23-81, ed. J. Puhvel. Los Angeles: University of California Press.

Whitaker, H. 1976. 'A case of isolation of the speech functions'. In *Studies in neurolinguistics*, Vol. 2, pp. 1-58, ed. H. Whitaker and H.A. Whitaker. London: Academic Press.

Winner, E. and H. Gardner. 1977. 'The comprehension of metaphor in brain-damaged patients'. *Brain* 100: 719-27.

Wong Fillmore, L. 1979. 'Individual differences in second language acquisition'. In *Individual differences in language ability and language behavior*, pp. 203-28, ed. C.J. Fillmore, D. Kempler and W.S.-Y. Wang. London: Academic Press.

Wray, A. 1999a. 'Formulaic language in learners and native speakers'. *Language Teaching* 32: 213-31.

Wray, A. 1999b. 'Formulaic sequences in second language teaching: Principle and practice'. *Applied Linguistics* 21: 463-89.

Wray, A. 2002. *Formulaic language and the lexicon.* Cambridge: Cambridge University Press.

Notes

* **Diana Van Lancker Sidtis**

I became a linguist because my Greek cousins talked their bubbly language at our family gatherings on religious holidays, and, as a very young child, I wondered how they did that. I took language and philosophy courses in college but only after graduating did I read Sol Saporta's *Psycholinguistics* and knew what I wanted to learn. I studied Anglistics at the University of Chicago and for the linguistics PhD pursued Indo-European languages at Brown University, mainly in order finally to learn Greek, even if it had to be ancient Greek. Another book influenced the course of study to an enthusiasm for systematic testing and observation: Eric Lenneberg's *Biological foundations of language*. From then on, following a move to Los Angeles, CA, the great mentor Peter Ladefoged led the way to scientific approaches in the UCLA Phonetics Laboratory. Thanks to an NIH postdoctoral fellowship at Northwestern University in Evanston, Illinois, Dr Jerry Canter and I alternated listening to classical music with developing innovative projects on familiar voice recognition and perception of idioms. He taught me the subtleties of designing clinical studies and the even more subtle art of interpreting results. In 1982 I returned to UCLA on my own NIH grant, pursuing voice perception studies with Jody Kreiman, who is now co-author of our book *Voices and listeners*. In 1988, several hardy students joined me in establishing a research laboratory in Fargo, North Dakota, where there was plenty of space and many chronic language impairments. There we discovered the preservation of famous proper noun recognition in severely aphasic subjects. Because I had paused to earn certification in speech-language pathology, clinical service had become an option; seeing patients again in Los Angeles was interesting and stimulating for research, but I missed teaching. The opportunity arose to teach in a temporary position at Carleton College in Northfield, MN, which became the scene of the accompanying chapter on teaching. Later, in 1999, my husband-to-be wanted to settle in New York, so I applied for the position of Chair of Communicative Sciences and Disorders at New York University, and since have enjoyed all the teaching I ever wanted.

[1] We called it 'NaSSlab' because of the crosslinguistic pun on the German word for 'wet'.

[2] Aphasia: a language disorder as a result of brain damage.

[3] Lenneberg (1967) distinguishes 'emotional' but not overlearned speech (p. 190).

[4] Prosody: intonation or melody of speech.

[5] Estimates by experts range from 200,000 to 500,000 formulaic expressions known to the native speaker, depending on classification criteria.

[6] Invented words that do not exist in the language

[7] E.g. the illocutionary force of 'Have a nice day' is not a command and 'She has him eating out of her hand' is not referring to eating or hands.

[8] Steven Pinker had visited the Carleton Campus earlier that year and had greatly impressed the student population.

[9] 'I'd like to say,' 'I was wondering if'.

[10] Sentences such as 'It broke the ice,' which carry either a literal or an idiomatic meaning.

[11] 'Birds of a feather!' means that persons with similar personal features associate with each other. Inferencing is required in all conversational interaction, but more so in formulaic language.

[12] 'country bumpkin', 'run amok', 'look askance', 'wreak havoc'.

[13] 'nick of time', 'pledge troth', 'hazard a guess', 'cut the mustard', 'fancy meeting you here'.

[14] 'trip the light fantastic', 'come hell or high water', 'don't take it so hard', 'far freaking out!', 'first come, first served', 'from here to kingdom come', 'funny you should…'

[15] 'chalk one up for…', 'give it everything you've got', 'let's give it the old one-two', 'let's give it the acid test', 'I gotta hand it to you'.

[16] Students remain anonymous in this report.

12 Teaching language acquisition

*Susan Foster-Cohen**

12.1 Introduction

Cute kids making adorable errors they will eradicate; adults making ones that they won't and which are generally less adorable; disturbing, heart-string tugging, fascinating patterns of disorder and delay; hot topics in sexy new neuroscience; mind-bending questions with implications for understanding the human condition, and heated arguments around models, methods and interpretation that leave the ordinary punter in the street at a loss to understand their ferocity… Language acquisition studies have it all. Moreover, students of linguistics, psychology, education, anthropology and both clinical and non-clinical therapeutic interventions recognize that language acquisition has relevance to their training and interests. As one of the most interdisciplinary of linguistics courses, language acquisition, particularly at the introductory level, is both a gift and a challenge to teach.

12.2 Linguistic preparation

Teaching an introductory course in language acquisition under the auspices of a linguistics department presents particular issues that often do not arise when it is taught in education, psychology or anthropology departments. Chief among these is helping students grasp enough of a linguist's understanding of language that they appreciate what the acquisition task is. This is a significant challenge for teaching students who have been attracted to a language acquisition course solely by a love of, and possibly a zeal to help, the youngest and most vulnerable members of their communities but are unsure of, and often scared silly by, even the most basic of metalinguistic descriptive categories.

One solution to the lack of basic linguistic terminological and analytical prowess among students is to insist on at least an introductory course in linguistics. However, this is not always practical. For one thing, while we might like to think that this would create a much-needed market for such an introductory linguistic prerequisite course, it is far more likely that it would decimate (or worse) the number of warm bodies in the language acquisition class. It would also turn away the student who might be drawn into linguistics precisely through the, more accessible, language acquisition course. In fact, I think it is important to treasure language acquisition courses precisely because they do attract the linguistically uninitiated and 'turn them on' to possible further, and more in depth, study of language.

So given that the 'linguistics-ly' unprepared are always going to be in our introductory language acquisition courses, how do we provide a course that does not bore those who do have a background, not frighten those who do not, and draw to the field those who never knew they had a facility for and interest in language acquisition in particular and/or linguistics in general? The trick, I believe, is to teach the necessary linguistics as you go along, and overtly postpone some, but crucially not all, of the more difficult material. This approach, of course, means deciding what the 'necessary linguistics' is for an introductory language acquisition course, and here we come up against the simplicity problem.

12.3 The simplicity problem

The simplicity problem is that it is entirely possible to select material for a language acquisition course that requires no, or very little, linguistics to understand. This is because there is a mountain of published material on children's language development that makes the assumption that language itself is nowhere near as complex as linguists argue that it is.

There are a range of reasons why researchers, generally though not entirely from outside linguistics, adopt this position. The most obvious is that it is because they come from disciplines that have paid and continue to pay little or no attention to linguistic discoveries about adult language and certainly not to those discoveries that require a considerable formal background to fully understand: generative approaches to syntax being the clearest example. Another is that in large quantitative research studies (often the gold standard of publication in human development studies) individual measures of language development (e.g. vocabulary size) are used to represent the whole of language leading researchers outside linguistics to assume they can treat language as if it were as simple as these empirical measures.

Another reason, I believe, for the field of language acquisition being replete with oversimplifications of language is that acquisition studies have tended to focus on the youngest learners. There is far more research available on the earliest stages of child language than on later ones. This has allowed researchers themselves to postpone consideration of the more complex data and explanations and often forget to come back to them. Research that puts the focus on the one and two-word stage of acquisition avoids having to engage the complexities of linguistics because it avoids the complexities of language. I am, in fact, constantly amazed at, and frustrated by, the number of well-respected researchers who purport to provide an overarching and sophisticated model of language development but who simply do not take that model beyond the two-word stage in any meaningful way.

I believe, however, that we do students of language acquisition a severe disservice if we capitulate to a simplistic view of language. Without an appreciation for the 'what' of language acquisition, we risk reducing the richness of the 'how' of language acquisition. We reduce the number and types of questions students might be encouraged to ask, and we prevent them from experiencing the thrill of being exposed to some extremely challenging ideas. As a result, I try to instil in students, from the introductory course level on, an appreciation for the complexity of language and of the language acquisition task. I also want them to have a sense that while some of the explanations we need in language acquisition may be easy to grasp, such as imitation of words, there are other aspects of acquisition that require more technical explanations. Understanding the errors that children make in their spelling, for example, is made possible through an understanding of morphophonemic regularities. Understanding why children do not proliferate acquired morphology throughout their systems requires an understanding of lexical semantics. Understanding why children make only certain errors with medial WH questions calls for an understanding of complex syntactic structure. None of these are beyond the capabilities of even beginning students if handled appropriately. However, a review of available textbooks will show how many of them shy away from these sorts of discussions.

There seems to be a fear of complexity. Or perhaps it is a fear of the invisible, since much of the complexity inherent in language and its development can only be made visible through theoretically driven empirical work that requires searching beyond the naturally occurring data. The net effect of avoiding complexity, however, is the creation of a false impression: that what you hear out of children's mouths or what they appear to understand (although comprehension generally gets short shrift everywhere in language acquisition research and teaching) is all there is to account for. However, by exposing students to aspects of language that are not available to the naked ear we can not only get them to appreciate the amazing task most children master before they even go school, but we can also get them to think about more sophisticated explanations for that mastery than the everyday ones with which they enter our classes.

Even the two-word stage can be made more interesting and challenging if a higher level of linguistic analysis and argumentation are incorporated. Moreover, if you introduce the multiplicity of ways in which language can be analysed using only the simple data of two-word utterances you make it easier to introduce the more complex notions needed for advanced syntax later in the course. If, for example, the notion of empty categories is introduced when discussing two-word utterances, then not only is the groundwork laid for continuity arguments, but the cognitive load of learning about later developments is appropriately reduced. I present students with a wide variety of ways of analysing two-word utterances: pivot-open, fixed phrasal, thematic roles, pragmatically controlled paratactics, partial tree construction, partial lexical insertion and so on. I find that showing students a tree diagram for a simple declarative sentence with only a single word filled in and asking them how they would know whether a child who said only that single word did or did not have a mental representation of the whole structure creates considerable discussion (after the stunned 'what on earth is she on about?' look, of course!) and we revisit the 'build up structures as needed' versus 'come ready equipped and just fill in the words' idea several times in the course. Positing this kind of complexity then leads naturally to looking at the poverty of the stimulus arguments and the continuity questions raised by different approaches.

12.4 Language acquisition in context

The flip side of the linguist's frustration with the simplification of language is the unwarranted isolation of language development from other child developments. For all the complaint that other disciplines do not understand the nature of language the way a linguist does, linguists are not infrequently remiss about putting language development in the context of other human developments that are precursors to or impact the course of language acquisition in some way. For this I largely blame the silo mentality of most if not all institutions of higher learning. Despite the apparent encouragement to collaborate across discipline boundaries, it is in my experience rarely genuine, and the students are the losers. Yes, language development is special, but it does not occur in a vacuum. At the very least students deserve to have us articulate at least some of the connections between language development and motor development, cognitive development, and social/emotional development. I usually spend quite some time in an introductory course on such contributory developments. (And of course there are other courses where language as contributory to other aspects of human development should be covered.) These include at least an outline of brain development, evidence of early sociability, the role of emotional security and physiological regulation in all human development, the development of social relationships with caregivers and other key people in a child's life, and the development of empathy and theory of mind. I have to say, by the way, that theory of mind is one of the all-time sexy ideas that can excite students at any level. By the end of my introductory course, students are recognizing it in a wide range of aspects of language development from inferencing in lexical development, to complex syntax to understanding the pragmatics of politeness to developing metalinguistic skills. It is one of the great unifying ideas of human development and keeps language development appropriately tied to both intellectual and social development.

Attention to the human development context of language acquisition also allows consideration of what happens when those developments do not happen optimally and the impact this has on language development. Starting from the assumption that language development is part of human development permits a focus on the variation in language development as essential to the course, rather than as an afterthought. Rather than focusing on typically developing monolingual children, ignoring much of the variation even between them, and treating language disorder and bilingualism as separate topics (as has been *de rigeur* in the past), we can begin to incorporate understanding of the wide range of developmental trajectories that children experience.

Over the last twenty years or so, language acquisition researchers, teachers, clinicians and others have themselves acquired a growing understanding of the huge amount of variability in children's paths to language, including both disorder and delay. We are now in a much better position to teach students about both typical and atypical variation in our courses and to demonstrate how porous the boundary between those two can be. We no longer need to settle for 'clip-on' discussions of language disorder or bilingual development as if these represented almost unwelcome deviations from the monolingual typical norm. Instead we have the knowledge (if not yet entirely the willingness) to integrate understanding of alternative paths for a wide range of developments with language acquisition into the more typical material and to use it to raise questions about the 'how' and 'why' of language acquisition in light of it. If children rescued from Eastern European orphanages continue to have language delays years after being adopted into caring families, what does that say about the relationships between language development and early social and emotional development? If vocabulary development is more robust under these circumstances than bound morphology, what does that say about the explanations needed for the development of different sub-components of language? If children with Down syndrome continue to show developments in their syntax during their twenties, what does that say about putative critical periods? If second-language or bilingual first-language development in infancy and early childhood is the norm for millions of children, how wrong have we got the picture if we have been basing our developmental schedules (and often high-stakes testing) on monolingual norms? If there is such a thing as perfect second-language learning, what qualities do the learner and/or their learning situation possess that makes this possible?

As the picture of what is and is not possible for language learners, what is and is not regarded as effective language learning (and how socially constructed versus biologically constructed is the notion of 'effective'?) broadens, those of us who teach language acquisition courses have a broader and deeper pool of material from which to choose. And for those whose students may take their knowledge into clinical and educational settings there is a humanistic need to ensure that this knowledge is presented. Developmental schedules, whether used by speech language therapists/pathologists or by teachers, are useful to a point, but not if they prevent a consideration of variable rates and paths of development that may, with support from knowledgeable professionals and parents, serve children's cognitive, social and communicative needs well. After all, all language development occurs because brain cells connect. There is no other mechanism. It is not as if learners of different types are humans of different types, although looking at politically controlled resourcing might lead one to an unfortunately different conclusion. And when attitudes translate into responses, we find ourselves again in issues around linguistic environments in which children grow and thrive (or don't).

12.5 What and how to teach

So, given that no language acquisition course can cover everything, what do you choose? And how do you ensure you make it relevant to students with little or no experience of young children, little or no experience of learning a second language (the case in New Zealand at least), who are growing up in a 'show me rather than tell me' world where concentrated reading is a significant challenge, and who have (dare I say it) paid for the course so they expect to pass?

When I first started in the field, introductory courses tended to be wide-coverage survey courses of the path of language development. Given the Internet age which encourages data gathering at the expense of insight and understanding, I have moved more and more towards not expecting students to memorize facts about development (ages and stages information) and more towards a focus on explanations for language development. I lighten students' loads of memorization and use assignments that cannot be answered using memorized material (also thereby making plagiarism more difficult), putting more and more emphasis on students' ability to understand the complexity of explaining development. So I give them take-home assignments of 500 words in which to say something intelligent about huge questions – What is the relationship between language development and cognitive development? Does child-directed speech have an impact on language development? Is there a critical period for language development? And so forth – and then give them the opportunity to flick me drafts by e-mail to which I will respond briefly. Many of them use that option for the first assignment but quickly get the hang of it and the request to review drafts drops off as the course progresses. Five hundred words, they soon discover, is harder than 5,000, and it concentrates the mind and the writing style, and certainly sorts the sheep from the goats.

Beginning students do, however, need to understand the broad lineaments of development, and I usually open a beginning course with an overview of development whose only goal is for students to ground their sense of two-year-old, three-year-old, four-year-old, ten-year-old and so on language. For many years I have done this overview using a combination of my own and published transcript data. This works fairly well, but more recently I have starting using short snippets of video data and this works far better. With video data much of the non-linguistic context of acquisition is absorbed without needing to be named: the development of motor and social skills can be seen instantly, and while students may be less focused on the actual specifics of the language, they are getting the gestalt of development.

From there we move through the phonological, lexical, morphological, syntactic, semantic and pragmatics arenas sampling big issues as we go. The trick is to select parts of language development that are both interesting and useful as well as ones that can form the basis of any further courses. So, when covering the development of speech from early babbling into first words, we also tackle the issue of how species specific this is and raise the whole issue of how linguistic Alex the African Grey parrot might be. When we look at developmental morphology, we look at cases such as Genie, where morphology is one of the major casualties, and Christopher, where morphology is a huge strength, and ask what they might tell us about the nature of morphology in relation to other aspects of language and communication from an acquisition point of view. Luckily there is quite a lot of available documentary video material to illustrate these sorts of issues, but there is real need for much, much more.

So, I make no apology for using the inherent fascination with children to enliven an introductory course in language acquisition. I have very real concerns for linguistics as a discipline, and I want to be sure I am doing my part to ensure its survival in our universities. Moreover, I would be extremely disappointed to see language acquisition courses lose their connection to the fundamental questions about human language and the human mind posed by linguists, Chomsky in particular, that were the reasons I got into the field in the first place, and for this reason I refuse to capitulate to the anti-theoretical linguistics attitude of many in my field. I frequently remember and try to live by Nobel Laureate Dick Feynman's adage that if you cannot explain a complicated idea to a nine-year-old, you probably do not understand it yourself.

Notes

* **Susan Foster-Cohen**

I went to Lancaster University in northwest England in 1972 to read English literature, but faced with the need to choose two other subjects for my first year I took a chance on linguistics. I quickly discovered that the scientific approach of linguistics made much more sense to me than literary criticism, and I ended up being one of the first to graduate from Lancaster with a BA in linguistics (actually, a double major in linguistics and English with as many courses in English language as I could manage).

The teachers who most influenced my undergraduate linguistics were probably Jim Hurford and Chris Candlin. Jim taught me syntax, which I found, and still find, hard work. But struggling with syntactic analysis made me a better teacher of it when I got the chance later on. Chris taught me sociolinguistics, which I took to easily, and he has been part of my linguistics journey across more than 30 years now, most recently as the commissioning editor of my edited collection on language acquisition with Palgrave.

My interests in language acquisition, though, grew out of 'the innateness question' to which Jim Hurford first exposed me. In his course I tried to get to grips with the philosophy of universal grammar, and later when I was choosing a doctoral thesis topic (still at Lancaster, though having made a detour through teacher training) this was what I really wanted to work on. However, being in a pretty radically anti-Chomskyan department (it had Geoffrey Sampson in it after all!), I ended up focusing on the very beginnings of language development under the misguided apprehension that looking at the emergence of language might tell me something about what was innate. It didn't of course, and what I ended up with was a doctoral thesis focusing on developmental pragmatics, work that was aided and abetted by Andrew Lock in the psychology department, who was both developmental psychologist and ethologist, and thought linguists just made language all too complicated.

I finally got serious exposure to cutting-edge generative syntax through an LSA summer institute in Austria in 1979 and then at the University of Southern California when my doctorate was finished. I was quickly seduced by the beauty of the big GB ideas that were emerging in the early 1980s, much to the disgruntlement of the developmental pragmatics folks who had hired me there, I might add. My stint in LA was followed by eleven years at Northern Arizona University as part of the programme in applied linguistics, teaching second-language acquisition and syntax mostly. My first-language interests were sustained through that time by writing textbooks, even though I wasn't doing much teaching in it. I like writing textbooks because they give me a sense that I have the big picture. I did, however, do research on Navajo-English bilingualism in school-aged children until I felt too much like an intruder into the lives of people who had been intruded upon far too much already. I also tried to bring my experience in pragmatics and my interests in syntax together and that's when I started working with Relevance Theory, which is the perfect combination of cognitive science and generative linguistics for me.

It was partly the allure of being closer to the London home of RT that made the offer of a position heading up an EFL department in Paris at the Institut Britannique de Paris (University of London) attractive; apart from the allure of Paris itself, of course. In France I continued to work with RT and spent some time exploring second-language acquisition in children. Then we shifted again, this time to New Zealand, and here I am having the chance to explore children's language disorder. Teaching and researching under the auspices of both the linguistics department and the communication disorders department with a focus on comprehension in children with disabilities from a Relevance Theory point of view is a long-term programme slowed only by my being the director of a therapy centre for infants and children with disabilities. I am, however, finally teaching a language acquisition course and bringing together all my interests and experience in typical and atypical first-language, bilingual and L2 acquisition. And, yes, there's another textbook gestating.

13 The value of linguistics to the ESL/EFL classroom practitioner

*David Mendelsohn**

13.1 Introduction

I have a friend who, when asked, 'What do you do?' replies, 'I teach linguistics.' This is invariably followed by the question, 'What is linguistics?' to which he replies, 'Linguistics is a discipline developed in order to keep linguists off the streets.' Sadly, it is my impression that there is a sizeable number of classroom teachers of ESL/EFL around the world who see little more value in studying linguistics than this.

Drawing on my extensive experience in this profession in several different countries, I have a very strong sense that classroom teachers on the whole have inadequate training in linguistics. This may at best result in them being guided as to what to teach, under the guidance of a lead teacher, but this does not mean that they know *why* they should do X and not Y. Moreover, teachers who have little or no linguistics training are 'at the mercy' of the more powerful members of our profession. Ours is a field in which different 'bandwagons' roll though town, and this often results in a change in methodology on the part of teachers. Unfortunately, these are not always well-researched or well-reasoned changes, but rather fads or fashions. But how is the teacher with no linguistics to know this? How are they to judge or to question what is viable, possible and logical? They are merely swept along as the bandwagon rolls through without a solid basis for doing what they are being told to do.

The purpose of this chapter is to make the case for classroom teachers of ESL/EFL to study linguistics. I will make my argument by providing two examples of how a knowledge of linguistics should inform and can benefit the classroom teacher. I will also discuss what happens when teachers have not studied linguistics. The arguments put forward below and the examples used, grow out of 45 years of classroom ESL/EFL teaching.

13.2 Example 1: The value of knowing linguistics for the teaching of pronunciation

The first example that I would like to describe relates to the need for ESL/EFL teachers to have studied some phonetics/phonology in order to teach pronunciation in the best and most meaningful way.

Many poorly trained teachers have studied very little phonetics and phonology, being scared of it, and do not know how to go about teaching pronunciation. I have several times seen untrained teachers simply avoid teaching pronunciation at all, and justifying this saying something like, 'I ran out of time.' This is at worst a rationalization, and at best is showing that they do not consider pronunciation an important skill to teach and they regard it as a luxury or 'peripheral frill'.

The result of the non-linguistics training of these teachers is that if they teach pronunciation at all – and that is usually because they are required to do so – they usually do it very poorly. Often all they do is what I call 'mindless, uncontextualized listen-and-repeat drills' without in any way making this meaningful or related to the information-structure of English.

Many teachers equate pronunciation with the ability to articulate the different segmentals of English – that the learners simply need to know how to articulate the individual sounds of English and all will be well. This inaccurate assessment leads to what I cynically call the 'Ship/Sheep School of Pronunciation' in which the suprasegmental features of English such as stress, rhythm and intonation are not taught at all, and the pronunciation work is largely variations of repetition of decontextualized expressions like, 'This is a ship. This is a sheep.'

Not only do I believe that the suprasegmentals need to be taught as well as the segmentals, but in fact I have argued for many years that the latter are *more* important. For the purposes of this chapter, I will consider stress, rhythm and intonation as the main components of the suprasegmental system (for two excellent examples of how to handle the teaching of suprasegmentals, see Gilbert 2005 and Grant 2001). I will discuss the importance of teaching stress/unstress, one component of the English suprasegmentals, in my second example. But there is more to stress than that: learners need to learn about the importance of correct word stress, and also primary sentence stress.

Correct word stress is very important for the production of comprehensible spoken English. I never tire of citing the following which I heard in a student presentation many years ago: 'My country's main export is "semen"' – cement, pronounced like 'semen', with the stress on the first syllable, 'Cement'. There could be no doubt from the shocked response of the other students that an embarrassing error in stress had occurred. Another example which makes my point clearly is when I was touring France many years ago, and the French guide at the Louvre kept saying things like: 'This is similar to the MoNAlisa', pronounced like 'analysis'. It took several repetitions of this mispronunciation to realize what she intended – Mona Lisa. These two examples show how important correct word stress is – after all, several psycholinguists claim that the brain catalogues and stores words according to their stress patterns, thus grouping 'Mona Lisa' with 'analysis' and 'cement' with 'semen'.

Another aspect of stress that needs to be taught is the rules of placement and meaning of primary sentence stress (often seen as an intonational rather than a stress feature) and how this links to information structure in English. Teachers often do not know the rules for the placement of primary sentence stress and the meaning that its placement carries.

I have seen teachers deal with the placement of primary sentence stress by having the students repeat utterances like the following:

My uncle from Havana's in the KITCHEN.

My uncle from HAVANA'S in the kitchen.

My UNCLE from Havana's in the kitchen

MY uncle from Havana's in the kitchen.

In my opinion, merely repeating these utterances is an example of virtually useless 'busy-work'.

The following is an example of how primary sentence stress relates to information structure:

'I bought a CAR.'

This would be produced with a fall from high (the largest pitch movement) on 'CAR'– the last lexical item in the utterance – the place to put primary sentence stress if there is no reason to place it elsewhere. This is the unmarked form. However, this would change if the conversation went as follows:

'I bought a CAR. It's a GREAT car.'

In 'I bought a CAR', we have the unmarked form – that is, the primary sentence stress appears on the last lexical item. However, in 'It's a GREAT car' we have to move the primary sentence stress to the new information 'GREAT', because it cannot occur on old or shared information like 'car'.

Placing the primary sentence stress anywhere other than on the last lexical item can also signal contrastive stress. Compare the following:

'I sold the FUTON' and 'I SOLD the futon' with the primary sentence stress on 'SOLD' – This second utterance means that I did not buy it or rent it or anything else.

Rhythm is another feature of the suprasegmental system that teachers need to understand. There is an equal amount of time (at least perceptually) between stressed syllables regardless of how many unstressed syllables (even zero) occur between them. The more unstressed syllables there are, the more these have to be speeded up. Rhythm is therefore determined by the juxtaposition of stressed and unstressed syllables. Many teachers I have observed fail to grasp this, and I would argue that it is simply because they had never been taught it. For example, compare:

1. 'The CAR was in a SERIOUS ACCIDENT.'
2. 'The CAR had a SERIOUS ACCIDENT.'
3. 'The CAR is DAMAGED.'

'was in a' in 1, 'had a' in 2, and 'is' in 3 need to be said in the same space of time so that the time between 'CAR' and the next stressed syllable in each case is the same despite the fact that there are different numbers of unstressed syllables in the different examples.

Classroom practitioners also need to know the rules of 'fast speech', that is, the way rapid spoken English is pronounced. They also need to know and to convey to their students that 'fast speech' is different from slow, deliberate speech, not a degenerate form of it, and that we do not necessarily pronounce words in the flow of regular speech exactly as the dictionary says. The following are some of the features that need to be understood. I have used the symbol + to indicate juncture, _ to indicate no juncture, ə to represent the centralized, unstressed schwa vowel, and ( ) to enclose segments that may be deleted in rapid speech. The following are some of the features of rapid speech, largely drawn from Mendelsohn 1994:

- Distortion of word boundaries – for example 'fish_n + chips'. This yields a unit more perceptually parallel to 'fishing' than to 'fish and'.
- Weak forms – for example, 'Tell them it's a piece for a fridge' would likely be pronounced with four schwas, as follows:
  'Tell_(the)əm+its_ə+piece+fərə+fridge.'
- Elision – the 'missing out' (Brown 1990: 66) of a consonant or a vowel. For example, 'las+year' for 'last year' and Brown's example:
  'The+nees_əv+thə+people' for 'the needs of the people'.
- Assimilation – when word-final sounds are not realized in their citation or dictionary form, but, under the influence of the following sound, and under the pressure of time, an articulation which is closer to the following sound is produced in anticipation of that sound. For example:
  'Be+a(k)_Kennedy+Airport' – 'be at Kennedy Airport'.
- 'He+hi(p)_Peter' for 'He hit Peter'.

- Gemination – when one word ends with a particular plosive (stop) and the next word begins with the same plosive, then these two sounds are 'run into' each other in rapid speech. For example 'Sto(p) picking_on+Val.' Note that the [p] is not released twice – once for 'stop' and once for 'picking'. Gemination can occur after assimilation like in the example of 'Be at Kennedy Airport' above.

It is my belief that my training in phonetics and phonology made it possible for me to understand, explain and teach the phenomena described above.

13.3 Example 2: The value of knowing linguistics for the teaching of listening comprehension

The second example is intended to show how knowledge of linguistics informs and guides the teacher in teaching one valuable strategy for listening comprehension.

Throughout my teaching career, students of mine have complained that 'Canadians talk too fast'. In fact, this is not the problem – the problem is that learners of English 'listen too slowly'. By that I mean that learners often cannot keep up processing spoken English because they try to listen to every word in the same way, assigning every word the same importance for comprehension. The problem is that they have not been taught the way spoken English is structured and how to utilize a command of English's stress/unstress system as a strategy for listening comprehension. (For a detailed discussion of how to teach strategies for listening comprehension, see Mendelsohn 1994.)

The argument that I am making is that learners need to be taught to distinguish between stress and unstress. At the auditory level, they need to learn that stressed syllables are 'louder, longer, more prominent in pitch and very precisely articulated' (Brown 1990: 54). In the first edition of her book, Brown (1977: 45) states that 'length is the variable that most students find easiest to control; and is a reliable marker of stress'.

Once they are able to distinguish stress from unstress, they need to do training exercises which lead them to the understanding that in English, as a rule of thumb, the content (lexical) words are stressed and the grammatical words are unstressed. And, more important than that is the final step, and that is to realize that if they focus on the stressed words, they will not only be able to 'listen fast enough', but they will be focusing on the essence of the message contained in the utterance. In other words, this will yield them a telegraphic version of the cognitive message being communicated.

For example, they hear the utterance:

'My video camera was stolen at the beach. Please claim the insurance.'

They need to separate out stress and unstress as follows:

> 'My VIDEO CAMERA was STOLEN at the BEACH. Please CLAIM the INSURANCE.'

In other words, they have teased out a telegraphic version of the utterance:

> 'VIDEO CAMERA STOLEN BEACH. CLAIM INSURANCE.'

This telegraphic version provides the essence of the message succinctly but still accurately, thereby enabling the listener, regardless of whether they are a native or non-native speaker, to process it fast enough for them to keep up.

Taking this approach will also enable the listener to disregard the 'empty verbal fillers' like *well*, *you see*, *in fact*, thereby giving the listener time to process the important content words.

An ESL/EFL teacher who has studied no linguistics would not be able to take their learners through the stages described above. The stages I am advocating are: identifying stress acoustically and learning that what they have is a manageable telegraphic version of the meaning of the utterance. What the teacher with no linguistics is likely to do with the teaching of listening comprehension is to simply have their students listen without teaching them how to go about it – largely because these teachers themselves do not know how to go about it. This, in my view should be classified as *testing* not *teaching* listening comprehension.

13.4 Linguistics and EFL/ESL teacher training

Having described two examples of how classroom teachers can benefit from studying linguistics, it is only fitting that some further thought be given as to why this situation exists and how it can be changed. We have a deep-rooted systemic problem: There is not enough linguistics being taught in teacher-training courses. Why is this the case and what can be done about it?

The first and strongest reason why so little linguistics is being taught in teacher-training courses is twofold: Those teaching these courses often have little linguistics knowledge themselves, and the profession is often happy to hire minimally trained or totally untrained teachers.

ESL/EFL teachers are often hired simply on the basis of their being native speakers of English. Some places require a university degree but a BA in English literature, sociology or whatever with no linguistics will suffice. This situation is most pervasive in EFL settings, in which that country's hunger for proficient users of English far exceeds the availability of well-trained teachers. This, coupled with the myth that, if you can speak English, you can teach English, creates a powerful force against the costly endeavour of teaching teachers linguistics.

What I find particularly upsetting in this situation is that this belief and this reality result in teachers who are non-native speakers being undervalued, or less-valued than native speakers, even when the non-native speaker is far better trained and equipped for the teaching position.

The vicious cycle continues, largely driven by financial considerations:

1. Why make courses longer and therefore more costly when those doing the hiring do not require it?
2. Why teach more linguistics when those doing the teacher-training do not believe it is necessary?
3. Why teach more linguistics when those taking these courses for teachers do not see the value of it?

1. ESL/EFL is 'big business', and unfortunately institutions like language schools often operate not according to the soundest pedagogical/academic principles, but rather with their eyes firmly on the 'bottom line'. Teaching more linguistics would require hiring costly experts and a lengthening of the course which, in turn, could drive prospective students away. Both the specialized hiring and the lengthening of the courses would not work to the institution's advantage.

2. Those doing the hiring seldom have an extensive knowledge of linguistics themselves, and so they easily convince themselves that if they have got to where they are without it, it could not be that necessary. In fact, they feel threatened by those with a knowledge of linguistics.

3. Many people argue that they do not see the value of learning a lot of linguistics. They claim to be doing just fine without it. This is the attitude, for example, of many 'backpacker teachers' – native-speakers of English who are travelling abroad and who land teaching jobs by dint of being native-speakers. There is really no motivation for them to take linguistics courses at all. This reason, coupled with the reasons listed above, makes a strong case against teaching linguistics. The sad part is that I have met many people who were 'backpacker teachers' and subsequently made a career of ESL/EFL teaching and who go to great lengths to argue the line that it is not at all necessary for ESL/EFL teachers to study linguistics. It is my contention that taking this position is actually a defence mechanism rather than a rational position.

What can be done about the fact that there is not enough linguistics being taught in teacher-training courses? There is an acute need for a change in attitudes to this issue in the profession. But the question remains: How do you change attitudes? I believe that the only way in which we will succeed in doing this is by setting standards that are nationally or even internationally observed, and educating accordingly.

There are many professions that have regulating/licensing bodies with responsibility to oversee quality and adequacy of training. Pharmacists are not pharmacists simply by calling themselves pharmacists or by getting a position in a pharmacy;

one has to be accredited as an architect in order to design and 'sign off' on a building, to cite just two examples. So why do we not have the same sort of system in our profession? Ideally, I would like to see these standards being set and monitored by the International Association of Teachers of English to Speakers of Other Languages (TESOL), but this is surely a pipe-dream. But oversight and professional standards at a national or a regional level are definitely possible. However, there has to be the will to create this and, even more difficult, to enforce it. In Canada we have taken the first steps to do this, with the TESL Canada Association having created a set of standards for individual teachers and for the accreditation of teacher-training programmes. It is still voluntary, but more and more institutions are realizing that if they do not come on board, they are going to lose clients. Such steps also require the non-hiring of untrained/inadequately trained teachers, and the taking of steps to enable such teachers already in the system to get up to speed. Moreover, a mechanism for programme inspection also needs to be created. All these proposals are difficult and costly, in addition to being very divisive in a profession such as ours.

Finally, for such a change to succeed, the linguistics courses must be seen to be necessary and relevant in the eyes of those who run the teacher-training programmes and in the eyes of those who take the courses. I have seen efforts to include linguistics courses backfire horribly. For example, I know of one case in which the teacher-training programme required of its students to take a number of pre-existing theoretical linguistics courses, intended for majors in theoretical linguistics. There was no attempt made by the administration or the professor in question to modify the course to make it more 'applied' – more relevant to the second/foreign language teaching situation. This is clearly essential if attitudes are going to change. As things stand, language teachers in training usually hate their linguistics courses and, moreover, are totally 'spooked' by them.

13.5 Conclusion

In conclusion, our profession needs to become more 'professional'. And one of the ways of doing this is by doing away with these fly-by-night very short courses, not hiring untrained teachers, and providing sufficient, relevant linguistics courses.

References

Brown, G. 1977. *Listening to spoken English.* 1st edn; London: Longman.

Brown, G. 1990. *Listening to spoken English.* 2nd edn. London: Longman.

Gilbert, J. 2005. *Clear speech: Pronunciation and listening comprehension in North American English.* 3rd edn. New York: Cambridge University Press.

Grant, L. 2001. *Well said: Pronunciation for clear communication.* 2nd edn. London: Longman.

Mendelsohn, D.J. 1994. *Learning to listen.* San Diego: Dominie Press.

Notes

* **David Mendelsohn**

David Mendelsohn is a Professor of Applied Linguistics and ESL at York University in Toronto, where he teaches undergraduate content-based ESL and graduate applied linguistics, particularly aspects of listening, speaking and pronunciation. He began his career as an EFL high-school teacher in Israel, and quickly realized the link to applied linguistics, and how further study in this field could inform and enrich his classroom work. This prompted him to do his MA in applied linguistics (University College of North Wales, Bangor), and his PhD in linguistics (University of Edinburgh). His 'guru' and mentor in virtually all his work has been Professor Gillian Brown of Cambridge University (formerly of Edinburgh), whose ideas and advice have been his inspiration and guide ever since she supervised his PhD dissertation.

Throughout his 45-year career he has taught both ESL and applied linguistics, showing how this can and should inform the work of the classroom teacher. He has authored, co-authored and edited seven books, numerous book chapters and articles, and has given over 200 conference presentations.

14 Games for exploring language origins and change

Alison Wray[*]

14.1 Introduction

I describe here four games I developed as seminar activities for my final year undergraduate module 'The Evolution of Human Communication and Language'. This module examined the social, psychological and physiological prerequisites for language in our species and the processes by which language might have arisen, including the order of appearance of the different components of language, the potential role of gesture, the immediate catalysts for its emergence, and the relative plausibility of monogenesis versus polygenesis. It also explored what would have happened to the first fully human language (if there were such a thing) after it became established, thus covering some aspects of language change.

The seminars were 50 minutes long and attended by 12-15 students, repeated up to four times to accommodate the entire class. Since seminars are not always well attended, I was keen to find a way to enhance the students' learning that was not reliant on who turned up and what they had or had not read. The students did not have to do any preparation for these seminars. I had extremely positive feedback, and excellent attendance. Ideally, the seminars would have lasted a little longer, not because the activities themselves require more time, but because there was so much scope for fascinating discussion after doing them.

Each game aimed to offer students some kind of hands-on experience of a process explored more theoretically and abstractly in the lectures and reading. The games were deliberately low-tech, partly for practical reasons, as I don't program and we did not have computers in the classrooms I used, but mostly because I felt it was important for the students to work directly through the processes rather than just punch in input and print out results. There is some excellent research into the evolution of language using computer simulations, and the games helped students understand what such simulations do, how computers have the advantage of being able to multiply the number of iterations of a process, but also how some of the qualitative decisions possible in a hands-on simulation might be difficult to replicate using a computer program.

The four games are:

1. **First five words**: At some point, presumably, our ancestors started using words. Which ones came first? (A discussion game)
2. **Limited lexicon**: What happens when you want to express more ideas than you have words and grammar for? (A competition between groups)
3. **Language contact**: A simulation of lexical borrowing. (A card game based on 'snap')
4. **Language diversification**: A simulation of the way in which phonological changes gradually turn one language into a number of dialects or languages. (A board game)

I often ran the contact and diversification games simultaneously, as it was a better use of time and materials. A disadvantage was that students didn't get the chance fully to understand the game they didn't play. On the other hand, seeing results from both games together helped students consider how the linguist is challenged when comparing languages that may have *both* diversified and been in contact.

14.2 First five words

14.2.1 Rationale

Research into the evolution of language has often addressed the question of what happened at various points of transition from 'no language' to 'language' (see, for instance, Wray 2002a). Although it is by no means agreed that there was a distinct point at which the first words suddenly came into being, imagining such an event is a useful device for exploring what words do in communication. In this game, a particular catalyst, different for each group, propels a clan of early humans into inventing the first five words of their language (Box 1). Groups of three to five people seem to work best. The exercise helps students think about what we use language for, and which words are most and least dispensable. Most groups begin by assuming that the first words would be labels for things (e.g. *food*), actions (e.g. *find*) and perhaps attributes (e.g. *hungry*), but the constraint of so few words may lead them to consider just pointing at anything concrete and imitating anything imitable, so they can use their precious five words for meanings less easily expressed in other ways. The idea of 'words' that express complete propositions has been central to my own research into language origins (Wray 1998, 2000, 2002b, Wray and Grace 2007), so I have been keen also to help students explore the potential there, particularly in relation to using language to manipulate others (see Wray 2002c).

Box 1 First five words – instructions for players

You are members of a tribe of anatomically modern hunter-gatherer humans, who do not yet have language. You communicate using noises and gestures but you have no 'words' or 'grammar'. Now, something has happened, which is putting severe pressure on your immediate survival, or on your ecological or social environment, and it is about to 'flip the switch' into the development of language for the first time. But what exactly will be the first things you need to say?

- *Briefly* (5 minutes) consider the catalyst situation you have been given. What would its practical impact be for a non-linguistic community? How could language help? What will you need to achieve in putting language to best use?
- Next (20 minutes), decide on just the first *five* words in your language. You don't need to invent forms for them, just consider what they should mean. Should these first words map onto something that is already communicated via noise or gesture, or should they express something new? Should you have five words that do similar things, or try to achieve different things with each one? Should your choices (for instance) name things, or describe things, or manipulate others, or express, say, quantity, a temporal or spatial relationship, a semantic detail such as 'future', or signal identity? They can mean whole sentences if you like, e.g. 'get away from me!', but if so, cannot be used to derive additional words ('get', 'away', 'from' or 'me').
- Next (5 minutes), consider how the meaning of the words will become established between you, and then across the whole group. Remember, there won't be any words to explain what the five words mean, or even to explain that you are inventing words!
- Feed back to the class about the decisions you made, and why.

Interesting discussion arises around how a community could ever come to agree about the meanings of words – particularly if they represent abstract concepts including displaced time and space, or absent objects or people – when they have no language to explain them.

I used four catalyst scenarios. It is fine for more than one group to work with a given scenario.

1. **Starvation:** You will die if you do not change where and/or how you live.
2. **Technological innovation:** People have started coming up with ideas for

new things to do and ways to do them, but it is hard to explain them to the rest of the group.

3. **Social change:** Your group is getting too big for everyone to know what is going on, who is whose friend, etc. by observation alone.
4. **Contact with outsiders:** You are mixing with outsiders with whom you do not share certain basic knowledge and practices.

Giving students different catalyst scenarios is a means of introducing more interest between groups at the report-back stage. It becomes a point of interesting discussion that some scenarios spark more manipulative language than others, some more socially oriented language. The game helps them explore the potential role of the environment, social relationships and physical need in driving humans to innovative communication. I am not meaning to imply that all these scenarios are equally likely as causes of the emergence of language in our species, but the exercise is less about finding 'the answer' than helping students think about what language does.

14.2.2 Preparatory materials

Very little preparation is required for this game. You just need copies of the instructions sheet (Box 1) plus a slip of paper for each group, indicating their scenario.

14.2.3 Typical outcomes

My groups varied hugely in how imaginative they were. If students can get beyond the idea that language labels objects, they can explore the opportunities afforded by even five words, as a springboard for developing more words and fuller communication. My students occasionally came up with a word for 'copy me'. Another smart choice would be a word meaning 'what shall we call that?' Many got stuck when it came to how the group would ever figure out a shared meaning, but that is a good discussion to have.

14.3 Limited lexicon

14.3.1 Rationale

Although it might seem that just getting words in the first place is the main hurdle in the emergence of language, there has been extensive discussion about what would happen next, and under what circumstances a language would extend its vocabulary beyond a small set of words and word classes. This game (Box 2) somewhat simulates the situation with a pidgin language, where rather little linguistic material has to achieve all the necessary communicative jobs. The space-station setting offers a little relief from always looking backwards in time, and reinforces the idea that the emergence of language probably occurred in humans not all that different from us today.

Box 2 A limited lexicon – instructions for players

The new International Space Station is truly international, and is staffed by 20 individuals from all over the world, working and living together for months at a time, researching the reproductive behaviour of different species of animals, and monitoring each other's health. For political reasons, no earth language may be used on the station, so the International Space Agency has devised a brand new basic language, LINSPAG (Language of the International Space Agency) that is equally foreign to everyone. Unfortunately, it only has 60 words.

Translate into LINSPAG the three sentences that you have been supplied with. You will need to use your imagination to find ways of expressing the meanings. Some things may simply not be expressible, but do your best to capture the message as accurately as possible. To do that, you need to stand back from the sentences, and think about what the core meaning is. You don't have to translate everything literally. In some cases, doing so would be incomprehensible to someone who didn't know the English original!

You can't add any details from another language (e.g. you may not put –s on to create a plural). The only 'grammar' you can use is: the hyphen to connect words if they are particularly closely associated (as in *the never-imagined disaster)*, and the comma, full stop, exclamation mark and question mark.

Example translations:

- *Where is the baby mouse?* might be written as: Rusto besod ris-plam (show-me location mouse-child)
- *I could eat a horse* might be written as: Bak rebost wolu-olit hamu (me preference many-big vegetable)

There will often be more than one possible way of translating the same thing. When you have worked out your translations, write them on the sheets provided (the same sentence four times on the same sheet, a different sheet for each different sentence). Don't write down the English, just the Linspag. You need to work in secret (i.e. keep your voices down), because once you have translated your sentences, another group will have to see if they can translate them back into English.

14.3.2 Procedure

The game is set up for four groups of around four people each, but it will also work with fewer or more, by excluding, or doubling up on, sets of sentences. Use differently coloured paper for each group, as it is then much easier to keep track of the translated slips. Each group has three sentences to translate (Appendix 14.1a), using the dictionary (Appendix 14.1b). Each translated sentence gets written out four times on the same sheet of paper (see Appendix 14.1c) – Group A has a sheet like this for sentence 1, another for sentence 2, another for sentence 3, all on, say, blue paper. Group B has sheets for sentences 4, 5 and 6, all on, say, red paper. And so on, for Groups C and D, making 12 sentences, each written out four times.

When the groups have written out their translations, tear each completed sheet into four strips, each with one copy of the translated sentence on, and distribute one copy to each of the other groups. Keep the fourth for yourself, if you want a record of the translations. Each group ends up with nine slips of paper, three in each of the three colours belonging to the other groups. Their job is then to translate them back into English.

You can get them to compete for the best translation back, though of course the main purpose is to discuss the challenges that arise.

14.3.3. Preparatory materials

- Instructions sheet (Box 2)
- For each group (A to D), four sheets of the same-coloured paper (different colour for each group):

printed on page 1 are the three sentences that this group will translate (see Appendix 14.1a for full list)

printed on pages 2, 3 and 4 are the instructions to write out FOUR times on the sheet the LINSPAG translation of a given sentence (see Appendix 14.1c)

- Dictionary sheet (Appendix 14.1b)

14.3.4 Outcomes

They will soon discover the impossibility of expressing certain kinds of exact meaning for which there is no word, and will have seen the semantic similarity between words and concepts usually kept discrete. Particularly interesting challenges arise with translating 'Karen' (there are no proper names in the dictionary), 'cooler system' and 'DVD player'. Sentence 2 is very hard to translate indeed. Many nuances cannot be translated easily (e.g. 'again' in sentence 8) which makes them think about the relative role of different words in conveying meaning.

14.4 Language contact

14.4.1 Rationale

This game helps students consider how languages influence each other. The languages are completely different at the start. Language contact is simulated by the matching of meaning cards during the game (Box 3). The procedures for dealing

Box 3 Language contact – instructions for players

The point of the game

The object of this simulation is to observe what happens when unrelated languages come into contact with each other. Each player begins with nine 'meanings', each with its own word-form. No forms are duplicated across 'meanings' or players. These forms, given on the player's grid, represent the language of a tribe. During the game, the tribes come into contact with each other and either pass on or accept a word-form from another tribe. Sometimes the new word-form simply replaces the old. Sometimes the two forms exist side by side, through the use of the new form for a related meaning. Watch what happens to your language and how, by the end of the game, its forms compare to those of the other players.

How to play

Each player has a set of nine cards with different meanings on, and a grid. There is also a set of 'spare' meaning cards. Put them to one side. All the players shuffle their own nine cards and hold the pile meaning-side down. The game is based on 'progressive snap', moving clockwise:

- Player 1 turns over the first card in his pile and places it, meaning-side up, on the table in front of him. Then Player 2 (to Player 1's left) places a card in front of *her* (*not* on top of Player 1's card), and so on round the group, so there are four cards on the table, all with their meanings showing. Then Player 1 turns over his next card and places it on top of the old one. So play goes on, with the player's new card covering up the old one(s).

- The players watch out for matching cards on the piles (see later).

- When all the cards have been used, each player picks up his/her own set, shuffles them, and starts again. At first, all players will have the same number of cards, but later in the game, some players will have more cards than others. If you run out of cards before other players, leave your final card exposed until all the players have finished, so everyone shuffles at the same time.

Whenever two cards match, stop and apply the procedures on the list. *It's important to remember whose turn it is next.* Don't read the procedures till the need arises. But then, do read all the bullet points for the eventuality described.

with matching meanings (Appendix 14.2a) lead to one language borrowing a word-form from another language, either to replace its own or to express a new, related meaning. Over the course of the game, certain forms start to dominate and others die out or survive only with a new meaning. The outcomes help students consider the problems associated with deciding when languages derive from a common ancestor and when they have simply been in contact. This can lead to discussions about what sorts of mechanism would, in real life, tend to determine which words got borrowed. The introduction of additional meanings helps students think about how meanings can fractionate to avoid synonymity, and how a word in one language can have a different, but related, meaning in another. It is rough and ready in linguistic terms but quite effective and surprisingly good fun to play.

14.4.2 Procedure

Each game can be played by up to five players. It is crucial that players write down the new form for their meaning whenever it changes on their grid (Appendix 14.2b). At the end of the game, they enter their final form for each word onto the results grid (Appendix 14.2c).

14.4.3 Preparing materials

- For each game you need two packs of cheap playing cards (A and B), with different back-designs or colour, so they can be easily re-sorted. Each game will require 45 cards from Pack A and 28 from Pack B. Print, in large clear letters, the game words onto sticky labels and stick one word onto the back of each card (Figure 1). Pack A consists of five sets of 9 words: *bird, blood, child, eat, egg, fight, head, love, water*. Pack B consists of 14 words, twice each: *anger, drink, face, follow, food, gentle, help, hot, hunt, life, new, rain, red, sing*. Each player begins with one set of nine cards from Pack A. The Pack B cards are the 'spare' meanings and are placed in a pile. For durability, cover the labelled cards with adhesive transparent plastic.
- Each player or group needs a copy of the procedures (Appendix 14.2a).
- Five different starter grids must be prepared per game. An example grid is given in Appendix 14.2b. See Table 14.1 for the start forms that go onto the different grids. Label each grid with the first two words, since they are hard to tell apart. The additional lines on the grid are for the extra meanings. The forms are short, to save space on the grids. I made them distinctive in their final letter, so it was easy to see which words had come from which language.
- Each group needs an overhead transparency sheet and pens, a computer file on a laptop, or a large sheet of paper and pen, to enter their final forms onto a grid (Appendix 14.2c).
- You also need two dice per game.

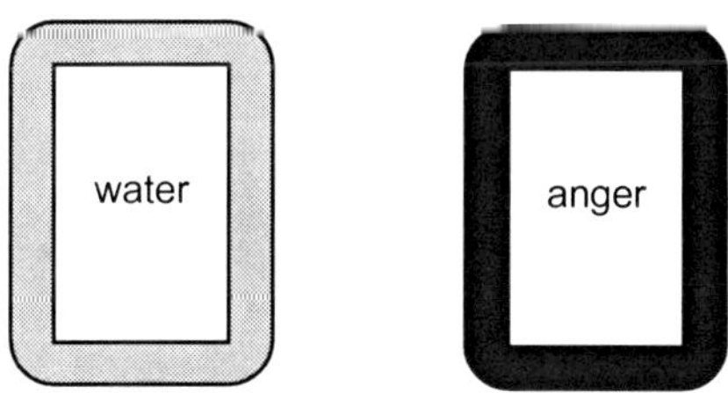

Figure 14.1 Example cards from Pack A (left) and Pack B (right) for Language Contact game

Table 14.1 List of start forms for Language Contact

	Meaning	Player 1	Player 2	Player 3	Player 4	Player 5
1	egg	But	Bas	Kano	Wom	Sir
2	bird	Wat	Lis	Abo	Ebim	Wur
3	fight	Ikot	Eses	Eko	Akim	Alar
4	blood	Pet	Omes	Seno	Sam	Por
5	eat	Sut	Mas	Muno	Mem	Okar
6	head	Lut	Apes	Pino	Imim	Mor
7	water	Asot	Kes	Leno	Elim	Usar
8	child	Kut	Bis	Emo	Pam	Lar
9	love	Mit	Sos	Olo	Ukim	Amar

Table 14.2 Illustration of Language Contact outcome

	Meaning	Player 1	Player 2	Player 3	Player 4	Player 5
1	egg	But	Kano	Kano	Wom	Kano
2	bird	Abo	Abo	Abo	Abo	Abo
3	fight	Eses	Eses	Eko	Akim	Eko
4	blood	Pet	Pet	Seno	Sam	Pet
5	eat	Mas	Mas	Muno	Muno	Muno
6	head	Lut	Apes	Mor	Mor	Mor
7	water	Elim	Kes	Kes	Kes	Usar
8	child	Pam	Bis	Emo	Pam	Pam
9	love	Ukim	Sos	Ukim	Ukim	Ukim
10	drink		Usar			
11	anger		Sam			
12	face	Olo				
13	new					Bis
14	hot			Eses		
15	rain		Asot			
16	gentle					
17	sing					
18	help					
19	follow					
20	hunt					
21	food	Wom			But	
22	life				Por	Seno
23	red			Por		Por

14.4.4 Outcomes

Each time the game is played, the outcome is different, making it useful to keep a copy of final grids for future comparisons. Table 14.2 gives a typical outcome after about 30 minutes' play. Typically, a given meaning will have one dominant form (e.g. lines 2, 9). Some languages will appear more susceptible to change than others (e.g. Player 5, with only two original form-meanings, plus one re-designated).

14.5 Language diversification

14.5.1 Rationale

In this game, everyone begins with the same forms, but gradually, under the influence of sound changes determined by throwing the die, the forms change away from each other (Box 4). The rules (Appendix 14.3a) usually apply to individual players, but sometimes everyone has to implement them. Any given rule will apply only to some of the words in the player's language, as defined by the detail of the rule. Since the words are changing all the time, rules have different effects according to when they are applied. Even though these rules apply chaotically and they are not intended closely to simulate real attested patterns of change in languages, the results of the game do seem to resemble, at least superficially, comparative word lists from real language groups, such as Indo-European or Bantu.

Because my students had relatively little knowledge of phonological rules, I was explicit in indicating what needed to be done to implement a change (Appendix 14.3a, middle column). Students with more experience can be given a notation based on the phonological theory they are familiar with and suitable for their level of competence, as exemplified in the left hand column, where descriptions based on generative phonology notation are given, though simplified to make them more practical for the purpose of the game. The meanings given to the words are, in fact, redundant, and just help players feel they are working with a language.

14.5.2 Procedure

Talk the students through the basic game, but tell them not to worry about the rules till they get to them. Remind them to mark word stress, since this makes a difference to the way the rules apply. For those not used to the phenomenon of sound change, the game slows down as the rules mount up faster than they can apply them. If they write down the rule letter in the next column, the group can take time out from rolling the die to catch up, knowing which rules to apply in which order. Players should be encouraged to help each other apply the rules. Not all students apply the rules accurately; this can be viewed as 'noise' – language has plenty of it. You can extend the game by having a new team pick up from where a previous team ended.

Box 4 Language diversification – instructions for players

The object of this simulation is to observe the process of diversification: when a single language splits into dialects and, ultimately, different languages. Each player has a grid with the same ten words and forms. This represents the language of your tribe at the point when it is the still same as the language of the other tribes. Your tribe's language will be subject to pronunciation changes, determined by the rules you apply during the game. The rules are lettered A to R and are on cards. All the languages in the game are potentially subject to the same kinds of changes, but not necessarily at the same time or in the same order. Watch what happens to your language and how, by the end of the game, its forms compare to those of the other players.

How to play

Put the laminated frame in the middle of the table. Shuffle the rule cards and lay out nine of them, letter-side up, in the spaces on the frame. Put the rest in a pile beside the frame. Play proceeds clockwise. When it is your go, throw the 10-sided die.

1. If you throw a number between 1 and 9 inclusive:

- Find your die score on the laminated frame to see which rule is in that position. This is the rule that you must apply. For example, if you throw an 8, go to position 8 on the grid, and read off the letter on that card.
- Place the play-marker stone on the rule card, to indicate to all players that this is the rule most recently selected.
- Write the letter code of the rule at the top of the first clear column on your grid. Find the correct rule on your rules list, and apply it to the (latest version of) each word in your language.

Note:
(a) Not all words will be affected by the rule.
(b) During the game you may need to apply the same rule to the same word(s) more than once, but the effect will not always be the same.

- For any word that changes as a result of the rule, write the new version in the appropriate column (see example below). *Take care to underline the stressed syllable.*
- Leave blank the cells corresponding to words that are not affected by the rule.

- Next time you apply a rule, start a new column – that way we can see clearly the effect of each rule.
- Always apply the rule to the most recent version of the word (i.e. read along the line to the most recently completed cell)

2. If you throw a 0:

- Throw the die again, until you get a number other than 0. Select the rule that occupies the space with that number, and remove it. Place it at the bottom of the pile of spare rules, and fill the space with the rule at the top of the pile. Play then passes to the next person, without you applying a rule.

3. If you throw the same number (between 1 and 9) as the person immediately before you:
[You will know this has happened, because the play-marker stone will already be on the rule]

- Instruct everyone in the game to apply that rule. They should apply it immediately, or if they are still applying their last rule, as soon as they have completed that.

Hint: to keep track of which rules you need to apply in which order, write the letter of the rule in the next available column.

- After instructing everyone to apply the rule, remove the rule card from the frame, and put it at the bottom of the pile. Replace it with the rule at the top of the pile. Play then passes to the next person.

4. If you get the same rule twice in succession:

- Don't apply a rule a second time to any words that have not changed since the rule was last applied.

5. How many syllables?

- Every vowel forms a syllable. If you are not sure which syllable a consonant belongs to, choose a strategy for deciding, and stick to it as far as you can (e.g. all syllables begin with their preceding consonant; syllables may end with one consonant, but no more).

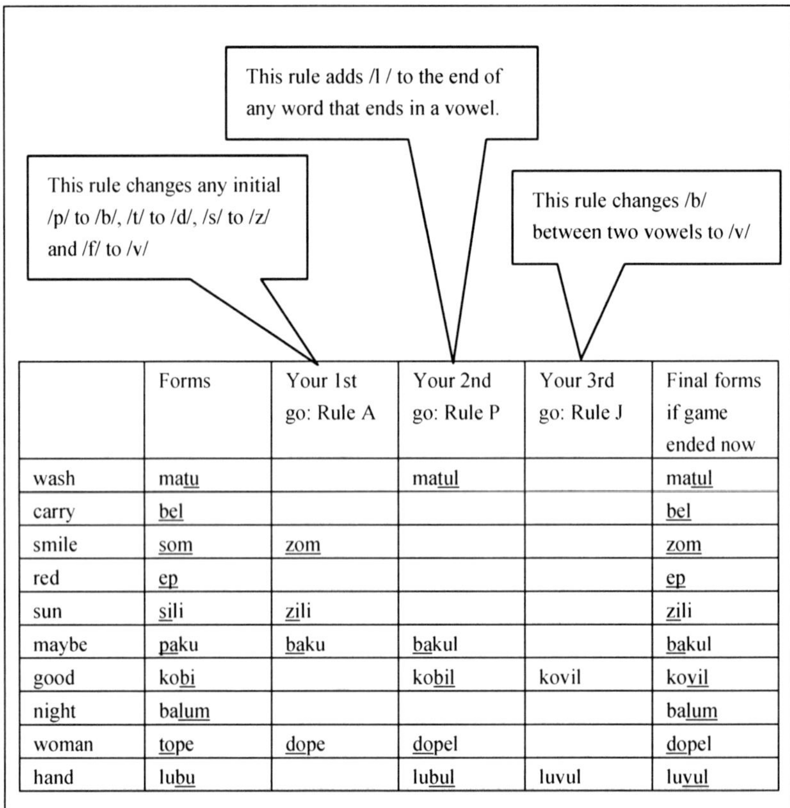

	Forms	Your 1st go: Rule A	Your 2nd go: Rule P	Your 3rd go: Rule J	Final forms if game ended now
wash	matu		matul		matul
carry	bel				bel
smile	som	zom			zom
red	ep				ep
sun	sili	zili			zili
maybe	paku	baku	bakul		bakul
good	kobi		kobil	kovil	kovil
night	balum				balum
woman	tope	dope	dopel		dopel
hand	lubu		lubul	luvul	luvul

14.5.3 Preparing materials

- Each game requires a set of 18 prepared playing cards, representing the 18 rules. For convenience, it is better to print labels reading 'Rule A', 'Rule B' etc. and to stick them on the backs of the cards (Figure 14.2), issuing the rule sheet separately, rather than to stick the rules themselves on the cards. During a game, everyone may need to apply the same rule at the same time, and it is easier for them to read off their own sheet of rules than off a single card. For durability, cover the labelled cards with adhesive transparent plastic.
- The 'game board' (Appendix 14.3b) should be printed onto an A4 sheet of coloured paper and laminated. The board contains 'slots' for nine rules cards – the rules that are active at that point in the game. Each slot is numbered, and the numbers need to be written under the slot as well as in it, otherwise, you cannot see them when there is a card on top. Alternatively a larger board can be made.
- You need one 10-sided die (also known as a 'lottery die') for each game. These dice have faces labelled 0 to 9 and can be bought from novelty and games shops.

You also need one ordinary counter, or pebble, per game.

- Each player needs a grid to track the changes in his/her language (Appendix 14.3c). All the grids are the same at the start but the forms change in each round. There is a tendency for the words to get longer, so they can be hard to fit into the spaces if the grid cells are too small.
- Each group needs an overhead transparency sheet and pen, a large sheet of paper for wall display and a pen, or else a computer file on a laptop, to enter their final forms at the end of the game onto the results grid (adapt Table 14.4 below by emptying the player cells). The grid needs to be large enough for the words to be written clearly.

Figure 14.2 Example rule card for Language Diversification game

14.5.4 Outcomes

Table 14.4 is an illustration of a game outcome, from a real game. (The rules used in that game were slightly different, so some changes may not be possible in the game as presented here). The longer the game goes on, the more distant the forms become, though it should always be possible to spot the common resemblance.

Table 14.4 Illustration of game final outcome for 5 players

Meaning	Original form	Player 1	Player 2	Player 3	Player 4	Player 5
wash	matu	matsu	mãttsu	matsu	mãtesu	mãtsuts
carry	bel	bel	bel	behel	bel	beb
smile	som	zõ	zõ	sõ	zõ	zo
red	ep	ĕp	ĕp	ĕp	ĕp	ĕ
sun	sili	zily	zilly	ziuhu	zily	zily
maybe	paku	baku	bakku	baku	baku	bakuk
good	kobi	gobi	gobbi	gobi	govi	gobi
night	balum	balũ	ballu	bahelum	batu	balu
woman	tope	tsope	tsope	tsope	tesope	tsope
hand	lubu	lubu	luvu	uhubu	luvu	lubu

14.6 Conclusion

As with any new board or card game, the rules and procedures, written out, can be pretty indigestible, but once you start playing, it becomes very easy. Typically, students look worried when I started to explain what they had to do, but within three or four minutes they were well into the game, and everything just worked. There are likely to be occasional questions or misunderstandings, so you need to circulate among the groups. Having graduate students as helpers is very useful too, as they can both help with clarifications and also stimulate discussion about the processes.

When using these games, modifications may come to mind that will make them more effective or linguistically more plausible. It is fine to make such changes, so that the games work optimally for your particular student population and teaching objectives.

Using simulation games worked very well for my students. Many commented in feedback that they wished more of their study had included educational games like this. On the other hand, one rather doleful student commented, ‘I can’t believe it. This is my last ever class at University, and I’m sitting here playing snap.’ Well, you can’t please them all.

Acknowledgments

I am grateful to Anthony Fox and Gerard O’Grady for help in formulating the phonological rules for game 4 in a manner appropriate for their purpose. Also, my thanks go to the various cohorts of undergraduates at Cardiff University who played these games and helped me refine their design.

References

Wray, A. 1998. ‘Protolanguage as a holistic system for social interaction’. *Language and Communication* 18: 47-67.

Wray. A. 2000. ‘Holistic utterances in protolanguage: The link from primates to humans’. In *The evolutionary emergence of language: Social function and the origins of linguistic form*, pp. 285-302, ed., C. Knight, M. Studdert-Kennedy and J. Hurford. New York: Cambridge University Press.

Wray, A. (ed.) 2002a. *The transition to language*. Oxford: Oxford University Press.

Wray, A. 2002b. ‘Dual processing in protolanguage: Competence without performance’. In Wray 2002a: 113-37.

Wray, A. 2002c. *Formulaic language and the lexicon*. Cambridge: Cambridge University Press.

Wray, A. and G.W. Grace. 2007. ‘The consequences of talking to strangers: Sociocultural influences on the lexical unit’. *Lingua* 117 (3): 543-78.

Appendix 14.1a. A limited lexicon – sentences for translation

Sentences Group A

1. I think the cooler system has packed in.
2. No, not under the box, *behind* it!
3. You lot can explore Mars if you want to. We five want to stay right here.

Sentences Group B

4. Karen is looking a bit peaky today.
5. It'll be my daughter's birthday tomorrow, and I'm really missing her.
6. Okay, who's nicked my DVD player then?

Sentences Group C

7. The mice were going at it like rabbits.
8. How do you make cabbage soup again?
9. I'm fed up with not being able to say what I really want to!

Sentences Group D

10. Not dehydrated parsnip paté again!
11. We need to send a message to the President because he's in hospital.
12. The rabbits we dyed crimson have reproduced better than the yellow ones.

Appendix 14.1b. A limited lexicon – dictionary

English–LINSPAG dictionary (thematic)

Me	Bak	Activity	Trig	Show me!	Rusto
You	Sobu	Dismay	Wagit		
Person	Hir	Location	Besod	Maybe	Blad
		Interior	Felib	Negative	Motik
Appear	Akas	Future	Gosit	What	Heb
Repeat	Mid	Obligation	Plag		
Cause	Ribit	Communication	Hamol	Light-coloured	Nash
Stop	Mast	Comparison	Bras	Dark-coloured	Primu
Go	Helit	Product	Stolu	Green	Ob
Recognise	Madu	Day	Dast	Red	Dek
Survive	Coss	Time	Hibat	Hot	Stom
Know	Emut	Event	Frol	Cold	Rido
		Preference	Rebost	Absent	Hemik
Mouse	Ris			Big	Olit
Rabbit	Pako	Many	Wolu	Small	Stoli
Machine	Stik	More	Mishi	Sick	Frib
Vegetable	Hamu	Here	Fleba	Incorrect	Ramiti
Water	Dila	Top	Hik	Simultaneous	Trimin
Container	Tumin	Bottom	Disku	Male	Gamin
Planet	Nast	Front	Mab	Female	Burik
Child	Plam	Back	Ebul	Important	Stig
		Towards	Flig		
				Yesterday	Abim

LINSPAG–English dictionary (alphabetical)

Abim	Yesterday	Dila	Water	Gosit	Future
Akas	Appear	Disku	Bottom	Hamol	Communication
Bak	Me	Ebul	Back	Hamu	Vegetable
Besod	Location	Emut	Know	Heb	What
Blad	Maybe	Felib	Interior	Helit	Go
Bras	Comparison	Fleba	Here	Hemik	Absent
Burik	Female	Flig	Towards	Hibat	Time
Coss	Survive	Frib	Sick	Hik	Top
Dast	Day	Frol	Event	Hir	Person
Dek	Red	Gamin	Male	Mab	Front

Madu	Recognise
Mast	Stop
Mid	Repeat
Mishi	More
Motik	Negative
Nash	Light-coloured
Nast	Planet
Ob	Green
Olit	Big
Pako	Rabbit
Plag	Obligation
Plam	Child
Primu	Dark-coloured
Ramiti	Incorrect
Rebost	Preference
Ribit	Cause
Rido	Cold
Ris	Mouse
Rusto	Show me!
Sobu	You
Stig	Important
Stik	Machine
Stoli	Small
Stolu	Product
Stom	Hot
Trig	Activity
Trimin	Simultaneous
Tumin	Container
Wagit	Dismay
Wolu	Many

Appendix 14.1c. A limited lexicon – translation sheet

Write your LINSPAG sentence here (don't write any English, just LINSPAG words). Write clearly because others have to read it)

SENTENCE NUMBER ONE

Write your LINSPAG sentence here (don't write any English, just LINSPAG words). Write clearly because others have to read it)

SENTENCE NUMBER ONE

Write your LINSPAG sentence here (don't write any English, just LINSPAG words). Write clearly because others have to read it)

SENTENCE NUMBER ONE

Write your LINSPAG sentence here (don't write any English, just LINSPAG words). Write clearly because others have to read it)

SENTENCE NUMBER ONE

Appendix 14.2a. Language contact – contact procedures

What to do when two cards (i.e. meanings) match:

- The two players roll one die each.
- If you roll the higher number, 'give' your word-form to the other player. That is, read the (latest) form for the word off your grid.
- If you roll the lower number, cross out your (latest) form for that meaning, and write the form from your opponent in the next column. If you already have that form for the meaning, then nothing changes.

> **Example:** Player 1's card shows the meaning 'blood'. Next, Player 2 plays a card with the meaning 'egg'. Then Player 3 plays his card, and it also reads 'blood'. Player 1's form is 'sa' and Player 3's form is 'ik'. They throw the die and Player 1 gets a 3, while Player 3 gets a 5. Player 1 crosses out 'sa' on her grid, and writes in 'ik'. Now both players have 'ik' as their word for 'blood'.

If the two die scores are the same:

- Both players keep their own word-form. But **they also adopt the other player's form**, with a new meaning. To do this, each player looks through the pile of spare meaning cards, and selects one. If possible, find a semantic connection between the chosen card and the original. Both players may end up choosing the same meaning, but they don't have to. They write the new meaning in the next spare row on the grid, and assign it the word form provided by the other player. The new meaning card is now part of their hand.

> **Example:** Player 1 and Player 3 match on the word 'blood'. Player 1's form is 'sa' and Player 3's form is 'ik'. They throw the die and both get a 4. Both players keep their own form for 'blood' intact. Player 1 looks through the spare cards and chooses 'red'. She writes 'red' on the next available line on her grid, and in the first column of that row writes Player 3's form ('ik'). Meanwhile, Player 3 chooses the new meaning card 'life'. He writes 'life' in the next available row on his grid, and in the first column writes Player 1's form ('sa'). Both players add the new meaning card to their card pack.

If three or more cards match:

- This will occur when two people have already thrown the die, and then a third player turns his/her card and it matches the two already down.
- The new player rolls the die with each of the players who have the same card—first with the person closest in a clockwise direction. As before, each encounter is based on the latest form, so the order of the encounters makes a difference.

If die scores match and the players have already swapped those very forms in a previous round:

- Leave the forms and meanings as they are.

If a new form, borrowed from another player, already exists in the player's set with another meaning:

- Adopt it anyway – now there is a homophone!

Appendix 14.2b. Language contact – example start grid for contact game

	Meaning	Start form								
1	egg	But								
2	bird	Wat								
3	fight	Ikot								
4	blood	Pet								
5	eat	Sut								
6	head	Lut								
7	water	Asot								
8	child	Kut								
9	love	Mit								
10										
11										
12										
13										
14										
15										
16										
17										
18										
19										
20										

Appendix 14.2c. Language contact – results grid

	Player 1	Player 2	Player 3	Player 4	Player 5
egg					
bird					
fight					
blood					
eat					
head					
water					
child					
love					
life					
red					
drink					
anger					
face					
new					
hot					
rain					
gentle					
sing					
help					
follow					
hunt					
food					

Appendix 14.3a. Language diversification – phonological rules

	Phonological description	Comprehensible description	Examples
A	{k, p, f, s} → [+ voice] / #_	If the word begins with k, p, f or s, change: k → g, p → b and f → v, s → z	pib → bib
B	V → Ṽ / N _	For any vowel immediately preceded by m, n or ŋ: Add the nasalisation symbol ˜ above the vowel	bamu → bamũ
C	i → [+ rounded] / l _	When immediately preceded by l: Change any i to y	lima → lyma
D	r → z / {V, C} _	Change any non-initial r to z	marak → mazak
E	V → [+stress] / _ (C) (C) #	Move the stress to the final syllable	kapak → kapak
F	VN → Ṽ / _ #	For any word-final n, m or ŋ: If the preceding letter is a vowel, write the nasalisation symbol ~ above the vowel and then delete the nasal consonant	bom → bõ, amin → amĩ
G	l → u / _ #	For any word-final l: Change it to u	bamil → bamiu
H	t → ts / _ V [+ stress]	For any stressed syllable beginning with t: If the next sound is a vowel, insert s between them.	tup → tsup, katu → katsu; *but* katu → katu, putke → putke
I	VV → VhV	For any two consecutive vowels: Put h between them.	bamiu → bamihu
J	b → v / V_V	For any b: If it is between two vowels, change it to v	babi → bavi
K	r → d / {#, V} _ V [+stress]	Any r at the start of a stressed syllable becomes d	marak → madak
L	Ø → N [+labial] / V _ C [+labial] N [+dental] / V _ C [+dental] N [+velar] / V _ C [+velar]	For p, b, t, d, k and g preceded by a vowel: Insert a nasal consonant between the vowel and the consonant, as follows: insert m between a vowel and p or b; insert n between a vowel and t or d; insert ŋ between a vowel and k or g	matu → mantu sigatsi → siŋgatsi

	Rule	Description	Example
M	$C \rightarrow \emptyset \,/\, V\_\#$ [−stress]	In any unstressed final syllable ending in a consonant, delete the consonant	pimas → pima ohutin → ohuti
N	$C_1 \rightarrow C_1C_1 \,/\, V\_V$	Double any single consonant between two vowels	hiku → hikku lidaluum → liddalluum
O	$CC \rightarrow C\,e\,C$	For any two consecutive consonants: Separate them by e	baddi → badedi sagatsi → sagatesi
P	$\emptyset \rightarrow l \,/\, V\_\#$	To any word-final vowel, add l	tope → topel
Q	$\emptyset \rightarrow i \,/\, \#\,(C)\,V$ [+stress]	For any word in which the first syllable is stressed: Add a preceding unstressed i	bom → ibom matu → imatu
R	$\emptyset \rightarrow e$ [−stress] $/\, V\_l$	For any vowel followed by l: Insert e between the vowel and the /l/, with the syllable break between the vowels.	bal → bael

Appendix 14.3b. Language diversification – game board

1	2	3
1	2	3
4	5	6
4	5	6
7	8	9
7	8	9

Appendix 14.3c. Language diversification – player's grid

PLAYER'S GRID: when top grid is full, write latest form for each word in first column of bottom grid and continue.

Meaning	Original form	Rule	Rule	Rule	Rule	Rule
wash	matu					
carry	bel					
smile	som					
red	ep					
sun	sili					
maybe	paku					
good	kobi					
night	balum					
woman	tope					
hand	lubu					

Con-tinue below

Meaning	Latest form	Rule	Rule	Rule	Rule	Rule	Rule
wash							
carry							
smile							
red							
sun							
maybe							
good							
night							
woman							
hand							

Notes

* **Alison Wray**

Alison Wray was introduced to linguistics at the age of 14 by her Russian teacher. After devouring books on the history of the Indo-European languages, she bought Eric Partridge's *Origins*, her favourite book to this day. Daringly ignoring warnings from her French and German teachers that linguistics was not what she thought it was, she applied to the University of York to read linguistics with German and Hindi. The course at York did not disappoint: the lecturers were enthusiasts, and the coursework was rich in research-based projects, with ample opportunity to experiment with 'doing research'. Graduating with a first, Alison did a year's voluntary work before returning for a doctorate under the supervision of Patrick

Griffiths, researching the evidence for and against the left hemisphere lateralisation of language. Keen to combine linguistics with her other passion, singing, on completing her doctorate in 1988 Alison became the researcher on the three-year *Singers' Language Project* in the Department of Music at York, funded by the Leverhulme Trust. There, she examined how singers cope with foreign languages, researched historical pronunciation for performances of early music (later acting as a consultant on over 80 CDs and broadcasts), and enjoyed being the only linguist in York with a piano in her office.

In 1991, Alison became a lecturer in linguistics at the University College of Ripon and York St John (now York St John University), where she learned her trade in the company of excellent colleagues committed to engaged and imaginative approaches to teaching. Changing later to a one-semester-on, one-semester-off contract, she combined linguistics lecturing with professional concert, opera and session singing in the UK and abroad. In 1996 she was appointed Assistant Director of the Wales Applied Language Research Unit, University of Wales Swansea, working with Paul Meara to support his excellent part-time distance PhD programme in vocabulary acquisition. She also began her research into formulaic language, and, linked to it, developed a theory of how human language originated. In 1999 she became a Senior Research Fellow at Cardiff University and, when the Fellowship transformed into a Senior Lectureship, devised her undergraduate module *The Evolution of Human Communication and Language*, using a range of creative approaches to presenting its complex ideas. Her empirical research has explored the role of formulaicity in extreme communication and language learning, and the genetic basis of language performance. In 2005 Alison was made a Professor of Language and Communication, and in 2007 a Research Professor. In 2008 she was elected to the Academy of Social Sciences. Since 2004 she has been the Director of Research for the Cardiff School of English, Communication and Philosophy, and increasingly works in the domain of researcher training and support. She continues to sing (but not in her office ... no piano).

15 Teaching *LING101*

*Koenraad Kuiper**

15.1 Introduction

Many a linguist has begun his or her personal relationship with linguistics with LING101 or its equivalent. But for every linguist that passes through LING101 and its successors – courses on syntax, sociolinguistics, semantics, morphology and mathematical linguistics – there are hundreds of students for whom LING101 is terminal. They are on their way somewhere else to become ESOL teachers, computer programmers, bureaucrats and real estate salespeople. So one question for anyone who teaches LING101 to such a class is what should such a heterogeneously motivated group know and how are they to learn it?

As with every other introductory course, this raises issues of what is core to the subject and what can be done without. Is the fact that bees dance to tell other bees where the honey is core knowledge that everyone who is interested in human language(s) should know? Do we need to think hard about whales and dolphins? Is Whorfian theory sexy or just seductive? In other words what can and should be crammed into a one-semester course?

Then there are other choices. There are so many interesting languages on the planet, a few of which students and teacher know; most of which they don't. Some have exotic properties such as having very few verbs. Some have their verbs at the end of the clause. Others have lots of juicy paradigms. Some have tones. Some have voiceless vowels and clicks. Some place stress on the last syllable of a word. Does one present students with the rich mix of all that or limit oneself to the mundane (but fascinating), the language inside the students' and one's own head, seeing the whole LING101 exercise as a way of getting students to look at their unconscious without them lying collectively on a psychiatrist's couch?

How much should be devoted to exposition and how much to analysis, to problem-based learning? Can a whole course be problem-based, building knowledge inductively or is there a place for telling students some things before they start their own explorations?

What place should the acquisition of terminology have and what terminology is necessary or desirable? One can hardly get away without nouns and verbs. Calling them Form Class 1 and Form Class 2 as C.C. Fries did is not going to work as well.

And then there are the students collectively and severally. LING101 may be taught to large classes of several hundred or to smaller groups in liberal-arts colleges, or the large class may be split into sections and be taught by TAs. What do these students already know when they enter LING101? Those lucky enough to have had an old-fashioned elementary school teacher somewhere along their past progress (I think of her as James Thurber's Miss Groby who hunted figures of speech 'as Palomides hunted the questing beast') may already know about nouns and verbs as may those international students who have studied English as a foreign language. Others may know nothing of the mysteries of nouns and verbs.

Linguistics also has many theoretical approaches (not quite as many as there are human languages but impressive numbers nevertheless). Does one teach cognitive grammar, principles and parameters, lexical functional grammar, or bits of all of these in LING101?

15.2 Curriculum development for LING101

15.2.1 Content

When you get a group of linguists together there is remarkable agreement about the domains that are central to linguistics. We agree that phonetics, phonology, morphology, syntax and semantics are core sub-disciplines without which one cannot proceed further. That kind of agreement does not exist in many humanities' disciplines. So linguists are lucky. LING101 needs to build a foundational knowledge of those central areas. That is what one gets in almost all LING101s. There is often more besides, but in a one-semester course, the choice is to devote more time to the core and so less to bees and dolphins, or more to bees and dolphins and consequently less to the core. The choice is not only made easier on the grounds of limitation of time but also on the basis of one of the oldest distinctions in the linguistics book: competence and performance. To offer a principled account of language use one needs at least a basic background in what is being used. So teaching knowledge of competence is pedagogically prior to teaching other more applied areas of linguistics such as socio-linguistics and psycholinguistics. That is not to say that the one cannot illuminate the other. Once students have a rough idea of free variation in phonology, the fact that free variation is not as free as all that in the social world is illuminating and helps the concept to stick. Department stores in New York can be useful here even if one has not been to Sax Fifth Avenue's, Macy's and Kleins' fourth floors.

15.2.2 Prior knowledge

One basic curriculum decision that must be made is what to assume students already know. In New Zealand, it is best to assume that students have no background knowledge at all, or if they do that it will enhance their learning one way or another. Given that the High School English curriculum in New Zealand has not taught the fundamentals of English structure for at least thirty years, the assumption that it is better to start from scratch is safe. The good news is that if one decides that the main language of exemplification is to be English, then one can assume that a great deal of tacit knowledge exists which can magically be conjured forth.

15.2.3 The language(s) of exemplification

The choice of the language(s) of exemplification has traditionally been influenced by the academic roots of linguistics. In North America, linguistics often grew out of anthropology and the study of indigenous languages of the Americas. The SIL manuals of Pike, Nida, and Elsdon and Picket are still wonderful treasure troves of exercises. In the UK linguistics more often grew out of English language programmes within English departments and thus they had a philological background. It is easy to take such traditions on trust. But they should be uncovered and then one can see that each has its advantages. Those LING101s which draw on a wide range of languages of exemplification make students aware of just how various languages can be and can make them less linguo-centric in their judgments. On the other hand, there are some things missing in the study of languages one does not know oneself, namely native intuitions. Looking at one's own language is already an imaginative leap that some students find hard. For example, when students are learning to transcribe their own speech into phonetics, many resist the idea that they elide perfectly respectable vowels and consonants. They have been taught that sloppy speech is bad and the moral opprobrium that attaches to normal connected speech is just as alienating and thus hard to overcome as the alienation effects of looking at exotic paradigms. Both have to do with becoming consciously aware of what is unconscious. But in the case of a native language, the speaker can at least recognize minimal pairs and (less happily) complementary distribution, because it comes naturally. One can point out that knowledge of where syllable boundaries are in one's own language is unerring, and yet there is nothing in the speech signal which indicates where they are. Focusing on English does not, of course, preclude the occasional foray into other languages by way of comparison. How can one teach syllable timing in contrast to stress timing without putting on a French accent and repeating stretches of *'Allo 'Allo* or Maurice Chevalier songs?

15.3 Curriculum delivery

As Sandy Chung shows in her chapter on syntax teaching in this volume and as Wray and Bloomer's problem-based text shows (Wray and Bloomer 2006), a large amount can be taught with carefully selected problem sets. This is particularly so with smaller classes where the instructor can provide constant feedback. But where a big first-year class is taught not in sections but in large lectures and small tutorials, exposition must play a part.

15.3.1 Lectures

It is tempting to think that a lecture is just a form of information transfer. But linguists know this is not the case. Speech simply does not come out of a lecturer's mouth and find its way into a student's ear without a great deal more going on before the signal gets into a form where it involves learning. So the question has to be asked, what is the difference between exposition in a textbook and exposition in a lecture? Sometimes not much. Effective lectures, however, have an interactive and affective dimension that is harder to get from a text. Students signal how a lecture is going by various kinds of silence and various kinds of back channelling. There is the silence of incomprehension, a kind of sullen demeanour linked to staring down at the notes, up at the overhead waiting for enlightenment. There is the silence of intense concentration when something is interesting and worth attending to. Books cannot hear these silences, nor can they respond to a question from someone or catch the satisfaction murmur when a third analogy makes the penny to drop. Are phonemes really like werewolves with different manifestations appearing in different environments? Is a wolf manifestation morphologically enough like the were-manifestation for them to be recognizably forms of the same individual? What about the butler and the murderer? Are they in complementary distribution, and if they are, are they one and the same person? Primarily lectures are about affect. Exposition is the vehicle but unless attitudes and feelings are uppermost, the lecture will fail since it is affect which motivates learning. Straight exposition is better done by a textbook (but it cannot recognize the person reading it).

There is a consequence to being a stand-up comic, an actor, producing affect. It is tiring. Professional actors are on stage for a maximum of two hours a night. They have to learn their lines by day and sleep in during the morning. Lecturing to a big LING101 has a major difference: no sleeping in and the script is extempore.

15.3.2 Problem-based learning

But lecturing to a big LING101 does not preclude analysis, discovery learning and problem sets. In lectures when things get difficult, a short exercise with feedback from the audience works wonders for keeping awake those who have had a hard night the day before. Also with a big lecture class in linguistics it is essential to have small group practical work. Here the problem sets prevail and student homework can be checked, small workgroups can get established and feedback is readily to hand. So the practical classes provide the balance necessary to put into practice what is provided with exposition in the lectures and text.

Some students need more practice and more problem sets than can be provided in a single practical session. Here learning management systems come into their own. Blackboard, for example, allows for numerous ways to present quizzes to students so that they can gain mastery through repeated attempts at the same conceptual or analytical material but with new stimuli. For example, derivational morphology can be got across by asking for the grammatical category of the base to which an affix attaches and what the grammatical category of the stem plus affix is. After 20 or 30 such questions, students get the idea that derivational affixes are part of the word-formation system, and many but not all create a different category of word from that of their base. LING101 at the University of Canterbury now has almost 40 of these quizzes. They took time to create but have proved very useful, particularly for the not-so-able student.

15.3.3 Theory

When you get a group of linguists together, although there is considerable agreement about the central sub-disciplines of the subject, how the facts are to be accounted for and what some of the facts are can get mightily contentious. It can lead to screaming matches on the platform at the Linguistic Society of America annual meeting. However interesting such an event would be for the students in LING101 to witness, it creates a problem for curriculum development. Should a syllabus be theoretically consistent throughout an undergraduate linguistics programme or should it be eclectic? The premise which seems to work best is to suppose that, until a student is familiar with one way of seeing and doing things, providing multiple perspectives can be confusing. Also it is better to move from a simple to a complex view of phenomena than present all the complexities at an early stage. For LING101, therefore, I keep it simple (for the most part). I try to keep it theory neutral (for the most part; although philosophers of science say that is just cheating: there is no theory neutral). But cheating a bit seems better than presenting Derrida, Kristeva and Barth to a first-year literature class when students have read only two novels.

Much of the conceptual material and attendant terminology that seems central for LING101 is assumed by most linguistic theories. Without knowing what a subordinate clause is and the distinction between lexical and auxiliary verbs one cannot get very far in any syntactic theory. In the first-year textbook Scott Allan and I wrote, there are about a hundred terms in the three glossaries. Most of these would not be contested, or if they are it is just that some other theory uses a different word for the same thing. Pronouns have antecedents. Inflectional morphemes form up into paradigms on the basis of their morphosyntactic categories and properties and so forth. In a sense, the conceptual and terminological choices are made by asking what areas of understanding all linguistic theories presuppose. These are the ones to teach in LING101.

15.3.4 Languages of exemplification

There is a problem with the interaction between the selection of a single language of exemplification and this latter desideratum. Some languages are better at illustrating some linguistic phenomena than others. Chinese languages are not good for illustrating inflectional morphology since they have none. English and German are not good at illustrating tone. Short excursions into foreign parts are therefore necessary.

15.3.5 Learning management systems

I have suggested that learning management systems can have a significant place in curriculum delivery. Here are a few more uses that can be made of them. Lectures can be recorded and played out to the campus network on a streaming video server. I have been doing that for five years by recording the PowerPoint presentation of lectures with a voiceover of the lecture providing QuickTime movies for anyone who was not at the lecture because their children were sick, they were at a sports tournament or they did not get up on time. They are popular with international students who need to hear it all again to make it make sense. Next year I will also load a large number of mp3s to be downloaded for use in mp3 players so that a small topic like the properties of words ending in *-gress* or the odd features of dvandva compounds can be heard while riding your bike to work. (It's not the latest pop track but the idea of being listed on iTunes and playing on an iPod is tempting. Classification in iTunes? Heavy metal?)

The availability of such learning avenues raises the issue of LING101 being offered by distance. If the lectures are available in video form, the quizzes can be accessed at any time, the textbook is assigned, what remains unavailable to the distance student is the face-to-face tutorial. Well, not necessarily. Skype and iChat can provide one-on-one and group tutoring opportunities (so long as everyone has done the homework).

15.4. Conclusion

The careful reader will have noticed that there is the odd *should* lurking in the foregoing. Choices always involve preferred ways of doing things. These tend to have a moral aspect to them. I guess these are my imperatives, and every teacher has their own. What is important to me is to find as many ways as I can of enthusing students, fascinating them in the minutiae of one of the most intricate systems humans develop. That does not always succeed. Let's face it, parts of speech are not all that riveting. But maybe the excuse for colonizing a piece of the mind of another person, in the case where the colonizer is a linguist, is that the language(s) has/have already done it before ever you came along.

References

Wray, A. and A. Bloomer. 2006. *Projects in linguistics: A practical guide to researching language*. 2nd edn; London: Hodder Educational.

Notes

* **Koenraad Kuiper**

I wanted to be a vet but once you have seen one case of bovine footrot, the next looks (and smells) little different. So I decided to train as a secondary-school teacher instead (which turned out to be anything but tedious). In my second year at university, a mentor suggested a course in English Language studies might prove useful. He was right. Half way through, Frank Brosnahan, who taught the course, marked one of my homework tree diagrams as wrong, but a week later said both his and my analyses were OK. But New York can't be both north and south of Cape Cod. I was hooked.

At graduate school at Simon Fraser University in Vancouver in the late 1960s, linguistics faculty were thick on the ground, offering everything from medieval theories of linguistics, through literary stylistics to current generative theory (and the corridors smelled sweetly). At least in the latter courses, if there were two tree diagrams, they both had to represent different semantically plausible formal semantic representations. In my current office there hangs a flying pig. Flying pigs can be dangerous.

After graduating and after three years high-school teaching, I moved to university teaching. I have had great teaching colleagues the last 38 years. We have team taught most classes (and the teacher training came in handy). Just as for Janet Holmes, there has also been a lot of administration: Dean, Head of Department, University Council, committees galore, but the teaching keeps your feet on the ground, and the memos and the policies and templates of the administration (even your own) in perspective.

16 'Beyond compare'[1]: Supervising postgraduate research

Janet Holmes[*]

I always remember my supervisor's smile and encouragement, 'Happy writing!'
At that time, I wondered how people could be happy and writing at the same time!

16.1 Introduction

Until the advent of Performance Based Research Funding in New Zealand,[2] it is probably true to say that postgraduate supervision was the Cinderella of linguistics teaching in New Zealand universities. The inescapable demands of scheduled classes from first year through to MA course teaching tended to shunt postgraduate teaching to the back burner, to be fitted in where it would least disrupt other activities. Though lip service has often been paid to the thesis student's right to 'regular' meetings with their (primary) supervisor, the regularity has often been more honoured in the breach than the observance, disrupted by intense teaching schedules, statutory holidays, vacation periods, and staff conference and study leave. And while, from the students' perspective, regular meetings with their supervisor are certainly desirable in principle, the need to earn additional income, and the natural reluctance to expose oneself to criticism for not having achieved one's objectives, tend to contribute to eroding the frequency of meetings.

In this context, it is worth asking what can be done to counter such subversive forces. What are the crucial components of good postgraduate supervision? And how can we ensure they are incorporated into the experience of our linguistics and applied linguistics postgraduates. In addition to my own personal experience and reflections, this short chapter draws on three sources of information to address these questions: (1) general research on the quality of postgraduate supervision (e.g. Harper 2005; Neale 2000; Morrow 2000; Dinham and Scott 1999); (2) feedback collected from linguistics and applied linguistics students at Victoria University; (3) discussions with a wide range of academics and linguistics scholars about these issues over the last three decades. The discussion is presented in four main sections: I first consider three areas which are generally identified as problems for postgraduate supervision – workload, choosing a topic and giving and getting feedback – and then I take a more constructive tack and outline one possible model for doing it well.

16.2 Workload

Workload is clearly one issue in relation to the quality of postgraduate supervision that individual academics can provide. The number of postgraduate students that any individual academic is expected to supervise varies enormously from one institution to another. Workload formulae which take systematic account of the number of students, their status as part-time or full-time, distance or on-campus students, and the proportion of supervision responsibility taken at different times by different supervisors are rare to say the least. Colleagues in the USA tend to teach mainly at (post)graduate level; the undergraduate teaching is largely undertaken by their students acting as teaching assistants. The picture in the UK, Australia and NZ is very different. Most academics are expected to make a substantial contribution to undergraduate teaching, and the extent to which a systematic workload allowance is allocated for postgraduate supervision is very variable indeed. In some cases, colleagues whose research is in popular areas for postgraduate thesis topics report concurrent supervision of up to 12 students (albeit some part-time), a total which could be regarded as constituting a full-time workload, and yet this is shouldered in addition to a substantial undergraduate teaching load.

It is not surprising then to find comments such as the following in postgraduate student surveys identifying aspects of the supervision process with which students were dissatisfied:

> Supervisors who read three pages of a chapter and then after half an hour's discussion say 'send me the next chapter when it's ready and come and see me the week after' (Harper 2005: 15).
>
> My emails would go unanswered for some time. I was expected to understand their home life (childcare) and work-life commitments and fit in around them (Harper 2005: 15).
>
> Supervisor is busy – therefore there is never enough time (Neale 2000: 7).

Those readers who are supervisors will no doubt feel sympathy with the staff members referred to in these quotations, while nonetheless recognizing that the students' dissatisfaction is reasonable.

It seems clear that if we are to ensure high quality supervision for our postgraduate students, an agreed workload allowance must be allocated systematically throughout the period of supervision. Postgraduate students cannot continue to be regarded as an absorbable 'extra' as they have often been in the past, an attitude that encourages staff to squash them into the interstices of other work, rather than to devote quality intellectual time to developing a postgraduate's scholarly abilities and assisting them to produce the very best research of which they are capable.

16.3 Choosing a topic

Given the small number of permanent staff available as supervisors, New Zealand linguistics and applied linguistics departments offer students a remarkably broad array of potential PhD topics, from language policy and language attitudes through all aspects of language learning and teaching, to the phonetics and syntactic analysis of the structure of the languages of Vanuatu using the most specialized current syntactic frameworks. In a previous, halcyon, non-competitive era of guaranteed university funding, academics would advise prospective postgraduate students to apply to the university with the highest level of academic expertise in their area of research interest. Those days have long gone, and staff at each university have been forced to develop expertise in a wider range of topics. In the current climate, good students are rarely sent elsewhere on the basis of inability to supervise their preferred topic alone (but see below for an alternative approach). Academic staff are often required to supervise in areas which stretch their expertise to its limits, a matter of concern on the basis of survey results of postgraduate students in other areas (Neale 2000; Harper 2005: 14).

Another important issue in relation to selecting a topic is the possibility of interdisciplinary collaboration between departments and supervisors. Really clear communication is a genuine issue in this situation, and it is crucial to establish who is primarily responsible for the student's progress. A related matter is cross-cultural research, and also that of research with indigenous groups and in areas of concern to non-majority group members. The ethical issues raised by research questions which venture into these areas require careful preparation which needs to begin well before a student is accepted for enrolment in many cases (see, for example, Smith 1999).

16.4 Feedback

The research literature provides abundant evidence that the topic that most preoccupies postgraduates is the amount, frequency and quality of feedback that they receive from their supervisors. Comments from exit questionnaires (Neale 2000), student surveys (Harper 2005) and constructive suggestions made by linguistics and applied linguistics students in a survey I undertook tend to tell a similar tale. Most students want frequent, full and focused feedback from their supervisors, and they want it promptly, that is, as soon as possible after they have delivered their written material. (See the Appendix for a summary of the points made by postgraduates who responded to my survey.)

Critical comments in the survey responses identified a range of unsatisfactory supervisory behaviours, from supervisors who told students they did not want to see anything in writing till it was in final form, to supervisors who simply did not make time to discuss material with students.

> I've only been able to have one meeting with my secondary supervisor since he took over and that took well in excess of a month to arrange through cancellations, his failure to prepare and his constant losing of material. Since that meeting, he has only answered one email and there has been no faculty support to confronting this neglect (Harper 2005: 15).

Hopefully this is an extreme, and I hasten to add that this supervisor was not in linguistics or applied linguistics.

On a more positive note, linguistics/applied linguistics students commented on the following helpful behaviours from their supervisors.

> I think the most important thing for me was positive feedback by the supervisors. Whether it was about the subject matter itself or writing ability, positive feedback gave me encouragement to keep writing.
>
> On the flip side, criticism, as opposed to constructive criticism, can be a downer. Research students spend a lot of time and energy in their studies and to have someone criticize their work without substantial reasoning or giving suggestions is very discouraging.

Another student said 'it helped when you gave such lovely positive feedback on any of my written stuff and set a new goal', and another noted that what helped most was 'quick feedback – keeps up the motivation…'

Some students noted unhelpful supervisory behaviour:

> the most unhelpful thing my supervisor did was to make comments about grammatical/stylistic details in early drafts when all I really wanted to know was whether my ideas/logic/argument made sense.

Others commented that they found it depressing when their supervisors wrote all over their drafts in red pen. This underlines the importance of focusing on the big picture from the beginning. The students' comments indicate awareness that the supervisor's role is to help them make an original and significant contribution to knowledge, the basic requirements of a PhD, and to assist them in locating their contribution in the scholarly field to which they are contributing. Stylistic issues should always be secondary, and are generally not an appropriate focus at the crucial early stages of a PhD.

One student enrolled in a PhD while working overseas commented on the motivating effect of their supervisor's requirements that they submit a written report every Friday stating what they had accomplished that week, however little: 'This means I always do just a bit more as I feel bad if I have nothing to report come Friday!'

It is also important, of course, to bear in mind that not all students are the same. In a survey of 25 postgraduate linguistics/applied linguistics students, two expressed a rather different perspective on what they expected of their supervisors. They saw themselves as mature researchers who took responsibility for their own progress, and in their view the appropriate role of the supervisor was as guide and mentor, to be called on when they judged it to be appropriate, rather than someone who was constantly setting them demanding writing deadlines which involved unwelcome and unhelpful pressure.

> I was always aware that I was expected to call the meetings, I set my own realistic short-term objectives and I took responsibility for my actions and inactions.

> My positive reflections on the research process to date can to a large degree be attributed to my retention of ownership of my work.

Such students need support so that they spread their wings and avoid being stifled by too much bureaucracy or a formulaic approach. Indeed, one could consider this as the ideal goal for all research students: to attain independence, taking responsibility for their own progress, and using their supervisor as a guide and advisor.

It is also worth noting that, not unreasonably, students do not welcome surprises at a late stage in the research process. One student commented, for instance, on how distressed they were to receive feedback 'about significant theoretical issues… in the final year which should have been received in the first year' (Neale 2000: 5). And another commented in response to my informal survey:

> I was very surprised when very late in the process my supervisor read over chapters and expressed concern with their content.

These comments suggest misunderstandings of various sorts about what kind of feedback was being provided at different stages. Clear communication is crucial at every stage of the supervisor–supervisee relationship.

Finally, while prompt, constructive and challenging feedback is essential to help correct misconceptions as well as to promote critical thinking and develop intellectual independence, it is also worth bearing in mind that the main supervisor is not the only source of useful feedback to a postgraduate student, a point developed in the next section.

16.5 One model for good supervision: support en route

Traditionally, like most students in the area of humanities and arts, linguistics/applied linguistics thesis students have a lonely row to hoe. For long periods at different points, they may be working virtually on their own – reading for their literature survey, collecting data, analysing data, or writing up. They often work at home, sometimes from choice, but frequently due to lack of desk space in crowded university departments. Rarely are there other students working in the same area of research. This is the model which still pertains in many humanities departments, namely, infrequent contact for postgraduate thesis students with others, whether students or staff.

But it is not the only model, and increasingly an alternative is developing, influenced partly by the fact that some sources of external funding encourage team work, but also by the perception by some supervisors of the advantages to their postgraduates of developing a community of researchers with which they can identify.

I will use Victoria's School of Linguistics and Applied Language Studies as an illustrative example here because it is obviously the school that I know best, but developments in linguistics departments in other New Zealand universities have, I know, taken the same general direction. We have not yet got everything right, but on the basis of the last decade's experience, we have a better idea of what we are aiming for.

16.5.1 Accepting students for postgraduate study

On the basis of sometimes rather painful experience, we have learned to be selective about who we accept as postgraduate research students. Those who have been enthused by the New Zealand undergraduate courses of inspired teachers like Scott Allan and who, ideally, have been actively encouraged to enrol in an honours degree easily make the transition to become excellent postgraduate thesis students. They are well prepared, and they often have a good idea of the topic area they want to work in. More challenging for our evaluation systems are applications from overseas, especially from universities whose grading systems are unfamiliar. Our current practice is to accept only those with excellent grades, but just as importantly, we also accept only those who are willing to work on a topic that fits within the research priorities of our school. In some cases, this means negotiating with good students to agree on a topic acceptable both to them and to their potential supervisors. Ideally this results in satisfactory identification for each student of at least two supervisors, as well as preferably an existing active research group to which they can be attached once they arrive.[3]

16.5.2 Developing a research proposal

While applicants provide a short research proposal with their application, the real work on their research questions begins when they commence work with their supervisor(s). In an ideal world, both supervisors will work with the student at the early stages, providing reading, and assisting them to narrow their focus to something manageable which relates to the supervisors' areas of research, with obvious ongoing benefits for all. Developing a research proposal for presentation to the school's research committee may take anything from three to six months, depending on a very wide range of factors. During this process, students may of course make use of a number of sources of feedback in addition to their supervisors, including other staff members, and, importantly, other students.

16.5.3 Regular meetings

Apart from providing feedback on written work (as discussed above), regular meetings between postgraduate students and their supervisors are important for planning and monitoring progress. One useful strategy recommended by experts in this area is to require the student to take the 'minutes' of meetings and to provide these in written form to the supervisor after the meeting. In this way, agreements and deadlines are documented, and any misconceptions can be quickly identified and cleared up. An initial timeframe documenting the stages of the research is required as part of the research proposal in most departments, and many students find it valuable to begin and/or end each session by referring to the stage that has been reached.

Another point made by some linguistics/applied linguistics PhD students in their survey responses is the importance of making it clear that *they* are the supervisor's priority during their consultation time: 'divert the phone, shut the door and put a note on it saying you are busy – this is *my* time!' wrote one student. Postgraduate students are paying hefty fees and they do not like to be marginalized or treated as interruptible.

16.5.4 PhD support groups

One useful way of obtaining unthreatening assistance during the various stressful stages of completing a thesis has proved to be the informal PhD support groups which have developed within the school. They come and go, and they take different forms at different times – sometimes predominantly social, grizzle and whinge groups, other times focused on the need to discuss tricky issues such as the most appropriate way of collecting data, or what alternative interpretations are possible of some complex material. One such group is largely self-organized in terms of how often it meets. The students (and occasionally staff) voluntarily opt for turns to raise issues they want to discuss, or bring along material for others to consider. They share references and advice about how to build a bibliography (evaluating tools such as EndNote and Zotero). Very recently, a technically sophisticated pair of students have taken the initiative of video-recording these sessions for the benefit of distance thesis students and for those who cannot get to a particular session. The videos are made available through a community group on Blackboard, the university staff–student interface now used in most courses. Students can provide feedback and thus continue to interact with the presenter after the event. This is a very valuable way of combating the isolation felt by many PhD students, especially those engaged in research at a distance.

Another model used at other universities is a schedule organized by a staff member where a different student presents a progress report at each meeting. In our experience, such meetings are always fruitful, even if the students' topics are very disparate. However, there are even greater benefits if the students' areas of research overlap, even if minimally. The sharing of insights and materials in this situation is immensely beneficial. This is another reason for attempting to limit the range of topic areas that staff are expected to supervise. The benefits of concentrating on areas of research strength are apparent in a myriad of ways.

A related initiative is the roundtables organized from time to time, usually in response to a visit from a researcher from elsewhere, where a group of students in the relevant area provide a brief snapshot of their research, and benefit from comments and feedback from the visitor. These sessions have the added benefit of providing an opportunity for students to make personal connections with a range of international scholars. These connections can make overseas conferences seem more hospitable events, and can foster career prospects.

16.5.5 Seminars and conferences

While focusing on a limited range of areas of research has many internal benefits in relation to the intellectual vigour of supervision, there are also benefits to be gained from broadening students' linguistic horizons. Again this is an ideal prescription, which we do not always live up to, but in principle all research students (and staff) are encouraged to attend weekly research seminars, as well as any additional seminars offered by visitors, with the goal of exposing people to alternative theoretical approaches and methodologies, and educating each other about the diversity and breadth of work in linguistics and applied linguistics. It is doubtless a counsel of perfection, but ideally students should emerge from postgraduate study not only as experts in their particular area of research but also well-informed about topics from a wide spectrum in (applied) linguistics.

Conferences obviously offer similar benefits on a larger scale. There has been some debate over the years amongst members of our school about the wisdom of encouraging students to attend conferences. Given the number of conferences currently being organized in areas of relevance to linguistics/applied linguistics students, it would be possible to do a David Lodge (*Changing places, Small world, Nice work*) continuous circuit. Some argue that too many conferences can distract students from getting on with their writing. Realistically, however, money is generally a practical constraint, and in my observation, students quickly learn for themselves to assess the benefits and disadvantages of conference attendance. Provided they are offering a paper, Victoria students can obtain faculty funding to assist with conference expenses, and most staff encourage their postgraduates to attend at least one local conference per year. Writing the paper ideally moves their research along, while the presentation exposes them to a wider range of opinions. (A practice run with their research group or PhD support group is common and beneficial to all.) In addition, postgraduates welcome the opportunity to meet others working in their research areas, and develop a feel for the breadth of the issues currently exercising (applied) linguists elsewhere. In my view, where funding can be obtained (e.g. through scholarships or research grants), there are also considerable benefits in students attending overseas conferences in relevant areas. The exposure to an even wider academic community is very valuable, as well as an opportunity to appreciate where their research fits into the bigger picture within (applied) linguistics. Conference presentations can also provide a basis for publications, and contribute to networking for elusive postdoctoral positions. In some cases, students return with a greater appreciation of their own situation and support structures, which is always welcome!

16.5.6 Location, location

Again the counsel of perfection is to attempt to locate postgraduate students working in related areas in shared and adjacent rooms, and ideally close to staff with similar interests. The benefits are incalculable, since it is the conversations which take place in the corridor, at the kitchen sink, or in the door jambs that many subsequently report helped them over a hump or reinvigorated their flagging energies. Because of intense space restrictions, we do not have a postgraduate social room, but we are in no doubt of the benefits such a place to socialize would offer. Even the limited opportunities for discussion provided to postgraduates by our morning tea room (where many turn up on different days) testify to the benefits of fostering community spirit among staff and postgraduates.

16.5.7 Life after the thesis

Once the thesis is submitted, it is tempting as a supervisor to heave a sigh of relief and move on to the next student needing support. But, of course, from the student's perspective a great deal more is required. Providing some (part time) research work which makes use of the skills they have developed is always much appreciated if it is possible, while they wait the interminable time it generally takes for a thesis to be examined and for the reports to be processed. Again this is more likely to be possible in a department which has research projects underway, and research teams to which a student can contribute. Encouraging seminar and conference presentations to give some publicity and exposure to the student's findings is important, as well as providing opportunities to start drafting material for publication.

Co-writing as a first step is an attractive option for many students who lack confidence in submitting to international journals, and this can provide a very valuable bridge to subsequent independent writing. Supervisors can also help by advising on how to select appropriate publishing outlets, and modelling how to respond to reviewers' critical comments with energy and enthusiasm, rather than collapsing in a deflated heap and burying the article in a bottom drawer. If the students' thesis will make a good book, the supervisor can advise on how to prepare a book proposal, making use of the examiners' comments in this task.

Another responsibility of a good supervisor is keeping an eye open for post-doctoral fellowships (which seem to be as rare as hen's teeth in linguistics/applied linguistics these days), as well as for possible academic jobs.

Finally, however, while all these aspects of support for postgraduate students (departmental culture, involvement with other students, academic satisfaction) contribute to the likelihood of prompt completion, the single most important factor is the quality of their relationship with their supervisor (Bair and Haworth 2004). Nothing can substitute for a trusting and intellectually stimulating relationship. Developing that takes time and good will, of course, and sometimes a lot of coffee and biscuits, but it is well worth it.

16.6 Conclusion

Performance Based Research Funding, and more specifically the inclusion of PhD completions as a source of additional research revenue for tertiary institutions in New Zealand, means that we now have a very concrete financial incentive to improve the quality of postgraduate supervision. NZ Ministry of Education figures for 2008 indicate that five years after enrolment more than 40% of masters thesis students and more than 65% of PhD students had not completed their degrees, and their estimate of long-term completion rates were no higher than 58% for masters and even lower for PhD degrees (State of Education in New Zealand 2008). This is in line with international figures which state that 40–60% of students who begin doctorates do not complete (Bair and Haworth 2004). We do not have specific figures for linguistics and applied linguistics, but I suspect our completion rates in New Zealand are somewhat better than average. Nonetheless, many of our students do drop out as the going gets tough. This chapter has identified some of the ways we can help reduce the attrition rate. In 2006, NZ universities were allocated a substantial amount for each PhD completion, and this amount doubled in 2007. This provides a good deal of leverage to those wishing to improve the standard of postgraduate supervision in their departments.

Just as important, however, are the academic benefits of excellent postgraduate supervision, not only in terms of the intellectual development of the student and the enhancement of their career prospects, but also to the supervisor who, in a good supervision relationship, is always learning, and whose own intellectual development and research skills cannot help but be enriched by such a relationship.

References

Bair, C.R. and J.G. Haworth. 2004. 'Doctoral student attrition and persistence: A meta-synthesis of research'. In *Higher education: Handbook of theory and research*, Vol. 19, pp. 481-534, ed. J.C. Smart. Dordrecht: Kluwer.

Dinham, S. and C. Scott. 1999. *The doctorate: Talking about the degree*. Research Report, University of Western Sydney, Australia.

Harper, J. 2005. *Worth their weight in gold: Tapping the potential of postgraduate students*. Report by Postgraduate Research Office, Victoria University of Wellington.

Morrow, J. 2000. 'Ensuring supervision quality'. *The Third Degree* 2 (1): 10-11.

Neale, J. 2000. 'Quality in postgraduate research: The thesis supervision "exit" questionnaire'. Paper presented at New Zealand Association of Research in Education, Waikato University, November 2000.

Smith, L.T. 1999. *Decolonizing methodologies: Research and indigenous peoples*. London and New York: Zed Books.

State of Education in New Zealand 2008. Strategy and System Performance, Ministry of Education. Available at: http://www.educationcounts.govt.nz/publications/ece/2551/34702/34656/7

Some additional useful references for postgraduates and their supervisors

Becker, L. 2004. *How to manage your postgraduate course*. Basingstoke: Palgrave Macmillan.

Churchill, H. and T. Sanders. 2007. *Getting your PhD: A practical insiders' guide*. Los Angeles: SAGE Publications.

Dunleavy, P. 2003. *Authoring a PhD: How to plan, draft, write, and finish a doctoral thesis or dissertation*. Basingstoke and New York: Palgrave Macmillan.

Eley, A.R. and R. Jennings. 2005. *Effective postgraduate supervision: Improving the student–supervisor relationship*. Maidenhead: Open University Press and McGraw-Hill Education

Evans, D. and P. Gruba. 2002. *How to write a better thesis*. 2nd edn; Melbourne: Melbourne University Press.

Finn, J.A. 2005. *Getting a PhD: An action plan to help manage your research, your supervisor and your project*. London: Routledge.

Hart, C. 2001. *Doing a literature search: A comprehensive guide for the social sciences*. London: SAGE Publications.

Locke, L.F., W.W. Spirduso and S.J. Silverman. 2007. *Proposals that work: A guide for planning dissertations and grant proposals*. Thousand Oaks: SAGE Publications.

Litosseliti, L. (ed.) 2009. *Research methods in linguistics*. London: Continuum
Marshall, S. and N. Green. 2007. *Your PhD companion: A handy mix of practical tips, sound advice and helpful commentary to see you through your PhD*. Oxford: How To Books.
Phillips, E. and D. Pugh 2000. *How to get a PhD*. 3rd edn; Buckingham: Open University Press.
Punch, K.F. 2006. *Developing effective research proposals*. London and Thousand Oaks, CA: SAGE Publications.
Rountree, K. and T. Laing. 1996. *Writing by degrees: A practical guide to writing theses and research papers*. Auckland: Longman.
Rudestam, K.E. and R.R. Newton. 2007. *Surviving your dissertation: A comprehensive guide to content and process*. Los Angeles: SAGE Publications.
Staines, G.M., K. Johnson and M. Bonacci. 2008. *Social sciences research: Research, writing, and presentation strategies for students*. Lanham, MD: Scarecrow Press.
Swales, J.M. and C.B. Feak. 2004. 2nd edn; *Academic writing for graduate students: Essential skills and tasks*. Ann Arbor: University of Michigan Press; Bristol: University Presses Marketing.
Thomas, R.M. and D.L. Brubaker. 2008. *Theses and dissertations: A guide to planning, research, and writing*. Thousand Oaks, CA: Corwin Press.
White, P. 2009. *Developing research questions: A guide for social scientists [electronic resource]*. Basingstoke and New York: Palgrave Macmillan.
Wisker, G. 2008. *Postgraduate research handbook: Succeed with your MA, MPhil, EdD and PhD*. Basingstoke and New York: Palgrave Macmillan.

Appendix 16.1

Notes distilled from feedback from current and recently completed linguistics and applied linguistics PhD students at Victoria University of Wellington 2006.

A good supervisor:

- sets up regular (weekly/fortnightly) meetings which should only be postponed if the student has a good reason (this is *much* better for most students than a system where the supervisor leaves it to the student to initiate meetings);
- gives the student full attention during regular meetings (i.e. so they don't feel squashed in between other obligations);
- actively involves both supervisors during the development of the research proposal and, as appropriate, also others working in related areas;
- checks time-line or progress sheet at the start or end of each meeting to provide a sense of continuity;
- demonstrates genuine interest in the student's subject area;
- has extensive knowledge of the general subject area (makes useful points, recommends relevant reading, shows insight, inspires confidence);
- requires the student to write something for every meeting; draft chapters are a good goal from the beginning;
- provides direction through student's summaries of each meeting and goal-setting for the next, i.e. requires student to record agreements, and email them to the supervisor;
- ensures a sound research proposal is prepared within a reasonable initial period;
- provides written feedback promptly on material the student has written;
- is available and reliable (responds swiftly to emails, etc.);
- engages with the student: provides constructive as well as challenging comments on the student's work, shows interest in the topic and also in the student personally; is positive and not patronizing;
- leaves enough rope to make mistakes, but not enough to hang with;
- assists with the student's professional development (gives advice on who to talk to, directs student to material relevant to the topic, organizes discussion sessions, provides opportunities for relevant tutoring, recommends and assists with preparation for conferences, supports and encourages publications, scholarship applications, faculty grant applications, etc.);
- shares opinions, ideas, contacts and 'inside' knowledge;
- gets the right mix of pushing and leaving the student to get on with it;
- provides encouragement and direction when the student is flagging;
- is available to provide prompt helpful feedback when pressure is on to complete;
- helps the student to produce publications and conference presentations from their thesis.

Acknowledgments

I would like to thank David Crabbe and Bernadette Vine for reading a draft of this chapter and for providing helpful feedback. I am also grateful to Brian King for his valuable comments on a revised version.

Notes

[*] **Janet Holmes**

I began my BA majoring in English literature at Leeds University with classes of over 300 students. I was attracted to the linguistics courses mainly because they had smaller enrolments and thus smaller classes which lent themselves to discussion. I got hooked on linguistics, entranced first by transformational grammar, which was then in its exciting infancy, and then by sociolinguistics which became a life-time passion. I was lucky to have very good teachers: John Strover, Tony Cowie, John Spencer and especially John Pride who was at the forefront of work in sociolinguistics at the time. He was appointed to a chair in English language at Victoria in 1969 and I was appointed as a lecturer in linguistics in 1970. The readings in the honours course we jointly taught formed the basis for the *Penguin Readings in Sociolinguistics*, one of the earliest sociolinguistics textbooks.

When I started teaching linguistics at Victoria University I was the only lecturer in the area. But with the support of those teaching English language, including the professor of English I.A. Gordon, linguistics steadily grew, and we first established a major, and then a department of linguistics, which has now been integrated into the School of Linguistics and Applied Language Studies.

Because I have never moved from Victoria, it could be thought that I have had a rather homogeneous career with little variety. Nothing could be further from the truth. Until very recently I taught a new course or at least a new series of lectures almost every year of my life at Victoria. I have experienced, and mainly enjoyed, many administrative roles including director of two boards of studies, head of department, head of school, dean, assistant vice chancellor, research director and convenor of many, many committees. In recent years, I have enjoyed establishing research areas first in corpus linguistics, and most recently in language in the workplace. Directing these has ensured my academic life has always been challenging and interesting. Overseas travel associated with my research has provided much-appreciated opportunities for discussion with colleagues. And finally the many postgraduate students who have come to work in the areas I teach and research have provided further enrichment as well as valuable feedback which informs the article I have written for this book.

1. The phrase 'beyond compare' is a comment by a satisfied PhD student on their supervisor (Harper 2005: 14). The quotation is taken from responses to a survey of 25 postgraduate students undertaken in the School of Linguistics and Applied Language Studies, Victoria University of Wellington. 2003.
2. Performance Based Research Funding includes PhD completions as one important source of funding for tertiary institutions.
3. The VUW School of Linguistics and Applied Language Studies, like other NZ university linguistics departments, encourages staff and postgraduates to work together in groupings with overlapping research interests where possible. Such groups may simply share reading material and discuss each other's work, while in some cases they actually work together in research teams.

17 Field methods: Where the rubber meets the road

Wes Collins *

17.1 Introduction: What to expect in this chapter

Field methods is a course that lots of linguistics students dread. It is kind of like a full physical exam. There's no hiding anything. We academics are a vulnerable sort. We don't usually mind showing what we know, but we are often quite reticent to broadcast what we don't know. And exposing what we don't know is basically what happens in a field methods (FM) course.

On the other hand, as the subtitle mentions, FM is where the linguistic rubber meets the road; where theory and practice come together. So you can get students that shine here that maybe have had trouble in other aspects of their linguistics training. Acoustic phonetics and syntax can be daunting, but these pale before the prospect of actually producing uvular fricatives or ergative case in a 'normal' stream of speech meant to communicate some semantic reality to another human being.

17.1.1 L2 acquisition

In this chapter we will consider what field linguists do and how to help train them to do it. In doing so, some of my own biases will leak out, first of which is that I think FM should include a strong language-acquisition component. Not all FM courses are taught this way. Indeed, I would venture that few are, particularly in graduate school. There is just too much data out there waiting to be discovered to waste time with one's own mouth and mind trying to pronounce and understand what the paradigms are begging to tell us. Speaking these data in some sort of relevant human context is often (usually?) considered irrelevant. But that is one place where the data people would be wrong.

Learning another language is a delight, and it is surprising what students can master in a semester (or preferably two) if expectations are high and there is some guidance. Even in FM courses that I have taken where language learning was not discussed, I made it a personal priority to learn to communicate – without notes – with our class language coach. Certainly there was a lot of repetition. How are you? How is your wife? How is your daughter? How are your two sons? How are you feeling today? Did you sleep well last night? We would go through this ritual every day, and I would add to it as I was able, making it a personal goal to learn and use at least two new sentences per week.

This may seem like fake conversation, but it isn't. After all, the phatic use of language is a legitimate use of it, where language is used simply to 'keep the friendship and communication channel open'. Language coaches delight to actually talk to someone in their language, contrived and predictable as the conversations may seem. Speaking someone's language sends a profound message. You matter to me. So much so that I am willing to stumble around in your language trying to communicate with memorized sentences. So even starting humbly is still starting. This is an important lesson for linguists to learn. I realize that computer linguistics students and psycholinguists and many others may never utter a syllable in a language other than English, but FM is the one place where we can try to get these students on board. Speaking another language is fun, meaningful and deeply satisfying. And it is the foundation of good fieldwork.

17.1.2 Good ethnography

Another of my biases is the privileging of good ethnography. Most of my students are committed to living long term among minority-language speakers, many of whom have no history of literacy. An important part of their training is in how to learn a language without the benefit of books, trained teachers and a class in 'Xish' 101. I realize that ethnography is something that does not usually get used when a student spends just a year or less *in situ*, but looking at the world as an ethnographer is a nice way to stay fascinated and engaged in life in general, and for those who have the luxury of long-term or oft-repeated contact with a group, I have found it a wonderful way to learn. So my FM classes promote the reading and teaching of good ethnography, particularly Geertz 1973 and Becker 1996 (1984).

There are entire courses in ethnography, so why try to jam the discipline into an already overflowing FM course? Fair enough. But there are also entire courses in phonetics, phonology, morphology, syntax and sociolinguistics. That does not keep us from tying them all together and including practical aspects of each in a single course. Indeed, it is just this eclectic nature that is the hallmark of a great FM course.

So those are two of my biases: L2 acquisition and ethnography. I mention them first because they are not part of most FM courses, and some would argue that they do not belong. And there is plenty to do in a FM course even without the additional emphases. Nevertheless, I consider them crucial to a great course, which leads me to the following confession. Students will not get everything they need for effective fieldwork from a single course (or two) in FM, but if they can capture the professor's own fascination with the language and culture they work on in class, and if they can come to see a relationship between theory and practice, and if they can get excited about life-long learning and the value and legitimacy of others' ways, I could wish for no more.

To language learning and ethnography, the other general topics I consider crucial to a solid course are an introduction to fieldwork and professional and personal organization along with some ideas on the FM course itself.

17.1.3 An introduction to fieldwork

In terms of fieldwork, several things are obvious. We need accurate data. Eliciting can be boring, but it is critical to successful fieldwork and an effective FM course. And if it is hard on us, just think what our poor coach must be thinking. By making the coach a collaborator rather than merely a data bank, we can humanize our quest and help build skills into our coach's life as well. Related to getting data and using it are issues concerning the ethics of fieldwork and elicitation. The writing or recording of some languages is considered taboo by tribal elders (especially among some North American Indian groups). This is a FM course, so we do not spend too much time on this issue (these tend to be languages we do not choose for FM), but we mention such a situation since we do not work or live in a vacuum, even in a FM classroom.

Another fieldwork skill is good recording technique. I ask students to record electronically a variety of language data, from phonetic utterances, in order to help distinguish (and analyse) phonetic segments, to a full (one- to two-minute long) text in order to listen to intonation contours and suprasegmental phenomena, and to gather sentences in some kind of context. Students also develop and record at least two language-learning exercises.

Computers. I give a single lecture on computer helps such as PRAAT and SIL's new software, but we do not require that these be used in class. Most of what I ask for in the course can be accomplished in Word – or in longhand. That may disappoint e-freaks, but it seems to me to be best to get ideas across that will span changes and improvements in software, without ignoring the help that these programs can give us.

Usually in an undergraduate programme, students will not have any fieldwork experience. That makes the professor the local expert and the disburser of practical advice. From never leaving home without duct tape, extra batteries and plastic bags to stashing away some Constant Comment tea bags and a deck of playing cards, the history of fieldwork has given us lots of ideas about how to survive and even prosper in the field. Practical advice extends to relationships (linguist–local, linguist–missionary, linguist–other linguist, linguist–political leaders, etc.) on the field. I do not spend a lot of time on this, since a FM course has its own purpose, but I do commit a lecture to all these practical concerns.

17.1.4 Professional and personal organization

It is pretty easy to elicit data – especially nouns. There are thousands of them, after all. But getting them into files where you need them and can access them is another story. Getting one's self organized and staying so are huge obstacles to good fieldwork. Section 17.4.2 discusses a number of ways to do this.

17.1.5 Don't forget these

To these four major topics I would add four more issues related specifically to a FM classroom setting: course assignments, class logistics, the advisability of a FM textbook, and the use of published sources.

Assignments. I include assignments in phonetics, phonology, morphology, lexicon, syntax and culture in my FM classes. I want the class to be fun, but it also has to accomplish some basics. I ask students for a write-up in each of these areas. At the end of the course, I help them choose one of their topics to present to the class in a FM colloquium.

Logistics. A problem we have in FM that other linguistics professors do not have is getting everyone the time they need with the language coach (without abusing the coach), while also providing time for students to watch the professor in elicitation sessions. Then there is both course content (mentioned above) to cover, as well as language-related issues that must be dealt with, as well as meetings between professor and students to make sure people are moving forward. Actually, a good FM course mimics fieldwork in general in that there is so much going on that getting and staying organized is one of the big challenges to success.

Textbook. Below I suggest the pros of using a textbook for a FM course. Since part of our course is aimed at discussing work 'on the field' I gravitate to books like Crowley 2007 and Bowern 2008 that discuss not just analysis and elicitation, but life and organization issues as well.

Using published sources. On the one hand, it would be nice to treat the language focused on in the course as if it were being discovered and described for the very first time, *ex nihilo*. On the other hand, consulting published sources is one of the ways we learn about languages and find areas for further research. I will discuss the use of these valuable sources of information in section 17.5.

17.1.6 A final word

Field methods is as much about personal discovery as it is about general linguistic discovery. Even in my own fieldwork, insights that I have made have often been made before me by someone else – usually Nora England, the 'queen' of Mam linguistics. When I shared this with my graduate advisor, Don Winford, his response was, 'That's great. You're obviously on the right track!' So just because insights have been seen by others, students should not be discouraged. After all, they are still insights.

One of my goals in FM is for the students to experience the fun of discovery. That they can effectively learn something of an L2 as young (and sometimes not so young) adults and enjoy the ride is important to me. Although it is highly unlikely that students will develop their observations from class into peer-reviewed journal articles, the fact that they are in touch with a new language as well as a new way to think about academics, where they do real-time, original research, is well within the purview of a good FM class.

17.2 L2 Acquisition

Effective communication goes beyond language, but the train of friendship certainly runs through the land of language. This strained metaphor is just to say that language matters in many, many ways.

This is especially true in today's globalizing world, where languages are being laid aside like leg weights in order for speakers to step up and compete in the real world of English, Spanish and a few 'super languages'.

But languages lost are a loss to all of us as we are deprived of understanding and hopefully interacting with yet 'another way to be'. Much has been written on this topic. Readers are directed to Krauss 1992, Crystal 2000, Nettle and Romaine 2000 and Grenoble and Whaley 2006 for starters. We do not take much class time to discuss the phenomenon of language shift and death, but it permeates the background as one of the reasons why FM is an important subject.

Of course, language death is not new. Languages have come and gone on the world stage since early time. In our own academic tradition, Boas' purpose for much of his linguistic anthropology programme was the 'salvaging' (Boas' term) of minority language data and cultural practices. Although linguistic salvage (now, less iconically, called 'documentation') is not the same as speaking the language, the chasm between dying languages and those which continue to prosper is one of moment-by-moment individual choices as speakers decide for themselves in real time which code will serve them best in light of present reality.

Over the span of the thirty years that I have worked among the Mam, I have seen attitudes change. Early on during our time in Guatemala, many refused to speak

Mam in our presence assuming that we would belittle them or laugh. Today there are many dozens of books in the language, along with bilingual schools, trained indigenous teachers, Mam institutions and events that celebrate local language and culture. Many factors have conspired to create this happy circumstance (although no one is assuming that Mam is somehow 'safe' from endangerment and shift), but certainly one ingredient has been the presence of a few 'prestigious' outsiders who have learned to speak and appreciate the language and its speakers.

So language is not merely about communication. Rather it is about life and culture and history and politics and the future. Helping our students understand, celebrate, and build linguistic and cultural diversity is clearly worth a pep talk from a FM professor.

So how does one go about learning a language? There are lots of methods, many having something to do with repetition. Since a recording and playback device is infinitely more patient than even the most Job-like of coaches, I recommend that students record some tool phrases early on and memorize them: a greeting and leave taking, assorted small talk, asking about one's family and health (if appropriate), telling about one's self, and so on (see Healey 1975 and Brewster and Brewster 1976 for details). Although these small-talk sentences may not be very helpful in terms of language analysis, they do provide a base upon which to build, what the Brewsters call a 'sticky little ball' that other insights can adhere to. To a sentence like 'I have two sisters' one can easily expand the context to 'I have three brothers', 'I have six cousins', and so on. These can then be inquired of: 'How are your two sisters?' 'How are your two brothers?' 'How are your six cousins?' For a more academic (and not uncontroversial) discussion of L2 acquisition, see http://languageinstinct.blogspot.com/2006/08/krashen-revolution.html.

Early on I request that students make a recording of a language-learning exercise. This might be something like learning the future tense paradigm such as.

prompt: I went to the store.	response: I'm going to go to the store.
prompt: He bought a bicycle.	response: He's going to buy a bicycle.
prompt: We ate lunch.	response: We're going to eat lunch.
etc.	

The idea here is for students to get the language coach to participate in preparing pedagogical materials that will help the student learn different aspects of the language. In exercises like these, after the prompt, the student provides the response. This is followed by the coach giving the correct response which is then repeated by the student. Again, see Brewster and Brewster 1976 for lots of detail and ideas.

Early in my time in Guatemala I worked on a Mam phrase, literally repeating it over a thousand times and listening to and mimicking it with the aid of an old cassette 'tape loop'. The next day when I proudly spoke the phrase in public, my coach said, 'you almost have it'. Years later, a Mam friend was commenting on my language ability telling me that I was 'almost normal'. Adult language acquisition is a humbling experience, good for the soul.

L2 acquisition is important for many reasons. It helps us establish intuitions about what sounds right and what doesn't. It encourages the language coach, which is important, as he or she is pouring their linguistic life into twenty students. It gives students a chance to learn acquisition techniques and to be successful in a controlled environment. It can be fun and very rewarding to communicate in another's birth language. And for locals, outsiders' speaking their language builds prestige in the language. In addition, it is hard to explain that we are linguists, those who study language, if we do not care about actually learning the local language.

And what other course will students have where L2 acquisition is even discussed? That is why I think it is appropriate to include in a good FM course: learn the language as best you can. Please!

17.3 Why ethnography?

Good ethnography is impossible to do in a FM course. Nevertheless, I believe it should be modelled and taught, so that students can recognize it. All my teaching is peppered with insights and experiences gained and from lots of contact with Mam Indians (some thirty years) and native Spanish-speaking university students from throughout Latin America. When we can ground what we teach in practice, it adds gravitas and reality to what we have to say.

Since the most powerful and persuasive evidence for claims about a group should come from an analysis of the daily life and interactions of members of the group, an appropriate research tool should focus on these aspects of living. This is what ethnography is, a privileging of the emic point of view, that is, how locals understand their own lives, or, as Malinowski put it, trying 'to grasp the native's point of view, his relation to life, to realize *his* vision of *his* world' (1922: 25, emphasis (and androcentric pronouns) in the original). In a summary of the ethnographic method, Zaharlick says:

> Ethnographers establish social relationships with others in order to learn from them their ways of life. Through firsthand, long-term, participant observation, using themselves as research instruments and using an eclectic approach to data collection and analysis, ethnographers view human events in the larger contexts in which they naturally occur… The knowledge and understandings gained through the ethnographic process are then presented in the form of an ethnographic report that describes in rich detail what it is like to be a member of that culture… A good ethnography systematically describes the flow of behavior in a way that allows others to comprehend at an emotional level the events set before them and to understand the context motivating these events (1992: 121).

This emotional connection with the reader is a hallmark of good ethnography. And the fact that the connection is by means of the participation (both competently, and sometimes incompetently) of the ethnographer in a new culture, helps to make these unknown people and their life ways come alive.

I have students read three articles for the course's emphasis on ethnography. Zaharlick's (1992) briefly explains the method, while Geertz (1973) and Becker (1996 [1984]) flesh it out. Good ethnography reads more like a novel than a treatise. In my view it is the most accessible of all academic writing.

My ethnography emphasis is meant to help raise cultural questions within the framework of what comes up in the daily data sessions and the insight gained through elicitation and observation. This is helpful for the short culture paper that the students write.

17.4 An introduction to fieldwork

Everett says, in essence, that fieldwork is basically work that is done in the field. This seems straightforward enough, but it has broad implications. How does one get to the field? What shots and vaccinations are needed? Do I need a visa? How can I stay healthy? Should I steer clear of politics (good luck!)? Will I have any privacy? Will I get culture shock? Do I have to eat grubs? Should I lend or give money away? How do I go about finding language associates to work with? How much should I pay them? What should I wear? Will people like me? Can I take pictures? What do they want from me? Do I need permission to allocate in a village? How will I ever pay for all this? There are approximately a million more similar questions.

Early in our life in the village the local Peace Corps volunteer got drunk, tried to leave a small diner without paying, got in a shouting match with the *señora*, poured what remained of his beer into the cauldron of soup, and spent the night in jail. When I saw him the next day he told me of his inebriation and incarceration, to which I responded,

> 'Oh yeah, I heard all about it.'
> 'How could you possibly know?' he queried. 'It was late last night.'
> 'Are you kidding?' I said. 'There are no secrets here.'
> He turned white. He thought that he had lots of secrets.

Most FM students plan to do fieldwork at some future date. Hopefully, the stories told about them will be a bit better than this one. They are about to become very public people, and very rich. They may not feel very rich, and they may prefer their privacy, but those notions are about to change radically.

We can help our students with the practical and emotional side of things. On these, perhaps more than on anything else, will depend a student's success in the field. If one cannot live there or be happy there, or fit in in some way, the research is unlikely to amount to much. On the other hand, if a student loves her or his allocation along with the people that live there and the language they speak and the culture they live out, then an individual can make a big impact and be impacted in a big way.

There are a number of articles that deal with what you need to consider before leaving the West for the East or the South. Crowley 2007 is a good choice as is Bowern 2008 and several articles in Newman and Ratliff 2001; see also Everett forthcoming.

17.4.1 Ethics

It is common to discuss in FM classes the ethics of research, both in terms of what we 'take' and what we leave behind.

When one is eliciting paradigms – to the henhouse, from the henhouse, over the henhouse, behind the henhouse – it is hard to think that there are ethical issues involved, and linguists aren't usually privy to the kinds of research that psychologists or sociologists do in terms of issues that might be embarrassing or sensitive such as sex, local politics, family relations and so on.

Nevertheless, there are ethical issues to deal with. One of the first is whether locals want or agree to the notion of writing down their language. As I mentioned above, it seems more likely that opposition to L1 literacy would come from North America than Latin America, Asia or Africa, but one should not assume that everyone will consider literacy like we do in the West. I admit to harbouring a highly pro-literacy bias when it comes to language vitality and revitalization, but not all share my enthusiasm.

Both Bowern and Crowley discuss ethics in some detail, so we won't belabour this issue here except to mention some categories of concern: We must treat people respectfully and explain as best we can what we are doing and how the products of our work will be used and disseminated. Participants need to understand as much as possible what we are doing and they must be allowed to abandon the project if they are uncomfortable with it for any reason. They should never be recorded on the sly (see Labov 1972: 61-62), and no texts should be published that could harm someone in any way ('The time my stupid neighbour and her ugly husband poisoned our cat').

The issue of paying a language coach is always an issue. It may seem amazing to us that someone would come to help us for several hours a day and not request or expect remuneration. We may feel that we are being set up and that after several months we will be asked to arrange for our coach to go to the States. One man I had recently met in Guatemala asked if I would lend him $50,000 to buy a truck. It can certainly seem that all proportionality goes out of the window when people begin to talk finances. A good resource is Maranz 2001, which deals specifically with Africa, although I have found it helpful in understanding facets of Latin American cultures as well.

The other side of ethics is what we need to leave behind. In some countries with a fairly small and inaccessible indigenous population, university linguistics students are sent out year after year to the same small towns and the same tired populace in order to elicit the same paradigms: my cow, your cow, his cow, our (inclusive) cow, etc.; please! Let us somehow work together to do something to help locals by meeting with local officials or leaders and see how we can help the community in some coherent way. In the small town where we lived we were able to make contacts for the construction of a small village library which has served the community now for over twenty years. The Guatemala government has provided a librarian, 'friends of the library' have donated books and equipment, and everyone feels pretty good about it.

I participated on a local 'community development committee' and helped design and erect a welcome sign in Mam at the entrance to the town. We participated in a programme to provide trash cans for the market area, to establish a playground for children and other projects which weren't simply giveaways, but projects in which outsiders and locals worked together to help meet local needs.

In addition, we published simple (and, much later, not-so-simple) booklets, other reading materials, both popular and academic, calendars, posters, and general publications, all aimed, in part, at building the prestige of the language.

The bottom line is that when we participate in community life, people rarely feel that they are getting ripped off. By giving as well as receiving, we participate to some degree in the daily give and take of local life. This is meaningful for all involved.

Be respectful of local custom. We are guests in a community and we should act accordingly. We are not only living for ourselves, but for researchers who may come later. If we are unappreciated, it is less likely that open arms will be extended to the next researcher, or the next.

17.4.2 Getting and staying organized

Organizing one's data is a factor of organizing one's self. Of course, there are many ways to do this. Most of my professor friends have a piling system that works for them, but when it comes to data, it needs to be more readily available than just motioning which pile it is on (or more likely, under).

The basic document of field work is the data notebook. This should be a bound (not loose leaf), lined notebook which basically documents a chronological listing of your linguistic life in the field. I recommend that researchers keep a parallel notebook, a personal diary, which should be cross-referenced to the data notebook. This book talks about your life in the field: your insights, feelings, concerns, experiences, interesting anecdotes and so on. Information in both notebooks should all be dated and pages should be numbered for easier access.

I do something that to many verges on the sacrilegious, linguistically speaking. I do not write directly in my data notebook. Rather, I write in a kind of 'pre-notebook' with circles and arrows, abbreviations, cryptic notations and other notes to myself that border on the illegible. Then within minutes (but never more than a few hours) of the elicitation session, I make a nice and neat recopy of the 'pre-notebook' into the data notebook. This works for me. If a datum is incomprehensible, having it in my 'actual' data notebook rather than my pre-notebook does not make it any more helpful. It simply means I need to re-elicit said information, understand it, and rewrite it in my data notebook. That way everything in my data notebook has been minimally processed.

The pre-notebook has a suggested small series of issues I want to deal with that day, but this can all change by the exigencies of the moment, what the coach feels is important, where our rabbit trails lead us and so on. By the time the information gets to the data notebook, it has been considered and minimally processed. So the actual data notebook is a record of what we really did at that session, not a compendium of what I had hoped to do.

Never write on the back of a sheet in the notebook. If the book gets damp, what is barely legible becomes hieroglyphic and otherwise useless. Also leave lots of space in and around your data for further annotation. Write only in ink, and annotations can be in coloured ink. Each section of the notebook should have some kind of title (dual and plural markers, prepositions, relational nouns, tense, etc.) and these titles or topics should go to an index (that you prepare) in the back of the book. The index need not be alphabetical while you are compiling it, but when the notebook is almost full and you are ready to move to the next one, it is helpful to consolidate the index of the previous notebook and to alphabetize it on the last few pages of the book. Also write an introduction at the beginning of the notebook to remind you of dates, places, language coach and general topics. If every page in the notebook is numbered, it becomes fairly easy to find data which was fresh when you wrote it, but that has become buried under new data, new hypotheses and the vagaries of your memory. This is also a reason why the notebook should not be a 500-page tome. How much easier to find data that are organized in smallish 75- to 100-page bound notebooks which have been duly, numbered, dated and from which an index has been created. Leave the first ten pages of the notebook blank as well for later annotation and an introduction.

From the notebook, exercises can be developed, lexical families can be established, sentence types pondered and so on. I use file folders to organize data that originate in my notebook. For example, if I get terms for wasp and bee, I can create a file of insects, or stinging insects, or good and bad insects, or bugs in general, or any kind of classification that is meaningful to me or my coach. This is a great way to learn vocabulary in some kind of context. The bug file can be extended to phrases (fly in the ointment, a hornets' nest, a beehive of activity, a bee in the bonnet, etc.). Meaningful sentences can become part of the file: Malaria is carried by the female anopheles mosquito. Flies on your food are gross.

Perhaps there are stories about bugs. Don't laugh. Jiminy Cricket entertained and taught many of us growing up, as did the 1950s' cult horror movie *The Fly*. These data and comments can all go in the file on bugs. And although these might be spread throughout the data notebook, they can show up in your files, neatly arranged and ready for further processing and memorization.

I have files on occupations, people's names (which I practised and studied daily), animals, trees, houses, construction, men's and women's activities and responsibilities, and hordes more. As I learned, the files became more phonologized (words beginning with ejectives, syllable types, phonotactics, etc.) and eventually more grammatical (sentence types, aspect markers, tense paradigms, etc.).

In all of this, the notebook feeds the files which contain the content of things I am trying to learn at any given time.

For ideas of types of things to elicit, see www.sil.org/Linguistics/Doing Linguistics/contents.htm

It may be clear by now that I am a list person. In the village, I also made lists of activities that I planned to accomplish each day: Memorize a short monologue and speak it to ten different people, spend 30 minutes repeatedly listening to a recorded text on planting corn, elicit a file on local ailments and diseases, help a local man put a roof on his house, add ten verbs to the dictionary file, spend 30 minutes practising helpful phrases and 30 minutes on self-prepared grammar exercises and so on.

By sticking to a schedule we can see our progress.

17.4.3 Computers

Computers are helpful in analysis and organization, and since these notions are part of the FM task, we should at least let our students know some of the things that are out there.

I recommend looking at the SIL website: http://sil.org/computing/catalog/ index.asp. The website lists over 60 software programs that are downloadable, many of which are free. A few to mention include AMPLE, which is a morphological parser; DDP (Dictionary Development Process), a program designed to input words as they are learned and which can be extended into a nicely formatted dictionary; IT (Interlinear Text) is a program that aligns text with glosses and which, based on user-inputted data, can semi-automatically parse new text.

Speech Analyzer is helpful for measuring phonetic segments, analyzing pitch, creating spectrograms and measuring fundamental frequencies. It is similar to Praat, which is another excellent phonetics tool. For a discussion and download of Praat, go to www.fon.hum.uva.nl/praat. Praat also offers a short tutorial.

At the SIL website, you can also download the IPA (international phonetic alphabet) for free. There is also a program called IPA Help which pronounces the IPA symbols.

The newest suite of programs from SIL is called FieldWorks Suite and it replaces Shoebox, LinguaLinks and Toolbox. It is not particularly appropriate for use in a FM course, but it is worth a quick introduction since it has a lot of helpful programs for field workers. FieldWorks includes programs for data analysis, as well as a vocabulary manager and a helpful electronic library of useful books and articles. It also has tools for cultural analysis, including the Human Relations Area Files.

17.5 Class logistics: working with everyone's schedule.

A FM class pretty much rises and falls on the strength of the language coach and one's interaction with her or him. I suggest that a course have one coach, or perhaps two (husband and wife?) that speak the same language. Of course, you could have three or four different coaches each speaking a different L1, but that means that the course has to be that much more abstract in order to cover everyone's needs as they attack different languages. If everyone is studying the same language it means that every question that arises in class is potentially relevant and interesting to all students. So the best-case scenario for a first-time, self-directed language-learning experience is one or two coaches but just one language. That way each student and the professor are all on the same page at the same time.

For the sake of argument, I will present two scenarios, one with 12 students spread over a 17-week semester of classes, with class meeting twice a week for two hours each session. The other scenario will be 20 students over the span of an academic quarter (12 weeks).

The course requires a certain amount of time for the professor to lecture. Students need time for elicitation, but we do not want them to burn out, nor do we want to burn out the coach. This kind of elicitation is very intense and tiring for both students and coach.

17.5.1 12 students, 17 weeks, 4 hours of class per week

Before taking FM, students should have had courses in basic linguistic disciplines: phonetics, phonology, morphology, syntax and sociolinguistics. So the FM professor isn't so much teaching linguistics as applying it to a specific language and situation.

Assuming two two-hour classes per week, probably Tuesday and Thursday, the first class each week should be dedicated to course content. This includes everything

I have mentioned up to now: the readings, discussions, presentations, anecdotes, any projects, group work, explanations, course housekeeping (assignments, due dates, scheduling) and so on. Brian Joseph, one of linguistics' most distinguished professors, spends a lot of time in each undergraduate class just helping students realize what his expectations are, where students should be vis-à-vis the syllabus and their readings, and how they should be progressing in the course. This is not time wasted. It needs to be invested. Insecure students do not learn very effectively, and a FM course has a way of bringing insecurity out of the shadows.

The other two-hour class should be divided into class content and professor elicitation and the regularization of data. Early in the course, students should elicit a word list of 100 to 200 items[1] just to start getting used to sounds and phonotactics. But before too much analysis is done, perhaps by the beginning of week 3, the professor should hand out a list of these same words which have been carefully corroborated by the language coach together with the professor. There is no real purpose served by having students try to garner insights from erroneous data. Nevertheless, it is good to have them in the hot seat for a while trying to transcribe real data from a real speaker.

For this reason I recommend that students not have free access to published materials on the language for the first three to four weeks of class. Eventually, however, I make these sources available (on reserve) to help students corroborate their findings. All data discussed in class has to have been elicited by the student with the coach (not gleaned from a book). They can get ideas from the books and articles of others, but they still need to confirm the data with the coach. There may be significant dialect differences, or differences due to socio-economic class, gender, home town, age and so on, so copying data from a book may not be accurate for the dialect spoken in class.

As the course continues, the professor should help students understand what it is they are getting. Everyone is served by having accurate data, so part of the second day each week should be committed to correcting or corroborating what the students have elicited. The language coach should be present. As much as 30 minutes might go to this each Thursday.

An additional half hour would go to the professor's elicitation. Here students watch the professor relate to the coach and elicit data in such a way as to resolve pending questions. This elicitation can follow assignments that students are working on, but the professor should elicit data for her or his own study, not just to corroborate student elicitation. For ideas on teaching elicitation techniques, see Vaux and Cooper 1999.

This leaves an additional hour of class time each week. If you have 12 students, break up the class into three groups of four students each. Each group will meet with the coach for an hour, and each student will guide 15 minutes of the elicitation session, searching for data to help him or her move forward in their understanding of the questions posed.

This means that there are two more hours that need to be scheduled outside of normal class time. Groups will need to meet such that each student is exposed to an hour of elicitation, including 15 minutes where she or he directs the entire small group of four. Of course, individuals in the group can work together if they want to, with all students eliciting in a similar field, or working together on the Swadesh 200-word list, but this isn't necessary.

Putting this schedule on the calendar is a challenge, since students have other classes and activities, and the coach has a life of his or her own as well. And groups should cycle through each time slot if possible. One hour will be during class time, while the other two will be outside of regular class hours. In this way, each week each student will be exposed to a half-hour elicitation session led by the professor, and they will spend an additional four 15-minute elicitation sessions in their small group, one of which is led by said student. The professor should visit these elicitation sessions occasionally in order to offer advice or help as needed.

With an additional hour, group size could be reduced from four to three and individual elicitation sessions expanded from 15 to 20 minutes (four groups of three students each), but I do not suggest going any further than that, especially for undergraduates. Filling a 20-minute elicitation session can seem like an eternity to students (although, once initiated, these sessions seem to race by), and expanding the coach's time adds to the cost and to the difficulty of the coach being available.

17.5.2 20 students, 12 weeks, 3 hours of class per week

For 20 students and 12 weeks, you could organize five groups of four with each student in charge of 15 minutes of elicitation time. You might consider four groups of five, with 12 minutes available to each student. This is too little time and too much changing from student to student for my liking.

In terms of a Monday, Wednesday, Friday format with just an hour (probably only 50 minutes) of class time, you have got to take advantage of available time. Demand that students be prompt. Two periods a week would be dedicated to class content and one to data regularization and professor elicitation. All student elicitation sessions would be outside normal class hours, which may cause a hubbub, but once students start learning and having a good time, my experience is that they will not complain.

But the coach might. With 20 students, he or she is looking at four or five hours a week with students plus an hour of class time. It will help very much if the professor and/or students can fill in the coach about course goals and why all the repetition is important.

17.5.3 Assignments

A FM course lends itself to assignments that can be nicely scaled to the abilities of each student, especially once you get past phonetics.

My phonetics assignment is to transcribe in fairly rich detail the Swadesh list of 200 words. With an hour of elicitation time and students working together, this can usually be done by the end of week 2. Here I am just looking for a list of phones.

The phonology assignment looks at several different phonological phenomena. Students write about phonemes and allophonic variation, syllable structure and phonotactics, word templates, stress patterns and so on. Depending on the language, I may ask students to look for certain items, or I may give them a degree of freedom for their own research.

For a morphology assignment, students choose what they want based on what they have found so far in class and in elicitation sessions. This may be a short paper on similar affixes (aspect, mode, tense, etc.), or something on deontics (could, would, should, must), deixis (here, there, now, then, you, me), evidentials (I heard, I saw, I see evidence of) or a host of additional possibilities. Is an animacy distinction expressed morphologically? Are there cases marked morphologically? Is there any sign of an ergative-absolutive case system? How are passives (or anti-passives) formed? And so on.

A paper on the lexicon is often among the most engaging. Students can look for body parts extended to other objects or phenomena: head, headwaters, the headmaster, headwaiter, the head of the class, the foamy head on a drink, head of the bed or table, the head of household. See also leg, hand, eye, face, etc. Words for concepts like 'to carry' or 'to hit' may be fascinating (as they are in Mam) depending on the language. Colours are interesting (Berlin and Kay 1969). Many languages use animal names to focus on certain aspects of a person's character or body (turkey, dog, fox, cow, bull, chicken, pig, weasel, monkey, among many others (including bugs)). Are there different numbers depending on what is being counted? Are there dual or trial forms of plurals? Are there classifiers in the language?

For a syntax write-up students can pursue question formation, word order, focus, phrase structure rules, clitics, anaphora, reflexive and reciprocal action, subordination, and on and on. The professor might choose one of these assignments to be a group project with a single paper submitted and a class presentation.

These need not be exhaustive studies, but when taken together it becomes clear that students have made a significant dent into what one would like to learn about a language.

17.5.4 Should you use a textbook?

I have been involved in a number of FM courses as both a student and a professor. Some used textbooks while others did not.

One of my FM professors is one of the world's great phonologists. His introduction to a FM class was basically, 'This is Abdul. Abdul how do you say "man" in your language?' When a professor is this committed to gathering data, a textbook is probably not necessary.

My own view is that a textbook can be a big help. When one is in the field, what is difficult is usually not data gathering, but living under the microscope of people so different from ourselves. When everyone heads off to bed just after sunset, what does one do for entertainment without electricity? These and many other practical questions were never entertained in that class with Abdul. Nor were issues of ethics, how to choose a language coach, what to pay, if anything, those who collaborate, and myriad additional questions.

I learned a lot in that class about the language studied and about elicitation techniques, but really nothing about, as the professor said, 'setting up a pup tent in the rain'. He doesn't 'do' rain.

It takes all kinds to move our science forward: those who work, as Crowley says, in 'armchairs' and those who tramp around with 'dirty feet'. To dirty feet we can easily add sick kids, physical danger, tropical parasites and diseases, and on and on. But hey, someone has to do it, as we come to understand better just how different languages can be and, at the same time, how similar they must be.

A textbook is not an absolute necessity. I normally teach FM with Spanish as the language of instruction, where I am unaware of a good textbook (although several chapters of Newman and Ratliff are drafted in Spanish). Nevertheless, I recommend a textbook so that the broad spectrum of FM issues can be dealt with, especially when a professor might otherwise concentrate only on data gathering. By recommending Crowley 2007 and Bowern 2008, it becomes clear that I am a 'dirty feet' kind of linguist. I have learned tons from 'armchair' linguists, but my own slant on data is that it is best collected in context and in the field, hence a course in *field* methods.

Vaux and Cooper 1999 is good, but it is a book basically about elicitation techniques and analysis. This is great and it is a good book for a graduate course. I would say the same about Bouquiaux and Thomas 1992 and Abbi 2001, although these last two are aimed specifically at Africa and India respectively.

I like Newman and Ratliff 2001, which has a number of neat articles including two by two of the truly gifted field linguists of our day, the late Ken Hale and Dan Everett. What I especially like about this book is the way each author shows his or her heart. The book is a nice mix of practical and analytical. I highly suggest the chapter by McLaughlin (the linguist) and Sall (the language coach). They present a parallel account from the writer's own perspective about how the project was going. The article deals with McLaughlin's dread of money issues and her role in the community, and Sall's reading of the same phenomena from an insider's perspective.

Another book that nicely straddles the fence between analysis and practical life on the field is Everett's *Linguistic fieldwork: A student guide* (forthcoming).

I suggest using either Bowern or Crowley as the class text enhanced by chapters taken from Newman and Ratliff and sections from Everett.

Two additional books that are loaded with practical advice about setting up an elicitation schedule are Healey 1975 and Brewster and Brewster 1976. They are somewhat dated, but they are loaded with helpful, practical information from the days before computers.

17.6 Conclusion

Field methods can be a great course. It combines the basic disciplines of linguistics: phonology, morpho-syntax and the lexicon. Yet it deals not only with the academic side of things, but the deeply personal. The course lends itself to group work (if desired), to as much depth as can be mustered in a semester, and to an integrated view of the importance and satisfaction of learning about a language.

Most students are nervous at the beginning of a FM course. By the time it is over, they have usually calmed down a great deal, and come to appreciate and enjoy this most human side of our science.

References

Abbi, A. 2001. *A manual of linguistic field work and structures of Indian languages*. Munich: LINCOM Europa.

Becker, A.L. 1996 [1984]. 'Biography of a sentence: A Burmese proverb'. In *The matrix of language: Contemporary linguistic anthropology*, pp.142-59, ed. D. Brennais and R.K.S. Macaulay. Boulder, CO: Westview Press.

Berlin, B. and P. Kay. 1969. *Basic color terms: Their universality and evolution*. Berkeley: University of California Press.

Bouquiaux, L. and J.M.C. Thomas. 1992. *Studying and describing unwritten languages*. Dallas: SIL.

Bowern, C.L. 2008. *Linguistic fieldwork: A practical guide*. New York: Palgrave Macmillan

Brewster, T. and E.S. Brewster. 1976. *Language acquisition made practical*. Colorado Springs: Lingua House.

Crowley, T. 2007. *Field linguistics: A beginner's guide*. Oxford: Oxford University Press.

Crystal, D. 2000. *Language death*. Cambridge: Cambridge University Press.

Everett, D. forthcoming. *Linguistic fieldwork: A student guide*. Cambridge: Cambridge University Press.

Geertz, C. 1973. *The interpretation of cultures*. New York: Harper Collins.
Healey, A. (ed.) 1975. *Language learner's field guide*. Ukarumpa, Papua New Guinea: SIL International.
Krauss, M. 1992. 'The world's languages in crisis'. *Language* 68: 4-10.
Labov, W. 1972. *Sociolinguistic patterns*. Philadelphia: University of Pennsylvania Press.
Malinowski, B. 1922. *Argonauts of the Western Pacific*. New York: Dutton.
Maranz, D. 2001. *African friends and money matters*. Dallas: SIL International.
Nettle, D. and S. Romaine. 2000. *Vanishing voices: The extinction of the world's languages*. Oxford: Oxford University Press.
Newman, P. and M. Ratliff. 2001. *Linguistic fieldwork*. Cambridge: Cambridge University Press.
Vaux, B. and J. Cooper. 1999. *Introduction to linguistic field methods*. Munich: LINCOM.
Zaharlick, A. 1992. 'Ethnography in anthropology and its value for education'. *Theory into Practice* 31 (2): 117-25.

Notes

* **Wes Collins**

Wes Collins lived with his family for 19 years under the auspices of SIL International among the Mam of Guatemala. After returning to the States, he completed his PhD at the Ohio State University in 2005. His introduction to linguistics and good teaching was with Hebrew professor Joe Kickasola at Ashland Theological Seminary in the early 1970s. Joe talked about Hebrew not simply as a field of study to be mastered, but as a social and cultural milieu out of which language naturally occurred.

Three decades later at Ohio State, Wes studied with a host of well-known scholars, two of whom stand out to him as prime educators as well as highly respected researchers: Brian Joseph and Mary Beckman. These professors brought broad experience home to the classroom along with the delight of discovery and a deep respect for and enjoyment of the teaching enterprise.

In response, Wes' goal is not only to teach well, but also to help students mine the wonder of our shared humanity through language.

[1] There is a Swadesh word list of 200 items. See www.df.lth.se/~cml/swadesh.txt, among other sites.

18 Metaphors we teach by: Sometimes they throw in a fish

Kate Burridge *

> I love metaphor. It provides two loaves where there seems to be one. Sometimes it throws in a load of fish (Bernard Malamud 1975, Interview in *Paris Review* (Spring); cited in Crystal and Crystal 2000: 246).

18.1 Backdrop

Definitions of metaphor have been many and varied over the years, to be sure, and it is not my place to investigate these here. The story I tell is based on a rather general and commonsensical account of the concept, but it does seem to be the one place where researchers and theorists, even those of very different 'flavours', reach agreement (cf. Cameron 1999: 3). When people use metaphor, they refer to one domain by using language expressions that are normally associated with some other domain. There is a transfer of meaning from one given context to another. This explanation of metaphor has strayed little from Aristotle's original account. As he put it back in the fourth century BC, 'a good metaphor implies an intuitive perception of the similarity in dissimilars' (Aristotle, *Poetics* Chapter 22, page 2335; translated by I. Bywater). As is clear from his various descriptions of metaphor in both *Poetics* and *Rhetoric*, Aristotle was definitely of the opinion that people will learn and grasp something far better when they experience it through a good metaphor: 'It is from metaphor that we can best get hold of something fresh' (Aristotle, *Rhetoric*, Book 3: 10, page 2250; translated by W. Rhys Roberts). I will be returning to Aristotle's writings on metaphor many times in this piece. I do not wish to be accused of trampling on Aristotle's footprints in the linguist's garden (to borrow an image used by Keith Allan to depict the failure of modern-day linguistics to acknowledge Aristotle's contribution; cf. Allan 2009).

Metaphor always involves the comparison of two items where there exists some sort of relationship. If this sounds vague, it is deliberately so, for there are many different kinds of relationships that can hold between these items. It is a matter of analogy. A straightforward example might be this. Let's say we call someone a *worm*. This sort of comparison takes salient characteristics from folk concepts about the appearance and the behaviour of the creature and these are then attributed to that person. A *worm* is 'someone sleazy, slimy, someone who crawls, a lickspittle'. We might want to convey a picture of a person who is totally loathsome in manner and character. Of course, taken literally, the statement is false. This person is not actually 'a worm'. But we are claiming that there is a semantic connection between this person (the figurative meaning) and a worm (the literal meaning) – all the colour and the expressive force of this insult derive from this relationship. Clearly, what metaphor does so well is to draw attention to certain features, while at the same time obscuring others (cf. Lakoff and Johnson 1981: Ch. 21). Such analogies as this one are taken from the real world, and when these analogies are conspicuous, they are dubbed a metaphor. To say 'he's a worm' quite obviously applies a term from the domain of animal behaviour to the domain of human behaviour.

Aristotle was probably the first to point to the ubiquity of metaphor. He wrote:

> In the language of prose, besides the regular and proper terms for things, metaphorical terms only can be used with advantage. This we gather from the fact that these two classes of terms, the proper or regular and the metaphorical – these and no others – are used by everybody in conversation (Aristotle, *Rhetoric* Book 3: 2, page 2240; translated by W. Rhys Roberts).

Our language is firmly founded in the world of our perceptions and conceptions, and as soon as we open our mouths or put pen to paper we produce metaphors. But most of them are conventionalized – they are automatic. As Lakoff and Johnson (1981: 139) express it, these are 'metaphors that structure the ordinary conceptual system of our culture, which is reflected in our everyday language'. For example, in English (like so many other languages) spatial activities give rise to mental verbs, such as those of understanding, supposing and deducing. *Understand* is transparent (from a verb meaning 'to step under'); *suppose* and *deduce* come from original Latin constructions with literal meanings 'under + put' and 'lead + down'. Expressions to do with seeing, hearing and touching also develop to become mental verbs; for example, *I see* and *I hear you* for 'I understand (you)' or *He finally grasped it* for 'He finally understood'. In these cases we are no longer conscious of the metaphorical links. Time has pushed them below the level of consciousness. Often the imagery is well and truly buried, as in the verb *comprehend*. It too comes from something that means 'to grasp, seize' but this is a metaphor from long ago, and one (like *suppose* and *deduce*) that has been borrowed from Latin. Most of what we talk about, it seems, is in terms of something else. Scratch the surface of many expressions and you will find a dried-out metaphor of this nature.

Over the years Keith Allan and I have worked on linguistic taboos (Allan and Burridge 1991, 2006). Taboos will always generate a rich exuberance of metaphorical language and the imagery here often falls well outside the conceptual system of the conventional metaphor. It is anything but routine and can involve language as diverse as street slang through to the poetic diction we normally associate with elevated literature. What our work has highlighted is the creativity and inventiveness of ordinary language users, not in the usual linguistic sense of creativity (in other words, the ability of language users to generate novel structures), but the poetic inventiveness of ordinary people in the figures they create to construct euphemistic and dysphemistic expressions. 'In classifying the vocabulary of defecation and urination, but more especially that pertaining to sex, the lexical evidence suggests to us that every avenue the imagination could reasonably take has been ventured upon; yet we cannot doubt that human minds will find new ones' (Allan and Burridge 1991: 76). The expressions range from the exquisitely lyrical to the disgustingly crass – many demonstrate an expressiveness and poetic ingenuity worthy of William Shakespeare. Clearly, metaphor, even marvelous metaphor, is not simply the stuff of great literature. Just look at current wine terminology that draws on figures like *big*, *full*, *deep*, *even*, *thick*, *flat* and *small*. This is the sort of bold imagery of poetry and fiction. Metaphor pervades our whole language and is undoubtedly one of the most significant forces behind linguistic change. We are constantly adapting familiar structures from our experiences to new purposes in our language. Whether we are inventing names for new concepts, adding to the names of old concepts, insulting someone, putting up a smoke-screen, even creating new grammar, metaphor is very often behind it all.

18.2 Metaphors at work

> Metaphor, moreover, gives style clearness, charm and distinction as nothing else can (Aristotle, *Rhetoric* Book 3: 2, page 2240; translated by W. Rhys Roberts).

In his work Aristotle emphasized the ability of metaphors to bring to mind new aspects of the world and new ways of understanding reality. He made much of the instructive value of metaphors through vividness and novelty of expression:

> Liveliness is specially conveyed by metaphor, and by the further power of surprising the hearer; because the hearer expected something different, his acquisition of the new idea impresses him all the more. His mind seems to say, 'Yes, to be sure; I never thought of that' (Aristotle, *Rhetoric* Book 3: 11, page 2253; translated by W. Rhys Roberts).

Great opportunities can be made of this aspect of metaphor in the classroom. Analogies that are taken from the real world – situations and concepts that are familiar to students – help them to cope with situations and concepts that are new and alien to them, and (with the right metaphor) in a way that is enjoyable and user-friendly.

Let me explain how it was that I first became aware of the usefulness of metaphors in the learning process. As a keen teacher of first-year students, it usually fell to me to give the introductory classes on phonology. It was something I always dreaded. Beginning students of linguistics always seemed to find the concepts of the phoneme, and particularly notions of complementary and contrastive distribution, very difficult. (As a fugitive from literature, I remember doing so.) Then I discovered the metaphor that said it all. In their introduction to linguistics, Crowley *et al.* (1995) explained the ideas in terms of the cane toads and the cane beetles of far north Queensland. Most Australians know the story well. And those students who were not familiar with it were interested to learn. Cane toads were introduced to Australia to wipe out the cane beetle, whose larvae were eating the roots of sugar cane and killing or stunting the plants. In 1935 more than 3,000 cane toads were released into the sugar cane plantations. The plan was a failure because, like the velar nasal and the glottal glide of English, the cane toad and the cane beetle are in complementary distribution. As it turns out, these introduced cane toads stay near the ground while the beetles live in the upper stalks of cane plants. In the course of the telling of this story, students acquire the concepts of complementary and contrastive distribution effortlessly and enjoyably. The ability of a novel metaphor such as this one to convey new meaning – cheerfully, clearly and colourfully – is what makes it such a valuable pedagogical device. The toads and beetles of far north Queensland added some theatre to the explanation of what are difficult and highly abstract phonological concepts.

As linguists I believe our task as teachers is made all the more difficult precisely because of the apparent familiar and everyday nature of the subject matter we deal with. It is after all just language. Quite simply, students feel they ought to understand and they quickly become discouraged (sometimes even hostile) when they don't. Outside the discipline of linguistics, there already exists an extensive non-technical vocabulary used by the lay public when talking about language; but unfortunately, the terminology is often too imprecise to be of real use for the systematic study of language and how it works. Linguists are therefore faced with having to narrow and redefine everyday terms like *sentence*, *word*, *syllable* and *grammar*, as well as add a barrage of new terms to overcome imprecision and to distinguish things that non-linguists ignore and, in consequence, ordinary language lacks terms for. The discipline of linguistics is perceived as intellectual hocus-pocus and all the more offensive because it seems to deal with an everyday domain. Metaphors help to bridge the gap. They help students see the subject matter in a new light and they stimulate discussion. Things normally invisible (all the more because they are so familiar) become visible.

In addition to the metaphors that must pervade my ordinary conversation as a matter of course, I have in my discussions about language made conscious use of a number of different metaphors over the years. Sometimes they appear singly; for example, allophones as slices of cake or books on a library shelf, euphemisms as fig leaves (an image I borrowed from Hugh Rawson 1981) and artful ones as diaphanous nightshifts (Keith Allan's description), language as an intricate folded rose (to explain its layers of complexity), the 'Great English Vowel Shift' as the Mad Hatter's tea-party (Aitchison 2001: Ch. 13) and, of course the usual suspects such as language as a game of chess (from Saussure 1974). In fact, anyone doubting the value of metaphor in education should consider that a number of years ago my own department changed the name of its first year unit from 'Language in Australian Society' to 'The Language Game: Why do we speak the way we do?' This hospitable metaphor of language as a game (which runs through the entire unit) has proved extremely successful in facilitating students' understanding of language. We have since doubled our enrolments.

Mostly I find myself making use of what is sometimes called the megametaphor, or metaphoric theme (thanks to Ludmilla A'Beckett for introducing this concept to me). For example, in 1998 Jean Mulder and I wrote a textbook on English 'Downunder'. This was intended as a first-year linguistics textbook based upon English in New Zealand and in Australia. We wanted to call it 'Feasting on English'. All examples were culled from culinary texts – cooking books throughout the centuries, food and wine magazines, books about food, health, diet and even etiquette. As we stated in the introduction, we couldn't imagine a more pleasant way of grappling with the English language than over knives, forks and a bottle of good wine. The metaphor of food provided the book with a nice consistency. Moreover, by drawing on everyday experiences, we could bring English alive and encourage the students to wallow in the day-to-day language that is all around them – everything from the instructions on the back of a cereal packet to the language of hangover cures. This was especially important for the texts from earlier periods of English. We wanted to show that speakers and writers of the past were part of a living, breathing speech community and that the language they spoke and wrote is the language we speak and write today. A tenth-century recipe for roasted swan, free from any literary ambition and stylization, brings the speakers and their language alive. But most useful was also the convenience of the occasional food analogy to help shed light on a difficult linguistic concept. I have always liked Jespersen's (1922) image of hypotactic sentences as Chinese boxes – but brown onions aren't bad either. The food metaphor is one I have revisited recently. The *Gift of the gob: Morsels of English language history* (Burridge 2010) is, like its predecessors, much like a degustation menu. Moreover, the 'gobbets' can be consumed randomly or consecutively – as the diner desires.

Work with Keith Allan on euphemism and taboo has also drawn constantly on a megametaphor, in this case that of language as shield and weapon. To speak euphemistically is to use language like a shield against the feared, the disliked, the unpleasant. Euphemisms can be used to upgrade (as a shield against scorn); to disguise (as a shield against the distasteful); they are used deceptively to conceal unpleasant aspects (as a shield against anger); and they are used to display in-group identity (as a shield against the intrusion of outsiders). Conversely, to speak dysphemistically is to use language as a weapon against those things and people that frustrate and annoy us, and whom we disapprove of, despise, dislike or plain hate (cf. Bolinger 1980 who also draws on the image of the loaded weapon). As we argued, it is not for nothing that there are laws of libel and that repressive regimes resort to censorship: language is sometimes the only weapon against brute force. Through these experiences it became obvious to me just how insightful these elaborate metaphorical themes can be – sometimes in ways not even anticipated by the metaphor-maker.

18.3 Language as a garden

> Ah, fie! 'tis an unweeded garden,
> That grows to seed; (Shakespeare, *Hamlet* [I.ii])

Recently, I have been having some fun playing with the links between gardens and language. I initially arrived at this gardening metaphor, when I was trying to find an image that would unite all of the little linguistic pieces I had written over the years for radio. These pieces were generated largely from talkback calls – observations on language and queries about language usage. Very often of course they involved complaints by callers about the language of others. (We are all of us born with a keen nose for the ill-chosen word and the grammatical error of our fellow speakers!) What united these pieces was the concern that people showed for the wellbeing of their language. This brought to mind a picture of English as some sort of garden that, if not carefully and constantly tended, would become unruly and overgrown. Shakespeare expressed it far more eloquently. Or as one of the passionate supporters of the apostrophe once put it to me in a grumpy letter (after I had suggested that English could well survive without the services of the possessive apostrophe): 'We shall have no formal structure of our language: it will become unteachable, unintelligible, and eventually, useless as an accurate means of communication'.

The garden metaphor helped me to organize my experiences of talkback radio. Clearly, what was involved here was prescription, but gardening provided a more gentle and more positive image; besides, as Deborah Cameron (1995) has claimed, the behaviour of speakers here is more complex and diverse than the dogmatic labels 'prescription' and 'purism' imply. She opts for the expression 'verbal hygiene' for exactly this reason. Like her verbal hygienists, language 'gardeners' can be found in all sorts of associations. They are the people found in language associations formed to promote causes as diverse as Plain English, simplified spelling, Esperanto, Klingon, assertiveness and effective communication – even something as esoteric as the abolition of aberrant apostrophes (such as *Canva's Hat's*) and the preservation of Old English strong verbs (such as *clomb* for the past of *climb*). But equally, gardeners are those folk who simply enjoy looking things up in dictionaries and usage books, who spend time thinking and talking about language, and who like punning and playing Scrabble or Balderdash. Like Cameron, I felt that a sense of linguistic values makes verbal hygiene part of every speaker's linguistic competence. We are all closet language gardeners of some sort. But it was also the sense of enjoyment that I wanted to get across, for clearly there is a tremendous amount of pleasure to be had pottering about in the garden – edging, staking, cutting back, keeping bugs at bay. Why else would R.E. Zachrisson (1931) bother to calculate that *scissors* could be spelt 596,580 different ways?

The garden is also an image that nicely caters for the arsenal of prescriptive texts (dictionaries, style guides, usage books, grammars) that give standard languages like English much of its muscle. These texts are the conservatories, the greenhouses and the hothouses that nurture our language, often artificially keeping alive features that have long perished in ordinary usage. Many people see these linguistic nurseries as working to protect and cherish endangered constructions, words, meanings and pronunciations. The neat lists and beautifully spun paradigms inside the dictionary and handbook provide the glasshouse counterpart to the outside 'wild garden'.

So where do linguists fit into this image of the garden? As they themselves will point out in any introductory lecture on linguistics, linguists study language, in the same way that botanists study plants and zoologists research the physiology, anatomy and behaviour of animals. And just as biologists cannot denigrate certain species in the plant world that the wider community views as weeds, neither can linguists disparage native speakers for, say, dropping an *l* in *vulnerable* or condemn as a 'linguistic atrocity' an expression such as *youse*. However, for those in the wider community, there is usually a very clear distinction between the unwanted plants in the garden and those that should be encouraged to survive. Accordingly, they view linguists as the seasoned gardeners whose task is precisely to advise on what should be trimmed, removed or promoted in the garden – linguists control the pests, build the hothouses and perform the topiary. The gulf to be bridged between these two camps is considerable.

The associated metaphor of the weed worked better than I anticipated, as I realized when I started to visit serious tomes on horticulture. Weed experts, I gather, have great difficulty coming up with a scientific account of the term *weed*. Even within technical works on weed management, I encountered definitions such as: 'a plant growing where we do not want it'; 'a plant whose virtues are yet to be discovered'; 'a plant growing out of place'; 'a plant that you do not want'; 'a plant you hate'. More precise definitions, apparently, are impossible – in fact not practicable. The difficulty is that weeds are context specific. It depends entirely on location and on time whether something is classified as a weed or not. And so it is with the weeds in our language. One speaker's noxious weed can be another's garden ornamental. A linguistic weed today can be a cherished garden contributor tomorrow. This is what I wanted readers to focus on and acknowledge. Whether they are in gardens or in languages, weeds are totally centred on human value judgments.

And there is another aspect to weeds – they are highly successful. Weeds share certain biological features that enable them to prosper. They have a prolific seed production and effective seed dispersal mechanisms, they spread by rhizomes and tubers which means they can regenerate from the smallest of fragments, and they are often unpalatable to browsers. In short, they are very hard to kill. So why, within one language system, do some 'weeds' end up flourishing while others eventually whither? Language change is typically marked by rivalry between different forms. What then are the capabilities that enable one feature to be triumphant and spread through the language? Hundreds of slang expressions are created by speakers each year. Most fall by the wayside but some succeed – why? Pronunciations of *sue* and *suitor* with initial [ʃ] were denounced in the eighteenth century as 'barbarous'. They were eventually eradicated. So how come the pronunciations for *sugar* and *sure* snuck through the weed controls? And what enables certain linguistic weeds to extend their perimeters beyond one social group to spread to others? One of the challenges confronting linguists is to determine the conditions that allow linguistic features to prosper in a particular language at a particular time. The weed metaphor provided the nice opportunity for discussing what has come to be known in linguistics as the 'actuation problem' (Weinreich *et al.* 1968: 102).

At first blush, there is one facet of weed behaviour that might focus people's attention wrongly. Clearly, there are truly noxious plants out there in weed flora that inflict (sometimes irreversible) damage on the landscapes they infest. As linguists, we would not want to claim that this pernicious behaviour of the weed fits in with our experience of language. Yet, there are aspects of language use that do have detrimental effects on people's lives and that we, as linguists, should expose – those qualities to do with manipulation through advertising and propaganda, the influences of language on our thinking and behaviour, linguistic discrimination and, in particular, official misrepresentation and obfuscation. The weed metaphor hopefully gave new meaning to these aspects of our language, and without the hysteria of some recent popular accounts such as Watson 2003. It is true, advertisers and politicians twist and warp language, sometimes outrageously, to sell their products or to persuade their audiences. But this is what we all do – bend language for our own ends. The words and constructions we choose always hint, suggest and insinuate. They never simply ditto reality. By its very nature, language has spin. Besides, there are many occasions where we don't want precise language, or even honest language, for that matter. We are expected to turn a tactful blind eye, perhaps, or tell a white lie. Most of the time we are polite, whatever we are feeling deep down. Without these weedy tendencies social interaction would soon grind to a halt. Speech communities are complex things and language must be able to reflect a vast range of social behaviour. Get rid of the weeds and the soil becomes impoverished. To steal a phrase from Mary Ellis' book on herbs, I wanted to get across the idea of the 'virtuous weed' (Ellis 1995).

Metaphors that come to us fresh can themselves create aspects of reality and suggest new methods of understanding. As hinted at earlier, my initial intention was that this metaphor would help to overcome the gap between the general public and linguistics. I am not sure whether or not it succeeded in the end, but it certainly has helped me to better understand the gap. Linguists can argue till they're blue in the face that all constructions are equally good and that change and variation are natural and inevitable features of any thriving language – it just so happens most others disagree. The feeling between the two camps is one of mutual distrust; linguistic experts fail to address lay concerns and lay activists show no interest in heeding linguists. In 1992 a newspaper article appeared which vividly conveyed the views of many in the wider community towards professional linguists: Laurence Urdang, editor of *Verbatim*, described linguists as 'categorically the dullest people on the face of the earth…rather than trying to present and explain information, they seem to be going in the opposite direction. They try to shield people from knowing anything useful about the language' (Burridge 2005: 162-64). Linguists find popular perceptions of language ill-informed and narrow-minded. The wider community feels let down.

It was after I read the great gardening debates of the eighteenth and nineteenth centuries that I started to see this divide in a different light. Gardeners during this time apparently fell into two camps over the question of what constituted a 'proper garden'. Was it a work of nature or was it a work of art? Suddenly it became obvious why I had such trouble getting my ideas across to talkback callers. For linguists, language is a natural (even if social) phenomenon, something that evolves and adapts and can be studied objectively. This stance is resoundingly rejected by others in the wider community for whom language is an art form, something to be cherished, revered and preserved. Understandably, they reject the neutral position of the linguistics profession. Others have written about this difference (Bolinger 1980, for example), but it took these gardening books for me to see it and properly understand it.

Gardens and standard languages have much in common. Both are human constructions and they share two fundamental characteristics. They are restricted by boundaries and they also cultivated. It is clear too that speakers of English believe in a standard language. They believe in, if not the existence, then the possibility of a totally regular and homogenous language system. Linguists have to realize just how powerful these beliefs are (sociolinguists probably have for some time). Non-linguists must also realize that we need to mess with the cherished standard if we are to develop a better and more constructive public discourse on language. To create a standard language or to build a garden is to enter into a partnership with natural processes. Languages and gardens are never finished products.

18.4 In conclusion

Lakoff and Johnson (1981: 3) go as far as claiming that the ordinary conceptual system of human beings is fundamentally metaphorical in nature. If they are right and all thinking is metaphorical, then it stands to reason that metaphors will be a good way to help us think. I spent much of this piece focusing on one example of a metaphorical theme that has been formed by a group of individual but coherent metaphors to do with gardening. Clearly, there is an advantage to metaphorical themes such as this, to organize and to draw together concepts in a coherent, efficient and (hopefully) pleasing fashion. Through *gardens*, *cherished flowers*, *weeds*, *hybrids*, *exotics*, *mulch*, *hothouses*, *fertilizers* and *blooming (English)* I found a way to unite what initially seemed a disparate bunch of articles about language. (There are also dangers – at least one of the books ended up on the gardening shelf of some bookshops!) The key metaphor (language is a garden) ended up sprouting an array of associated metaphors that I hoped were informative and memorable. Moreover, it took me down paths I had not foreseen. When such themes activate other metaphors in this way, they help to unfold a topic and also to draw attention to different aspects of the topic. This can be in ways not even anticipated by the creator of the metaphor.

I do not research how metaphors work and I cannot provide evidence from learning outcomes to support the notion that metaphors are valuable pedagogical tools (though see Cortazzi and Jin 1999, who make a fairly convincing case that metaphors can raise language awareness). I can only go by what I have observed in the classroom and from feedback I have received in the way of phone calls and emails from radio listeners. Literal language might be more precise and less ambiguous, as critics of metaphor have argued, but it is metaphorical language (particularly, the non-common-or-garden variety) that creates new insights and new exciting means of comprehending reality. Metaphors highlight reality and also generate aspects of reality that go beyond literal language. Metaphors offer two loaves where there seems to be one: they might even throw in a fish.

References

Aitchison, J. 2001. *Language change: Progress or decay.* Cambridge: Cambridge University Press.

Allan, K. 2009. *The Western classical tradition in linguistics.* 2nd expanded edn; London: Equinox.

Allan, K. and K. Burridge. 1991. *Euphemism and dysphemism: Language used as shield and weapon*. New York: Oxford University Press.

Allan, K. and K. Burridge. 2006. *Forbidden words: Taboo and the censoring of language*. Cambridge: Cambridge University Press.

Barnes, J. (ed.) 1984. *The complete works of Aristotle*. The revised Oxford translation; Bollingen Series 71. Princeton: Princeton University Press.

Bolinger, D. 1980. *Language: The loaded weapon*. London: Longman.

Burridge, K. 2004. *Blooming English: Observations on the roots, cultivation and hybrids of the English language*. Cambridge: Cambridge University Press.

Burridge, K. 2005. *Weeds in the garden of words: Further observations on the tangled history of the English language*. Cambridge: Cambridge University Press.

Burridge, K. 2010. *Gift of the gob: Morsels of English language history*. Sydney: HarperCollins Publishers.

Burridge, K. and J. Mulder. 1998. *English in Australia and New Zealand: An introduction to its structure, history and use*. Melbourne: Oxford University Press.

Cameron, D. 1995. *Verbal hygiene*. London: Routledge.

Cameron, L. 1999. 'Operationalising "metaphor" for applied linguistic research'. In *Researching and applying metaphor*, pp. 3-28, ed. L. Cameron and G. Low. Cambridge: Cambridge University Press..

Cortazzi, M. and Lixian Jin 1999. 'Bridges to learning: Metaphors of teaching, learning and language'. In *Researching and applying metaphor*, pp.149-76. ed. L. Cameron and G. Low. Cambridge: Cambridge University Press.

Crowley, T., J. Lynch, J. Siegel and J. Piau. 1995. *The design of language: An introduction to descriptive linguistics*. Auckland: Longman Paul.

Crystal, D. and H. Crystal 2000. *Words on words: Quotations about language and languages*. London: Penguin.

Ellis, M. 1995. *Growing and using herbs in Australia: Virtuous weeds*. Crows, Nest, NSW: Little Hill Press.

Jesperson, O. 1922. *Language, its nature, development and origin*. London: Allen & Unwin.

Lakoff, G. and M. Johnson 1981. *Metaphors we live by*. Chicago: The University of Chicago Press.

Rawson, H. 1981. *A dictionary of euphemisms and other doubletalk*. New York: Crown.

Saussure, F. de. 1974. *A course in general linguistics*, ed. C. Bally and A. Sechehaye; trans. W. Baskin. Glasgow: Fontana/Collins. [First published 1915].

Shakespeare, W. 1938. *The complete works*. London: Clear-Type Press.

Watson, Don. 2003. *Death sentence: The decay of public language*. Sydney: Random House.

Weinreich, Uriel, William Labov and Marvin I. Herzog 1968. 'Empirical foundations for a theory of language change'. In *Directions for historical linguistics*, pp. 95-195, ed. W.P. Lehmann and Y. Malkiel. Austin: University of Texas Press.

Zachrisson, R.E. 1931. 'Four hundred years of English spelling reform', reprinted in *Studia Neophilologica* 1.

Notes

* **Kate Burridge**

I fell into Linguistics quite by accident. As a fledgling undergraduate, I had an interest in individual languages, but never dreamt there was a separate academic discipline that dealt purely with human language. My school experience was at the time when educators had begun to turn their backs on the explicit teaching of language. So when I started my first linguistic unit in the second year of study (at the time simply to flesh out my degree), I was thrilled by what I had encountered. There were many inspirational teachers at this time, but Shelly Harrison stands out. His lectures, in particular, showed me how exciting it was to think about language in a scientific way – very different, as I found out, from the sort of unconscious knowledge I had as a native speaker of English.

After completing a BA Honours degree at the University of Western Australia, I proceeded to the University of London where I did a PhD on syntactic change in medieval Dutch. During this time, I audited as many units as I could manage and again I was blessed with inspired teaching. Geoff Horrock's lecturing brilliance almost turned me into a formal syntactician and what I learned in Paddy Considine's comparative philolology seminars will never leave me (especially those under the trees in Gordon Square fuelled by the bowl of Pavlovian jelly babies!). Of course, my acolyte feet were at all times expertly guided by my supervisor Theodora Bynon.

Since becoming a full-time academic (now in the linguistics programme at Monash University), I have spent a good deal of time engaging with groups outside the university – public lectures (for schools, festivals, charities and a range of societies and institutions) and involvement with the Australian Broadcasting Corporation, preparing and presenting weekly programmes on language for radio and television. Encounters with the public teach me a great deal these days, and I find this sort of work is a constant source of ideas. Like the classroom, these venues are often the starting point for new research projects. The teaching–research nexus is something I have always believed in.

Index

Lightning Source UK Ltd.
Milton Keynes UK
UKOW030905120513

210536UK00002B/24/P